COMPARATIVE POLITICAL ECONOMY OF EAST AND SOUTH ASIA

Comparative Political Economy of East and South Asia

A Critique of Development Policy and Management

R. C. Mascarenhas
Reader in Political Science and Public Policy
School of Business and Public Management
Victoria University of Wellington
New Zealand

First published in Great Britain 1999 by
MACMILLAN PRESS LTD
Houndmills, Basingstoke, Hampshire RG21 6XS and London
Companies and representatives throughout the world

A catalogue record for this book is available from the British Library.

ISBN 0–333–73574–9

 First published in the United States of America 1999 by
ST. MARTIN'S PRESS, INC.,
Scholarly and Reference Division,
175 Fifth Avenue, New York, N.Y. 10010

ISBN 0–312–21843–5

Library of Congress Cataloging-in-Publication Data
Mascarenhas, R. C.
Comparative political economy of East and South Asia : a critique
of development policy and management / R.C. Mascarenhas.
    p. cm.
Includes bibliographical references and index.
ISBN 0–312–21843–5 (cloth)
    1. East Asia—Economic policy.   2. East Asia—Economic conditions.
    3. South Asia—Economic policy.   4. South Asia—Economic conditions.
    I. Title.
HC460.5.M35—1999
338.95—dc21   98–38454
                                                                    CIP

This book is printed on paper suitable for recycling and made from fully managed and
sustained forest sources.

10   9   8   7   6   5   4   3   2   1
08   07   06   05   04   03   02   01   00   99

Printed and bound in Great Britain by
Antony Rowe Ltd, Chippenham, Wiltshire

Contents

Preface

This study of the comparative political economy of East and South Asia is a product of my long association as an academic interested in research and teaching in the field of Third World (TW) development. I regard this book as a contribution to the field of development policy and management and I hope it will enhance the understanding of the political economy of the region. This work, like my earlier work, reaffirms my position on the role of the state in the economy. It is a position that is unfashionable in an era of neo-classical market dominance and an issue over which policy-makers and academics are ideologically divided. In my view the state and market ought to be complementary, not competitive. Among academics working on TW development, particularly East Asia, the complementarity view is becoming widely acceptable.

Comparative studies of the political economy of two regions – economically developed East Asia and politically developed South Asia – are seen as outcomes of their unique historical experience. Comparing two diverse regions has been a difficult task, forcing me to be selective in the range of countries covered. I have chosen to focus on Taiwan and Korea in East Asia and India in South Asia, countries on which abundant primary and secondary material is available.

In working on this study I have gained insight into the political and administrative systems in these countries and their problems in achieving developmental objectives. Successful achievement of development depends essentially on the quality of policies and their effective implementation.

In any academic research one aspires to adopt a balanced and critical view. Such a view is difficult to achieve in a comparative study involving two regions and the perspective adopted is likely to suffer from imbalances or even unconscious bias resulting from the author's personal circumstances. If that imbalance has crept in, it can only be seen as human. Opportunity to receive feedback from academics working in similar fields is something I look forward to. An academic in this part of the world has to envy the collaborative academic culture which is so much a part of the North American scene. This work has been meticulously edited by my wife Iris. Thanks are due to her and to my daughters Arati and Antara – the former for editing two chapters and the latter for typing two of them. Brenda Bongiovanni of the School of Business and Public Management helped with the preparation of tables and with setting the work on the computer. My thanks to her for her readiness to help whenever requested. My thanks also to Linda Walker who prepared some of the graphs.

R. C. M.
Wellington, New Zealand

1 Development: a Comparative Study

I INTRODUCTION

Development entails a process of comparing progress from an initial to a desired state. That process of development is not always certain even if it is deliberate or planned. The fact that variation exists between countries and within countries suggests that the process of development is uncertain and is governed by both controllable and uncontrollable forces. Furthermore, the uncertainty of outcomes of the development process is likely to be greater in societies whose economic, technological and organizational capacity is less developed when compared with ones that are developed. To highlight this, Sen (1984) quotes Marx who describes it as 'replacing the domination of circumstances and chance over individuals by the domination of individuals over chance and circumstances' (497). That statement implies that human societies are categorised into two groups, those capable of dominating their environment (physical, social and economic) and those who are victims of their environment. It is that relative capacity to manipulate the physical, economic and social environment that distinguishes one country's development from another's. In order to distinguish countries on the basis of relative technological, economic and organizational capability, we adopt comparative studies within which the following categories of countries have been developed: the First World (FW), Second World (SW) and the Third World (TW). While comparative researchers examine patterns of similarities and differences, in this study I focus on a few countries in two regions in order to understand the process of development.

Efforts to enhance that capacity to manipulate the environment are impeded in TW countries by the extensive interrelationship between the economy and society. Effective development entails a transition from a less differentiated to a more differentiated stage at which individuals and collectivities can enhance their capacity to influence the physical, social and economic environment. Creating that capacity is the purpose or goal of TW development – but that process is difficult because of 'social embeddedness', which argues that behaviour and institutions are constrained by ongoing social relations (Granovetter, 1985). For institutionalists the idea of embeddedness suggests that individuals' development of interests is influenced by culture, religion and society. The following is an illustration of such social embeddedness: 'The cycles of cultivation practised by farmers in Maharashtra (India) neatly fit into the yearly round of weddings, festivals and pilgrimages. New methods of cultivation can soon disrupt this social calendar' (Sachs, 1988). It is in such a context that economic and social change in TW countries is difficult, because it disrupts village corporate and social life through the entry of new methods, new technology and markets. Such a disruption of stable social relations is one that concerns the moral economists (Booth, 1994).

The influence of social relations (embeddedness) has to be seen from different perspectives. When positive it can be a social asset, when negative it turns into a social liability. This can take the form of personal relations and networks that can be effectively used to promote economic activity. However, when such networks are used to promote certain types of behaviour, they can become antisocial and unproductive. When trust and social relations are used for positive enhancement of the community, they are described as social capital (Coleman, 1988). The various perspectives on development of TW countries recognize the importance of interrelationships between the economy and society and emphasize the need to direct attention to political, institutional and historical factors hitherto neglected in development studies. To comprehend these factors, political, institutional and historical, I adopt the political economy approach.

II   APPROACH TO THE STUDY

Interest in studies of the TW has been revived following a slump during the late 1970s and early 1980s. The revival has been triggered by recent research on East Asian economies which have created interest because of their extraordinary performance when compared with the rest of the TW. Such studies have not only brought about a revival in TW research but have also adopted a different approach. Similarly, this study of the comparative political economy of East and South Asia adopts the 'new institutionalist' approach.

II (1)   Comparative Political Economy

The political economy or statist approach adopted in this study examines the role of the state in promoting political and socio-economic development. To understand the process of how that role of the state has been instrumental in promoting development, it also becomes necessary to understand the relationship between the state and the economy. Such an approach helps to explain the comparative performance of these countries. Unlike the 'state versus market' options hotly debated in the 1950s by the structuralists and the neoclassical economists, the current perspective relates to the appropriate mix or complementarity of market and government necessary to achieve late industrialization (Amsden, 1989, Wade, 1990, Mascarenhas, 1996, Evans, 1996).

Political economy recognizes that TW markets are not developed, raising several issues identified with dualism. If markets have to be developed through state intervention, then the capacity of governments to carry out functions fundamental to the economy, such as maintainance of law and order, justice, property rights and contracts, is essential. To guarantee this, both political legitimacy and stability of governments are essential (Lal and Myint, 1996).

In this study of comparative political economy of two regions, I raise questions about the ability of East Asian governments and why they were able to adopt appropriate types of state intervention while other countries failed to do so. In so doing, they (East Asians) have evolved what academics describe as 'the developmental state' (Johnson, 1982) 'the disciplined state' (Amsden, 1989) and 'the governed market' (Wade, 1990), which offer alternatives to the dominant neo-classical paradigm where state and societal forces (particularly business) are portrayed as antagonistic or adversarial in contrast to the co-operative relationship of guided development. If the former assigns a more distinctive role for the state in development, the latter views the state as a hindrance to a competitive economy. The neoclassical concept of the market based on rational economic behaviour rejects or ignores the historical, cultural and contextual factors. Schatzher (1995) comments:

> In recent years neoclassical economists have seized the commanding heights of the terrain of development economics with their injunction to 'get prices right'. But this school neither deals adequately with institutions nor seriously analyses politics. Bates seeks to remedy this by demonstrating that 'the study of institutions provides foundations not only for the study of markets but also for the study of political economy' (1414–1415).

Evidence from studies on TW development suggests that their performance is related to the capacity of governments to govern. This means that a country needs to develop political and administrative systems capable of deciding developmental objectives appropriate to its resources. Further, it needs to translate such objectives into policies and programmes and achieve them through effective implementation. In this study I critique the strategies adopted in development policy and its management, adopting the comparative political economy approach. In doing this I examine the differences between the type of regime (democratic or authoritarian), type of administrative system (generalist administration or technocratic) and the influence of historical and contextual factors. The success of East Asian countries is attributed to the distinctive institutional characteristics identified with a strong state, in contrast to the soft state characteristic of South Asia where little is demanded from its citizens (Myrdal, 1968, Blomkvist, 1992). In reflecting on such differences I consider (1) the influence of Japanese colonialism on Taiwan and South Korea and British colonialism in South Asia and (2) the introduction of democratic institutions prior to industrialization in South Asia, which was a reversal of the process in East Asia.

The political economy approach is consistent with the comparative studies recently undertaken in the field of development studies and can be classed as comparative political economy (Fields, 1995, Mascarenhas, 1996). In their use of the term 'political economy', Lal and Myint (1996) emphasize the political, historical, institutional factors that affect economic growth and income distribution. They take account of organizational factors affecting the workings of the market, administrative and fiscal machinery of government and the political factors affecting economic decision making (7), concluding that both markets and the government administrative and fiscal system in TW countries are incomplete and that any study of their functioning needs information that is not easily available. The other aspect to the political economy approach is the examination of political factors influential in economic decisions (Lal and Myint, 1996, 8).

II (2) Institutional Approach

In this study of the comparative political economy of East and South Asia I adopt an institutionalist approach to examine problems and issues of political and economic development (Hall, 1986, Fields, 1995, Mascarenhas, 1996). The institutionalist perspective in development studies recognizes the influence of historical, social and resource constraints specific to Third World countries and examines the development of political and administrative institutions to cope with such constraints. In recent years researchers have become actively involved in studying the relative successes or failures of TW development, and have focused particularly on the role of the state versus market as instrumental to the success of East Asian countries (Johnson, 1982, Amsden, 1989, Wade, 1990). In examining these issues I view institutions as constraints on policymakers.

The institutionalist perspective on economic policy emphasizes the organisational features of the state that affect the ability of social groups and political elites to realise their objectives. The state is conceived as a field of organizations, rules, and norms that sets limits on what political actors can achieve. Institutionalism is a theory of the constraints on political behaviour (Haggard and Moon, 1989–90, 230).

While the institutionalist approach in social science is currently on the ascendancy, it is necessary to identify the particular institutional perspective one adopts. Hamilton and Biggert (1988) examine three distinct approaches. Using the market or economic approach, the cultural approach and the political economy approach, they evaluate the efficacy of each to explain the industrial arrangements and strategies respectively adopted by Japan, South Korea and Taiwan. Having examined the three approaches, the authors conclude that both market or cultural explanations offer useful insights into certain aspects but are insufficient on their own to understand their effective functioning. According to them, a realistic view is provided by a 'political economy approach which incorporates elements of the market and culture explanations but does so from the point of view of the historically developed authority relations that exist among individuals and institutions in each society' (Hamilton and Biggert, 1988, S53). Further:

> The authority explanation deals with organisations themselves and conceptualizes them broadly as patterned interactions among people, that is, as structures of authority. It aims at understanding how these structures come into being, how they are maintained, and to what consequence. As such, it attempts historically adequate explanation and therefore differs from both general cultural theories and specific, predictive economic models (Hamilton and Biggert, 1988, S76).

The broadly-based institutional approach adopted in this study builds on recent research which has identified distinctive state–economy relations within both East Asia and South Asia (Hamilton and Biggert, 1988, Fields, 1995, Mascarenhas, 1993). Accordingly, a study of the historical evolution of institutional structures in both East and South Asia is helpful in explaining differences in development. There are two aspects to this. While the first focuses on the evolution of institutions and the historical, cultural and ideological constraints on the choice of policy elites in their efforts to promote development, the second studies the response of people to various changes arising out of the policy choices made by such policy elites. In looking at state–economy relations in both East and South Asia, one needs to look at various institutional arrangements adopted to understand the variation in response (Hamilton and Biggert, 1988).

In adopting a comparative political economy approach with an emphasis on institutions, I am interested in understanding the relationship between the type of political and administrative systems and the relative development performance of TW countries. Research on the TW in the 1980s and the 1990s has focused on the importance of the role of the state in development. In focusing on types of political and administrative systems as vital to arriving at appropriate policies (policy efficiency, Mascarenhas, 1982) and their effective implementation, this study explains the differing outcomes, thus offering a variant to the otherwise dominant influence of economic factors in studies on development. The historical institutionalist approach adopted in this study examines (1) the capacity of governments to formulate development policy and implement them, (2) what type of strategies policy-makers adopt to achieve development, taking into consideration resources and constraints, (3) the distribution of power between political elites and the administrative elite, and (4) the relationship of policy-makers and various societal interests (Pontusson, 1995).

Debates on development have brought forth a variety of explanations. While the state–society interrelationship in development has been a popular theme, that focus has shifted from society-centred to state-centred with the recent studies of East Asia (Haggard and Moon, 1989–90, Amsden, 1989, Wade, 1990, Fields, 1995). I intend in this study to examine the role of the state and its institutions in TW development and their centrality in understanding the comparative performance of the East Asian and South Asian economies. This entails a discussion on institutional arrangements such as the forms of policy structures and their implications for policy outcomes.

In attempting to explain why East Asian governments adopted appropriate types of state intervention while other TW countries failed to do so, some studies adopting a narrow focus have concluded that political arrangements have been used to insulate policy-makers from powerful groups, resulting in a technocratic or authoritarian state. However, a variety of other explanations – such as historical, cultural, religious and situational factors that explain the reasons why East Asian and not South Asian economies adopted appropriate economic policies – have been overlooked.

While focusing on the relationship of the state and the economy, one must consider the significant role played by social relations in traditional societies, where religion, culture and history continue to be important. In other words, any attempt to bring about socio-economic and political change through specific strategies of state intervention needs to incorporate social relations. Students of East Asian economies reject the notion that their economic miracle is exclusively a result of market forces; in promoting the concept of the 'developmental state' (Johnson, 1983, Amsden, 1989, Wade, 1990), they recognize the significance of social relations otherwise known as social embeddedness or social capital in economic development (Granovetter, 1985, Coleman, 1985, Fields, 1995, Evans, 1996).

Neoclassical thinking disembeds the market by excluding the influence of factors like history, culture and social relations (Fields, 1995). That political and economic behaviour is embedded suggests that it is influenced by ongoing social relations. Fields (1995) writes: 'Economics, like all forms of interaction, is embedded in the ongoing and evolving structure of social relations. Therefore, the institutional embeddedness approach provides an interpretive and analytical middleground between utilitarian and cultural explanations for economic behaviour and enterprise organization' (Fields, 1995). Using such an institutional approach, Fields (1995) develops the concept of embedded enterprise and provides a framework which explains economic outcome through the intervening variable of institution. The more socially embedded the institution, the more likely it is that norms of behaviour will be governed by trust and reciprocity and less likely by self-interest (Granovetter, 1988).

Using social embeddedness or social capital as a base, Evans (1996) develops the concept of synergy or network between public and private organizations. This synergy or complementarity is a network of ties that connects citizens and public officials across the public and private divide. In other words, networks which trespass the boundary between public and private are regarded as valuable social capital.

As TW societies are predominantly agrarian and less influenced by market forces, they are more likely to function on the basis of trust and reciprocity. Moral economists warn that the entry of market forces will lead to a process of disembeddedness. For moral economists the overlap between the traditional or subsistence economy and society is indistinguishable. A stable traditional society responds better to changes from within through a process of adaptation rather than to change which is imposed from outside.

The cultural perspective once sidelined is being considered again as a partial explanation for the success or failure of TW countries. The cultural explanation provides researchers with a frame of reference within which they can see how values, attitudes, and practices have influenced the process of development in TW countries. Further, it questions the traditional versus the modern school which advocates the replacement of traditional with modern values in the process of development. Culturalists believe that tradition and modernity can co-exist and promote this combination as a valued social asset for East Asian economic success. In the context of East and South Asian development, the cultural perspective highlights the varying influence of Confucianism, Hinduism, Buddhism and Islam.

However, the extent of overlap between social and economic forces varies from country to country. It is assumed that the process of differentiation as a consequence of development gradually reduces the extent of overlap between the economy and social forces. In other words, traditional TW economies are more socially embedded than FW industrialized economies (Granovetter, 1985, Fields, 1995).

While East Asians have achieved considerable economic success, they continue however to be influenced by historical and sociocultural forces, thus questioning the linear progression thesis – that interrelationship between the economy and social forces declines with development. The institutionalist approach recognizes that the degree of embeddedness has been greater than that acknowledged by the neoclassical theories of the market (Fields, 1995).

III EMERGENCE OF DEVELOPMENT STUDIES

The evidence of the negative consequences of the growth model of development in the 1960s alerted researchers to the importance of non-economic factors. In recent years recognition of the interrelationships of social relations and the economy has led to interesting developments in the discipline. It was realized then that policies to achieve growth were not to be equated with development. A new phase in thinking from growth to development has changed the emphasis from GNP to basic needs like education, health and housing, and this shift in the focus of TW development from growth to development has necessitated an interdisciplinary approach. The process of becoming interdisciplinary has involved a constant debate between different schools, the liberal or neoclassical, the statist and the dependency, resulting in innumerable studies (Smith, 1984–85, Bartlett, 1996).

This study recognizes the growing divergence in development performance between TW countries as an outcome of institutional, historical, cultural and political factors, resulting from the adoption of different policies. Such divergence between East Asian, South Asian, Latin American and Sub-Saharan African countries, when observed by analysts in the 1970s and 1980s, reactivated the debate between different schools in development studies and raised the need to examine the underlying reasons for such variation.

It thus became inevitable for different social science disciplines to use their distinctive perspectives to understand the various aspects of TW development such as the economy, the polity, history, religion and culture within a unified framework. However while retaining that distinctive perspective, there is also the need to co-operate with other disciplines, so as to provide a more comprehensive or complete perspective. Thus:

> whatever the attraction, rhetorically of interdisciplinary studies in the United States, the various fields of the social sciences jealously insisted on their autonomy, on an identity based on a body of theoretical propositions over whose integrity they stood guard. In this context, development studies represented virgin territory, not only for the unification of the social sciences, but more immediately for the carving out of new, discrete domains of analysis (Smith, 1984–85, 540).

This failure to bring about a truly unified social science approach to the study of the TW caused much disillusion, particularly at a time when the TW was faced with acute problems.

Disillusion with the early work of developmentalists led to the emergence of the 'dependency school'. The dependency school viewed the problems of the TW as a product of the international division of labour. According to this view, private investment through multinationals creates a dual economy within TW countries, a modern sector responding to international demands and a subsistence sector linked to the past (Smith, 1984–85, 546). The problems faced by the TW are caused by the international division of labour, dating back to colonial days, and cannot be attributed solely to lack of resources, skills or capability. This line of analysis adopted by the dependency school was reinforced by the predominantly American interest in development, the cold war, continued dependence of the TW on western capital and western markets for export of primary goods and the rapid growth of authoritarian regimes in Latin America and Africa. The impact of the dependency school on development studies in the mid-1980s is summed up thus:

> The dependency perspective is not only coherent and complex, but it is capable of conceptual self-criticism and development. In the wake of the demise of developmentalism, it offers an alternative paradigm of study. The fact that it has not only survived sharp internal dispute, but it has actually grown in conceptual acuteness as a result, is the most conclusive evidence that as a school of thought dependency approach has come of age (Smith, 1984–85, 550).

While largely confined to the Latin American academic scene, the influence of the dependency school has dissipated with globalization, the end of the cold war and the democratization of TW regimes.

IV   THE PLAN OF THE STUDY

By adopting a broad-based perspective, this study in the political economy of development compares the economic miracle of East Asia with the political miracle of South Asia. If some academics and political leaders advocate that political development must be preceded by economic development offering East Asia as a model, this study looks at South Asia where some countries have attempted both political and economic development in tandem. In comparing the two models, it is not our purpose to offer value judgements on which of the two is better. That depends on each country's priorities. What is important, however, is to recognize that they are different paths to development involving different processes and that they offer different lessons for adoption.

The study is an interpretive analysis of divergent approaches to understanding TW development, covering a period of four decades. It is a comparative study of East and South Asia, with emphasis on South Korea and Taiwan in the former and India in the latter. The focus is on the choice of development policies and their implementation, using both primary and secondary sources, and is interdisciplinary in nature.

The study spans eleven chapters (including Chapter 1) and can be grouped into three parts. Part One covers four chapters. Chapter 2 examines the problems and constraints faced by TW countries. The chapter poses the magnitude of the problems, the range of expectations created and the lack of resources and capability to cope with the problems. The facts clearly expose the naïvety of policy-makers, academics and donor countries.

Chapter 3 is a broad overview which poses the issue of 'why development?'. The objective of catching up with the industrial world suggests an element of imitation influenced largely by the then fashionable growth model in development economics. The outcome of those early efforts was some growth with serious social consequences, leading to a redefinition of development. The chapter reviews the different schools and their contributions to the field of development studies.

Chapter 4 analyses the debate on the state versus the market as alternative explanations for the success of East Asian economies. The debate naturally focuses on revisionists who distinguish effective from ineffective state intervention and advocate guided development in which both state and market play a complementary role. It emerges as the central theme, particularly in the context of donor-dictated structural adjustment policies.

Chapter 5 follows the same theme with specific focus on both East Asia and South Asia as alternative models. In this chapter I examine a variety of other explanations for relative performance of the two regions. In moving to a broader frame of reference I examine the historical experience and the importance of political development, an aspect insufficiently studied in the analysis of East Asian economies. This opens an unresolved debate on the relationship between democracy and development.

Part Two of the study, which consists of two chapters, covers the area of development policy and management. Chapter 6 discusses the process of developing policies and their implementation. It highlights the significance of different political systems and their ability to arrive at policies and implement them. It adopts the concept of implementation analysis so as to anticipate the likely problems of implementation. This aspect is emphasized because of the nature of TW political and administrative systems where limited political input goes into the policy-making process with opposition emerging at the implementation stage.

Chapter 7 is a review of various approaches to the development of capability for administering development. Here it is important to note the underlying conflict between administration of law and order from that of administering development programmes. In the context of colonial inheritance, TW bureaucracy, particularly in South Asia, is more attuned to the former role and less concerned with the latter. The continuance of the law and order orientation precludes the emergence of the other orientation (i.e. development). The chapter also reviews the various strategies to develop such capability.

Part Three of the study, which includes three chapters, delves into different areas of development like policies of technology development and industrialization, strategy on public enterprises, agriculture and rural development. Chapter 8 analyses various industrial development strategies, ranging from export substitution and import substitution to basic industry.

Chapter 9 discusses the role of public enterprises in the process of industrial and economic development. It is viewed in the context of a limited private sector, with state entrepreneurship seen as a vehicle for creating markets in the early stages of development. In the context of structural adjustment I also discuss the prospects for divestment in the TW.

Chapter 10 discusses the problems of agriculture and rural development in the context of their significance to TW development. The significance relates, first, to its importance in terms of numbers of people dependent on agriculture, and, second, to its position as an area where the social structure plays a major role in people's attitudes and values to programmes of development. The two areas that receive particular attention are (1) the green revolution and (2) land reform. The success or failure of the latter will have a bearing on the direction of future development in both East and South Asia. Rural development involves policies aimed at generating non-agricultural incomes through state-initiated rural development programmes. Here I reiterate the importance of adopting a distinct rural development strategy to suit the type of problems and the social structure.

The final chapter sums up the study.

2 Development: Problems and Constraints

I INTRODUCTION

The emergence from colonialism to independence after World War II of several Asian, African and Latin American countries drew the attention of academics and policy-makers to significant gaps in the knowledge and understanding of these countries and led to a concerted effort to study them, their economy, polity, society and culture. Such studies revealed the chasm between them and other countries that, over a period of time, had exploited opportunities and resources and moved ahead in the economic and political spheres, achieving a developed status. The measures adopted for comparison were economic indicators like gross national product or equivalent levels of growth, level of political development, technology and modernization of society. Assuming a desire on the part of the newly independent countries to aspire to that 'developed' status, such studies focused on possible paths to guide these countries towards that goal.

While the industrialized countries have had a head start, having reached their current level of development through a gradual process of accumulation, the less industrialized who aspire to imitate their forerunners have had to force that process of economic and social change. A significant contributor to that process in the FW was the market, by which I mean the underlying interaction between consuming households, productive enterprises, credit institutions and the government (Arndt, 1988, Jagannathan, 1987). Such an institution has had to be created in the TW by the state. Even so, obstacles exist between the essential institutions of the market, preventing the free flow of information and serving in the long run to distort the market. That is, TW countries operate in what is called a 'dual economy', where there is both an organized and an unorganized sector. Efforts to create a market are hampered by lack of resources like capital, skills, organization and entrepreneurial ability.

It was assumed that TW countries would overcome their backwardness through appropriate policies aimed at encouraging mobilization of savings and investment and promoting industrialization through the provision of capital, machinery and technical skills. Encouraged by the success of the Marshall Plan in rebuilding the war-torn economies of

Europe, advocates of such a strategy overlooked the existence of very basic differences between the two sets of countries. Europe's long history of industrialization and developed skills required capital only to rebuild. By contrast, the TW in large measure has not actually moved from traditional subsistence agriculture. The absence of skills therefore meant that capital investment on the lines of the Marshall Plan was unlikely to produce the same result as in Europe and Japan. Besides, the strategy adopted was not appropriate to the resources, skills, capabilities and needs of TW countries, and this became evident during the mid-1970s.

Having briefly introduced the subject of this study, I intend in this chapter to examine the process by which TW countries have developed policies and strategies to promote development. The chapter is divided into five sections. Section II discusses the historical background to the understanding of TW problems; section III examines why TW governments adopted the policies at a certain point in time i.e. having emerged from colonialism following World War II. Section IV is a critique of state intervention which traces the shift in development policies from state intervention to more market-oriented liberalization sponsored by international lending agencies. The final section is a conclusion.

II   HISTORICAL BACKGROUND

The countries categorized as TW happen, with some exceptions, to have experienced colonialism of one type or another and gained independence since World War II. Generally described as traditional – because their attitudes and values have been and continue to be influenced by religion, ethnicity, tribal and familial relationships, which together impact on their general view of life and its environment (Foster, 1973, Darling, 1979) – such economies, being predominantly agricultural, rely on the export of primary produce. Thus, the historical, social, economic and cultural influences on these countries are quite distinct from the influence of the industrialized world which has gradually developed from a traditional to a modern technological society.

Excessive population with limited resources in most TW countries leads to problems like unemployment, urban drift arising from limited opportunities in agriculture and related occupations, and insatiable demands for primary and secondary education, housing, transport and health. When faced with similar problems, the FW overcame them through increased agricultural production, the industrial revolution, and, most important of all, exploration to meet the demand for resources

(Brockway, 1996). This desire for exploration gradually led to the colonization of countries across the globe, a trend which appears to have ceased only recently.

The growing gap between the industrialized (First World) and the less industrialized (Third World) is evident fom the comparative data. For example, the ratio of per capita income between FW and TW is 1:10 (i.e. $ 800 to $ 8000). When the data are further disaggregated, one out of every five in the TW earns below $200. In the richest of the FW countries, per capita income is 50 times that of the poorest TW countries. With higher per capita incomes, the expenditure in FW on education and health is 100 times and 150 times that of TW countries respectively. Average life expectancy is 22 years more than TW countries. A comparison of the occupational composition of population reveals that the percentage employed in agriculture in TW countries is 64 while in the FW it is just 10. One third of the TW population, estimated at 800 million, lives in poverty. An estimated 870 million are illiterate and 500 million are unemployed or underemployed. Statistics for children are equally disconcerting: 130 million children are unable to attend school, 450 million children suffer from malnutrition, 12 million children die before the age of one and 250 million live in slums or lack real shelter (Dube, 1984).

Such acute conditions of poverty can only be confronted by major population control programmes and significant increases in food production. Notwithstanding the acuteness of problems faced by TW countries, the policies to overcome them have had considerable success. Life expectancy for TW countries has increased from 35 years in 1950 to 56 years in 1994. The per capita caloric supplies increased from 1,940 during 1961–63 to 2,473 during 1988–90, an increase of 27 per cent, which is a remarkable achievement in less than three decades. 'The absolute increase exceeded that for all of previous history. This was achieved while population grew far more rapidly than it ever did in the developed countries' (Johnson, 1997, 8).While economic growth in the TW in general has been higher than that of the FW in the last 30 years, such growth has unfortunately been eroded by population increases caused by increasing birth rates and declining death rates in TW (Sundrum, 1983).

Basing its view on past experience, the United Nations Development Programme (UNDP) is confident of banishing poverty in the world by the early 21st century. The basis for this is that developing countries have halved child death rates since 1960, reduced malnutrition by one third, and raised school enrolment by a quarter (*The Hindu*, January 13, 1997). While these figures are encouraging, after four decades of development the gap between the rich and poor countries is glaring.

The world distribution of wealth shows that 20 percent of the world population owned 82.7 per cent of the world gross product, had 81.2 per cent of world trade, 94.6 of commercial loans, 80.6 of domestic savings and 80.5 of world investment. Very little left for the remaining 80 per cent of the planet's population. The tendency too was quite alarming, because the disparity between the income of the richest 20 per cent and the poorest 20 per cent doubled between 1960 and 1990 (Kilksberg, 1994, 184)

A striking aspect of the early outcome of development policies is the uneven result between TW countries. The differential performance has led to a recategorization from FW and TW into several different categories. The World Bank now adopts a different set of categories accepted as more realistic to distinguish between TW countries. The new system incorporates the use of GNP per capita as a basis to differentiate between countries: low-income ($635 or less), lower middle-income ($ 2,555 or less), upper middle-income ($7,911 or less), and high-income economies (over $ 7,911). According to this system, countries once grouped as TW are now differentiated across a wide range. While some East Asian economies are listed as high-performing economies, a large number of South East Asian and South Asian economies are spread across both middle- and low-income economies (World Bank, 1993).

To adequately appreciate the situation described above, it must be viewed in the historical context of European exploration, colonization and subsequent independence. European exploration in the fifteenth century in search of spices and silk led to encounters with many more hitherto unknown commodities. Their introduction into Europe and the resulting demand for them fuelled further exploration and, eventually, colonization. In particular, it became necessary to produce in greater quantities a variety of crops such as cotton, sugar cane, tobacco, tea, coffee, cocoa, opium and indigo which could not be grown in the temperate climate of Europe (Brockway, 1996, Havinden and Meredith, 1995, Biswas, 1984). These plantation crops were then introduced and produced in countries in which agriculture had, until then, been primarily for subsistence. A shift in agriculture from traditional to commercial crops was possible only through some control over these countries. Colonization enabled the colonizers to link the agricultural crops grown in these colonies with industrial production back home. Effective production involved the importation of skills and thus the new systems inevitably led to the disintegration of indigenous skills and the gradual destruction of the link between local agriculture and social structure (Sundrum, 1983,

52–59).The term 'monoculture' or 'monoeconomy' symbolises that process whereby a country's entire resource is linked to an external economy. That outcome is termed 'dependency' by some developmentalists and can take various forms. Irrespective of the intentions of the colonizers, which incidentally differed from the British to the Dutch and from the French to the Portuguese (Panickar, 1953), the ultimate outcome was the creation of the distinction between industrialized economies and agricultural economies, and between FW countries and TW countries.

As people from temperate regions sought tropical areas to grow certain types of food crops, so climate also must be considered an important factor in understanding development. For countries dependent on agriculture climate plays a critical role (Biswas, 1984, Ram, 1997). The distance of a country from the equator is used as a physical measure of the infrastructure and as the strongest predictor in long-term economic success (Hall and Jones, 1997, 176, Ram, 1997). A country's geographical location is considered important for achieving development. TW countries are identified as tropical, are predominantly agricultural, their soils are poor in organic material and they are more likely to be exposed to floods and drought. Because of the unpredictability of the weather, people are reluctant to take risks, tend to suffer from poor health due to endemic diseases and lack enthusiasm to work hard. Perceiving their life as governed by chance, they tend to become fatalistic, developing an 'image of limited good' (Foster, 1973 see Chapter 9).

What significance does religion assume in this study of TW economies? Much as one would like to avoid traversing this area, it cannot however be overlooked, particularly with the extensive literature beginning with Max Weber's *The Protestant Ethic* and the more recent discussion on Confucianism and its probable influence on NIEs. Christianity, the predominant religion of the FW, is practised in a private capacity and thereby contributes to individualism. By contrast non-Christian religions, being more communal in character, do not draw clear distinctions between religion and society and religion and state. This effectively retards the process of creating an environment which is fundamental to the development of individualism, freedom, capitalism and market and which could contribute to growth and development (Sundrum, 1983).

Development, according to Sundrum (1983), is the process of developing the economic human being and is reflected in the growth of the market and the development of capitalism in industrialized economies. Therefore the challenge for TW countries is to free individuals from social barriers which confine them to predetermined or particular economic roles in society. A typical example is the caste system which checked social mobility and change by assigning specific economic roles to certain castes.

'India's notion of "otherworldiness" with little concern for material goods; her philosophical contemplation of the abstract as the highest ideal to be achieved through renunciation of the material world and the existence of caste as a social and economic feature of society have contributed to the western perception that here is a country with a culture and people distinct from the west' (Subrahmanyam, 1996, 22–23). Having made the comment, Subrahmanyam cites Myrdal's (1968) observation that:

> The failure of India to escape the quicksands of tradition and endemic poverty could be largely attributed to two factors: on the one hand, social institutions, notably caste, which ensured that change and social mobility were kept in check, on the other, the fact that the Indian state lacked the degree of autonomy and agency required to impose change on society. This latter part of the formulation led to the well-known slogan of the 'soft-state' with its ambiguous political overtones (23–24).

The emergence of entrepreneurial behaviour is linked to periods of historical change which bring about a change in social values. An example of this is the decline in authoritarianism with the overthrow of feudal lords in the Tokugawa regime in Japan, thus bringing about change in societal values (Tabb, 1995, 65–68). In countries which have not experienced such social upheaval the perpetuation of the authoritarian personality influences child rearing practices and constricts innovative or entrepreneurial behaviour (Hagen, 1966). Traditional societies need to experiment with new ideas and new techniques of production. The economic growth of the FW after the industrial revolution is a direct result of such maximizing behaviour of the economic human being. Policymakers in the TW working on a much-needed strategy of development which focuses on changing the socio-economic and political behaviour of people have met with relative success.

III   STATE INTERVENTION: CONTEXT OR TIMING

In the absence of the private sector that could provide the entrepreneurial skills and capital, state intervention remained the only option for achieving development in the TW. Its proponents realized that the FW, then facing a major post-war recession, had found the market mechanism incapable of assisting in its economic recovery. Influenced by their imminent emergence from colonialism, the obvious alternative model appeared to be the planned economy of the Soviet Union (the Second World). The success of the Soviet Union as an ally of the west in World War II, followed by achievements in industry and technology, instilled confidence in the TW's attempts at state intervention. This assessment by TW policy elites and their advisers (who were generally products of European universities) was encouraged by Keynesian economics as intellectual support for the adoption of state intervention (Arndt, 1987, 57–58).

While the historical context offers an explanation for the adoption of state intervention by TW governments, they were probably encouraged by an administrative system inherited from colonial governments. As already stated, state intervention was the only option in economies which lacked any semblance of a market. In addition to this lacuna, TW countries lacked basic economic infrastructure like transport, communications and education, the development of which was perceived to be a responsibility of government. According to Arndt (1988) market forces are too slow to meet the needs of TW countries as their problems demand rapid economic change. Other important reasons offered by Arndt (1988) for state intervention are the achievement of a desirable distribution of income, protection of the environment, protection of the traditional culture and other aspects relating to the quality of life.

It is important to recognize market variations that exist between and within TW countries (Jagannathan, 1987). Solomon (1995) analyses TW markets into five categories: the market for personal services, the market for perishable produce, the market for agricultural staples, the market for manufactured consumer goods and lastly the capital goods market. Of these, Solomon regards both the consumer goods market and the capital goods market as having some resemblance to the organized sector in FW economies. While the consumer goods market suffers less from market fluctuations and more from the uncertainties of government intervention, which 'takes the form of spasmodic and inconsistent sallies into various sectors of the economy', the capital goods market is the least developed. It is also largely state-dominated and has an element of foreign capital imports which are constantly threatened by pressures of economic nationalism and political uncertainties (Solomon, 1995, 92–93).

While such variations in the development of markets exist, policymakers cannot overlook the consequences of what the dependency school refers to as the dual economy – i.e. the simultaneous existence of both modern and a subsistence economy (Smith, 1984–85). While these consequences have to be anticipated, policy-makers need to recognize a variety of options that are available for utilizing informal markets in the development process, also called social assets or social capital (Jagannathan, 1987, Evans, 1996). The growing emphasis on markets and the ideological thrust of the 1980s has concerned moral economists. Historically, the TW economy has been characterized as dual or subsistence economy where mutual relations are based on reciprocity. According to the moral economists, any extension of the market while enhancing, opportunity contains the prospect of upsetting the socio-economic structure of the village economy (Booth, 1994)

The adoption by TW governments of state intervention to cope with problems has to be viewed in the context of the past and current role of the state in the FW. Although markets are credited with contributing to the current state of industrialized capitalist economies, there is no doubt that the state has contributed in great measure in the past and continues to contribute to that development. That role of the state is essential in the early stages of development but that role understandably undergoes change in later stages of capitalist development. How significant that changed role is to economic development remains a question of interpretation (Brusser-Pereira, 1994).

The state's active role in economic development has led policy elites to place undue emphasis on growth with the aim of catching up with industrialized economies and reducing the economic divisions between rich and poor countries. Contrary to expectations the existing socio-economic structure of TW countries has turned into a fertile breeding-ground for growing inequality fuelled by policies for economic growth without distribution adopted by the new regimes. The social consequences of growth through industrialization are neglect of the countryside, which is the dominant sector of these economies, resulting in rural unemployment and urban migration straining existing services like housing, sanitation, education, transport and health.

A question that comes to mind is: would these problems caused by the first phase of economic development have occurred if an alternative path to development been adopted? By this I mean an economic strategy more appropriate to the needs and capabilities of TW countries. What is not clear is whether the objectives sought were the cause of the social consequences of growth or whether the process adopted for achieving growth was faulty.

India, one of the earliest to gain independence, adopted planning to promote industrialization and soon became a role model for other emerging countries (Grindle and Thomas, 1989). Much emphasis was placed on planning and investment in basic industry and the establishment of public enterprises. However, insufficient consideration was given to organizational and administrative capability as such an active role for the state in industrialization would have necessitated extensive human and institutional resources, as well as extensive mobilization of financial resources.

In adopting such a strategy TW countries which had achieved independence from colonialism sought to protect that independence by seeking to become more self-reliant. Pursuit of such economic independence led governments to adopt import substitution. The adoption of an import substitution industrial strategy involved investment in basic and heavy industry, leading these governments to overlook agriculture and labour intensive industries which, according to economists, should have been the natural focus for TW economies (Oshima, 1987).

India faltered on that path because of a bureaucracy supported by politicians and business resulting in rent seeking (Bhagwati, 1990; Raj, 1973; Myrdal, 1968). In what became a restrictive regime of bureaucratic controls, a certain type of business entrepreneur thrived, with an outcome quite contrary to that seen in Taiwan and South Korea (Amsden, 1989, Fields, 1995, Wade, 1990). Acclaimed for the appropriateness of their policies of state intervention, their achievements have nevertheless come at the cost of democracy.

Faced by the greater inequalities and increased poverty without development caused by the policies of growth, TW governments started to re-examine their development strategies. Concern arising from outcomes of the growth strategy prompted policy-makers to emphasize basic needs, such as housing, health, education, sanitation and drinking water. TW governments realized the need to establish a minimum standard of living for all. Viewed by some TW countries as a retrograde step from their ambitions of catching up through modernization, this shift to basic needs was a departure from the growth model and found to be irksome, coming as it did from western sources (Arndt, 1987) (see Chapter 3 for a different perspective).

IV   A CRITIQUE OF STATE INTERVENTION

In its first two phases, development policy dominated by the state emphasised growth and basic needs. Critics question state intervention on the grounds that government was the problem rather than the solution.

Blame for the current state of TW economies has been attributed by them to the policies of state intervention. In their view these have resulted in high levels of debt, poor economic performance, high levels of inflation, excessive unemployment and inefficient public enterprises. An alternative suggested is its replacement by the market, based on the micro-analytical maximizing framework and modern macro-economic and trade models (Fishlow, 1991). This represents a shift from the closed import substitution to a more open export-oriented economy based on the success of countries like South Korea and Taiwan. As the justification for this shift in policy is arguable, I think there is a need to bring a balance to the debate on the virtues of the market and the weaknesses of state intervention.

The apparent swing in the profession from the whole-hearted espousal of extensive government intervention to its rubbishing seems to be an example of unbalanced intellectual growth, although perhaps development economics is no more subject to this kind of fluctuation than other parts of the subject. There are problems and virtues of both state intervention and the free market. The problem should not be viewed as one of simple choice. There is no doubt, however, that whether one sees a very large or very small role for the market depends on how one judges the seriousness of the problems with markets and planning which we have been describing. In my judgement the problems of the market are particularly severe (relative to those of state intervention) in the areas of health, infrastructure (roads, communications, power, water and so on), education and social security. Those of planning appear most sharply when the government gets heavily involved in production activities outside the infrastructure (Stern, 1989, 621–622).

Advocates of the minimalist state support greater reliance on markets based on evidence of inadequate design and implementation of government intervention. They do this:

by invoking an implicit and sometimes explicit institutional setting where enforcement of public decisions is often so costly or problematic as to be infeasible

where interest group organisations diffuse benefits and create inefficiencies through rent seeking

where bureaucratic structuring leads to abdication of national interest in favour of sectoral advantage (Fishlow, 1991, 1735).

Neo-liberalism based on the broad strategies advocated and referred to as the 'Washington Consensus' (Williamson, 1995) fails to recognize that the shortcomings of the TW have been caused to some extent by inappropriate policies largely prescribed by policy-makers who lacked necessary skills, by the existence of political instability, the lack of administrative capability, excessive investment on armaments, and the problems caused by the two oil crises. While all these factors contributed to the state of affairs, the underlying determinants for differences in the levels of economic performance rest with institutions and government policies. Hall and Jones (1997) state: 'Our hypothesis is that an important part of the explanation lies in the economic environment in which individuals produce, transact, invent, and accumulate skills. The infrastructure of an economy is the collection of laws, institutions, and government policies that make up the economic environment. A successful infrastructure encourages production. A perverse infrastructure discourages production in ways that are detrimental to economic performance' (174). 'Countries that have successfully developed the infrastructure that favour production over diversion have typically done so through effective government' (Hall and Jones, 1997, 175). Too many bureaucratic restrictions and too few incentives have, according to Bhagwati, (1988) created a culture of controls. Diversion in the form of rent seeking becomes the natural response in what is regarded as an unfavourable environment encouraged by a 'soft state' (Myrdal, 1968).

The performance of TW governments has to be judged on (a) their capacity to exercise authority over citizens through the machinery of government and (2) their capacity to extract support in the form of resources within society to achieve national objectives. The exercise of authority and the willingness of citizens to support it depends on the overall performance of government, which, in turn, is reflected in the state of the economy. 'What destabilises regimes are economic crises, and democracies, particularly poor democracies, are extremely vulnerable to bad economic performance' (Przeworski and Limongi, 1997, 169). TW governments have had to expend excessive resources to exercise authority when their legitimacy has been questioned. When legitimacy of governments is questioned, governments tend to adopt policies to win over powerful segments, and that might mean a reluctance to adopt unpopular tax measures to meet the costs of such policies, ultimately leading to bankruptcy and indebtedness (Snider 1990, Raj, 1973).

The reason for the dramatic shift from state intervention to market-oriented policies in recent years can be explained on the grounds of political or economic crisis (perhaps international indebtedness) or pressure from external forces influenced by the economic performance of NIEs. Their success has been used to promote economic liberalization across the TW overlooking the historical and other factors which have been instrumental (Discussed in Chapters 4 and 8). Factors that have been overlooked include the cultural ethic of a region influenced by Confucianism, the impact of Japanese colonialism, access to special treatment during the cold war period and finally the agrarian transformation that laid the foundation for late industrialization. Those who attribute success to policies of open trade and competitive markets (and recommend it to others) have overlooked the above factors, as well as the significant role of effective state intervention in that process (Amsden, 1989, Wade, 1990).

In their adoption of such a narrow focus to explain the extraordinary performance of East Asian countries, the neoclassical economists appear to have ignored the political economy of development. Increased reliance on the market is described as structural adjustment. Relevant questions raised by academics are: Why have such structural adjustment policies been undertaken? Why has this occurred only in the last decade? Why are these policies being pursued extensively in so many developing countries? (Bierstakes, 1994, 10).

The shift from state intervention to market liberalism has led some critics to question the continued relevance of Development Economics. Sen (1983) does not see the emergence of economic liberalism and the resulting structural adjustment as an indictment of Development Economics. He states:

> Development Economics was born at a time when government involvement in deliberately fostering economic growth in general, and industrialization in particular, was very rare, and when the typical rates of capital accumulation were quite low. That situation has changed in many respects and, while that may suggest the need to emphasize different issues, it does not in any way invalidate the wisdom of the strategies then suggested (Sen, 1984, 404).

Having defended the contribution of Development Economics to the understanding of development problems, Sen then states:

> Perhaps the most important thematic deficiency of traditional development economics is its concentration on national product, aggregate income and total supply of particular goods rather than on 'entitlements' of people and the capabilities these entitlements generate. Ultimately, the process of economic development has to be concerned

with what people can or cannot do…, it has to do in Marx's words, with 'replacing the domination of circumstances and chance over individuals by the domination of individuals over chance and circumstances (1984, 497).

Sen (1984) and Goulet (1992) emphasise that development has to do with 'qualitative improvement in any society's provision of life sustaining goods, esteem, and freedom to all its citizens'. The counter-movement urges the need for alternative values which include the primacy of basic needs, elimination of poverty over more growth, reduction of dependency, protection of the environment, respect for individual rights, local culture and local communities. In assessing the achievements, the balance sheet shows both gains and losses. The gains are better living standards in terms of food, shelter and jobs, greater technological progress, greater differentiation through specialization and increased freedom of choice, greater tolerance and diversity and global interdependence. The losses are excessive desire for material goods, disruption to local culture and values, increasing debt, growing social alienation, and increased pressure on existing resources (Goulet, 1992).

V CONCLUSION

In reviewing the problems and constraints of TW economies and the strategy of state intervention to combat them, this chapter provides a background to what is to follow in this study. In the course of four or five decades we have observed the significant changes that TW countries have undergone from growth to development, and from development based on state intervention to market liberalism. This process has resulted in varying outcomes extraordinary in the case of East Asia, reasonable in the case of South Asia and dismal in the case of sub-Saharan Africa.

Such wide ranging divergence raises fundamental questions on categorizing countries into developed (FW) and underdeveloped (TW). Categorization such as this assumes a unidirectional progression on the lines of the development of western liberal democracies. Furthermore, such academic analysis fails to recognize that these countries have emerged from different historical experiences; that they have inherited different political and administrative institutions; that their material and human resources vary, and that they have been influenced by varying cultures, religions, and physical circumstances that have had a significant bearing on their development outcomes.

3 Development: Changing Objectives

I INTRODUCTION

Excessive emphasis on growth in the 1950s and 1960s in the TW resulted in unintended social and economic consequences and to eventual misgivings about the direction being taken by development. Realization of the limited success of development after two decades of active state intervention led to serious examination of fundamental objectives. By the early 1970s increasing evidence of the failure of this narrow economic approach had become a cause for concern among governments in the TW, leading to much debate.

We find two varying responses to this situation. The first was to enlarge the concept of development and adopt a broad-based multi-dimensional view incorporating economic, political, cultural, environmental and social objectives (Goulet, 1992, 468, Sen, 1984). This approach would, it was felt, emphasize values like freedom and equality and provide fundamental basic needs like education, housing and health with economic growth. The second was to narrow the focus by adopting market-oriented policies, supposedly adopted with success by the NIEs. Either response necessitated a re-examination of development objectives on the part of governments.

This chapter examines those issues. In section II, I discuss the importance of adopting an interdisciplinary approach to development studies. Section III discusses the concept of quality of life and well-being as development objectives as an answer to the growth strategy of the early period. In section IV the compatibility between traditional societies and modernisation is raised. In section V, I argue for political development as an important objective, thus critiquing the authoritarian models of East Asian development. Section VI sums the chapter with a conclusion.

II THE NEED FOR A DIFFERENT APPROACH

The marked shift in development objectives in the 1970s demanded an interdisciplinary problem-oriented perspective and led to the emergence of Development Studies as an academic pursuit (Smith, 1984–85). While recognizing that problems facing TW countries are multi-dimensional, the interdisciplinary approach to TW development assumes an understanding of relevant information, knowledge and methodology from different disciplines. The term 'interdisciplinary' suggests that the use of concepts or a methodology from various disciplines can bring about greater variation in the application of concepts. It implies an approach where two or more disciplines integrate through cross-fertilization of ideas and may involve considerable overlap in areas like culture and religion. Further methodologies and concepts of several disciplines may be combined to understand problems and help solve them (Streeton, 1975). However, early efforts in development studies attracted criticism for their 'inability to articulate a unified model of comparative political economy . . . lacking any broad-based comparative historical perspective into which problems of mid-20th century development could be placed' (Smith, 1984–85, 540).

Research on TW countries has until now failed to recognize the significant influences of history, culture and religion over traditional societies (Bartlett, 1996). For TW countries in search of a future vision of society, culture 'is a social legacy the individual acquires in a group, a storehouse of pooled learning, a set of techniques for adjusting both to the external environment and to others . . . then we move to the heart of why economics as it is practised cannot adequately explain economic development' (Tabb, 1995, 23). It is therefore important to adopt an interdisciplinary view of development and a new focus for development studies.

The evolving field of Development Studies heralds an awareness among social scientists that the problems faced by TW countries are not likely to be solved by adopting the experience of the FW. That assumption rests on the recognition that the economies of developing countries, their societies and culture are basically influenced by human attitudes, behavioural patterns, a sense of values and morals which differ from the developed world. The differing response of TW societies to economic, political and social problems has led to them being characterized as traditional. Originating from the need to adopt a different approach, what this subject really demands is a distinctive discipline (Streeton, 1975). If one accepts that human behaviour and attitudes are a product of the environment, then central to this approach to development is the need to develop the capability of TW societies to change from a situation of being dominated by chance and circumstance to the position of being able to shape one's physical, social and economic environment (Sen, 1984). Essentially, the suggestion that development depends on the capability to respond to environmental pressures and challenges is an acknowledgement that each society is a product of its environment. One's skills and one's capacities can only be viewed in terms of one's environment. The coastal fishing village, the rain forest regions, the mountainous terrain, and the deserts are all different and demand different skills. Such skills have been evolved by local people over the centuries. The process of development is the achievement of that capacity to use the resources and skills already available in that environment, i.e. the capacity to solve problems. However, in development policy terms, development is the creation of conditions in which people can live longer, be better nourished, acquire literacy and numeracy skills and be better housed, all of which are termed 'entitlements' by Sen (1984). When these conditions are available individuals within a society can be encouraged to develop capabilities in order to achieve these entitlements.

A society or country is distinguished from another by the relative entitlements and capabilities that exist within it to manipulate the environment. Instead of seeking the universal goal of growth, the development strategist focuses on relative capacities that recognize diversity.

Growing acceptance of the shift in emphasis from economic growth to quality of life or human wellbeing (Das Gupta, 1988, Goulet, 1992, Sen 1984, Dreeze and Sen, 1996) has led to the incorporation of the concept into UNDP reports in the form of the Human Development Index (HDI) 'as the enlargement of people's choices. It is an extension, enlargement and deepening of the now somewhat unpopular basic needs approach. Thinking about poverty has evolved from economic growth as the performance criterion to employment, income distribution, the informal sector, and via basic needs to human development' (Streeton, 1995, 25). HDI includes indicators like life expectancy, adult literacy, years of schooling, etc. Commenting on the UNDP Human Development Report (1996), Reddy writes

A rapid expansion of the economy seems to be the sole objective of modern societies. But economic growth, high incomes and the commodities that high incomes can buy are not ends in themselves. What matters for people – and how the standard of living should be judged – is the freedom they have to lead the lives they value. Their freedom of choice is indicated by the 'capabilities' they enjoy – in the form of good health, knowledge and the ability to participate in community life (*The Hindu Magazine*, Madras, August 25, 1996, 1).

A new indicator, introduced by the UNDP, is the Human Deprivation Measure (HDM) which goes beyond the general perception of poverty. Once measured in terms of earnings below what is required for minimum subsistence, the concept has changed over the years to include access to health, education and housing. According to this, health deprivation is measured by access to safe drinking water and the weight of children under the age of five. Education deprivation is measured by adult literacy and the opportunity for children to attend school. By these standards over 500 million in South Asia suffer from deprivation in health and education (*The Hindu*, May 12, 1997). (See Table III-1).

The emphasis now placed on quality of life (Lane, 1996) is attributable to disillusionment with the consequences of growth like increased poverty, growing inequality and the concern for distributive justice. According to Qizilbash (1996) these are issues of 'ethical development'. Attainment of these new measures, however, seems a distant goal for many TW countries. In recent years, technology missions have been set up in India to carry out projects as varied as polio immunization, the provision of clean drinking water through the installation of tube wells, increased milk production and improved basic communication. The initial success of such missions offers hope, despite the enormity of human deprivation in South Asia.

Another encouraging trend is the movement from an orthodox conception of economic growth to a broader vision of development through the recognition of social capital (i.e. norms and interpersonal networks) within communities. While traditional ties of community were once viewed as an impediment to modernization, these, now termed social capital, are seen as a valuable economic asset (Evans, 1996).

When one has the capacity to choose one's response to challenges from the environment, then discretion enters into the process. Individuals in developed societies are better able to exercise discretion than individuals in less developed societies where such capacities are limited. In broader societal terms, discretion is exercised through the process of organizational differentiation when specialization occurs at different periods of development. Societies where such differentiation has not occurred, i.e. those that lack a specific type of organization to respond to a specific type of societal function, are inherently less capable of solving problems. However, the real differences that persist between the FW and the TW are differences in the quality of national management, i.e. the ability to develop policies and effectively implement them (Discussed in Chapters 6 and 7).

Table III-1   Human Deprivation Measure (HDM) for South Asia

Country	Population (millions)	Health Deprivation Measure		Education Deprivation Measure		Income Deprivation Measure		Human Deprivation Measure (HDM) value	
		%	(total millions)	%	(total millions)	%	(total millions)	%	(total millions)
Bangladesh	115	31	36	73	84	48	55	61	70
India	902	32	288	53	479	25	226	40	361
Pakistan	133	58	77	65	86	34	45	57	76
Sri Lanka	18	44	8	17	3	22	4	31	6
South Asia (average % total)	1,168	35	409	56	652	28	330	44	514

Source: UNDP Human Development in South Asia, 1997.

Mancur Olson (1995) considers the indigenous characteristics of TW countries to be unfavourable to effective large-scale organization. Large-scale organization, he claims, ought to be an essential element of development. Other reasons cited by him as unfavourable for the development of large-scale organisations in TW countries are:

(1) scarcity of capital caused by low rate of savings and antagonism to foreign private capital;
(2) primitive level of technology which tends to encourage small-scale operations and not large-scale production;
(3) low level of per capita income, which tends to favour small-scale enterprises because of the small size of markets;
(4) small markets governed by the cost of transportation and communication in addition to per capita income;
(5) poor transportation and communication which tend to encourage firms to rely on local factors of production. Any extension of production geographically is beset with co-ordination and cost problems.

As a consequence of the above, Mancur Olson (1995) says that one can 'expect the skills, attitudes, and expectations of people in traditional societies derived from and geared to small institutions rather than large ones'. He concludes that:

If the above is true we should expect that the characteristic institutions of traditional societies would be both small and unspecialized. The prevalence of extended families, tribes, clans, manors and communal village organization tentatively suggests that the prediction is correct (1995, 98).

If the underlying characteristics of TW societies are perceived as impediments to development, the target or objective of TW governments should be to overcome these impediments. Overcoming them, however, need not necessarily be dependent on developing large-scale organization. Evidence of the success of industrial districts in countries like Denmark, Sweden, Italy and Germany can serve as encouragement for a co-operative relationship between government and the private sector (Humphrey, 1995). Described as synergy, such co-operation is seen to be emerging in the TW (Evans, 1996).

III   DIRECTION FOR TRADITIONAL SOCIETIES

TW countries are often described as traditional to distinguish them from the modern. This distinction can lead to the traditional being seen as negative and the modern being seen as positive. And when modernization is equated with development, the obvious conclusion is that TW countries need to adopt the modern values of the FW. In striving for this there is an implicit encouragement to imitate the values of that other society. In the early stages of Technical Assistance, experts from industrialized countries unwittingly sought to introduce methods and techniques from their countries into the TW. In doing so, they failed to understand the context or the rationale for the continuation of existing practices. Subsequent research has shown that the utmost caution is necessary when introducing technical and social change, particularly in TW countries where traditional methods are embedded in society, culture, values and religion (Foster, 1973, Fields, 1995).

While social change is an important ingredient of any process of development, such changes have to be selective and have to be built into existing institutions that are favourable to such change. Japan and Turkey are examples of countries which adopted modernization on the strength of their traditional culture and institutions. A creative approach needs to be adopted keeping in mind that 'wherever one wants to go there is no alternative but to start from where one is' (Bhatt, 1977, 50).

The direction for TW development lies not in discarding the traditional in search of the modern but in beginning with existing levels of knowledge and technology. The strategy therefore lies in identifying (a) households, (b) natural resources, (c) traditional skills and traditional technology, and (d) the structural-institutional context. This involves an active search to improve traditional technology and then undertake the creative adaptation of modern technology. Therefore, according to Bhatt (1977), 'the problem of development is the problem of learning; the process of development, of living is the process of learning from mistakes' (Bhatt, 1977, 54).

The initial task faced by those favouring the new development strategy was the rectification of the mistakes of the earlier growth strategy. Current development studies centre around the recognition of the need for greater participation in development through decentralization with reform of political institutions and public services. Agriculture has become a primary focus and is recognized now as an essential component of this strategy with the provision of agricultural support like credit, extension services, irrigation, fertilizer, power, improved seeds, price support and access to assured markets.

In the long run, development which involves internal transformation of societies has to encounter deeply entrenched values and attitudes that, over the centuries, have been obstacles to economic and social change in traditional societies. Similar to the influence of the Protestant ethic on the emergence of entrepreneurial behaviour in the FW, TW societies need to accept and adopt new ways of personal behaviour. 'New ways demand and make new people. Time consciousness must become time discipline, the organisation and character of work, the very relations of person to person, are transformed. These changes do not come easy' (Landes, 1955, 83).

IV THE ESSENTIALITY OF POLITICAL DEVELOPMENT

Leaders of TW countries placed emphasis on early economic growth, which, for various reasons, did not materialize. Under-achievement led to disenchantment and the mobilization of discontent, resulting in civilian and military dictatorships in many countries. Supported by both power blocs, the unfortunate outcome of this was the emphasis on regime security which led to diversion of resources to armaments, neglecting both political and economic development. In 1985, 57 out of 143 TW regimes experienced seizure of power by either military or civilian bureaucracies. Riggs (1992) comments that 'when regimes created by constitutional or legislative design fail to establish and implement relevant public policies effectively, pre-existing socio-cultural systems, notably those based on families, clans and tribes and religious affiliations play a residual role, providing a basis for solidarity and action by peoples who have lost confidence in their own governments' (2). The emergence of such non-democratic regimes cannot however be attributed solely to economic failures. Their emergence at the height of the cold war was partly encouraged by the two power blocs. With the decline of the power of the Soviet Union in the 1980s one observes a renewed emphasis on democratization in the 'New World Order' (Do Chull Shin 1994).

If authoritarianism emerged as a result of economic and political failure of regimes in TW countries, its existence has been instrumental in the success of East Asian economies justifying its continuation. East Asian regimes retain power within a small elite which until recently restricted all forms of democracy, dissallowed the unionization of labour and discouraged any form of political activity which was likely to question the authority of these governments. Combined with such an authoritarian approach, the judicious use of state intervention was instrumental in achieving economic development. Thus regime security and economic growth have assumed priority over political participation and received the endorsement of reputed economists identified with the neo-liberals (Colclough and Manor, 1991, 314). Discussing the success of these economies, *The Economist* asked 'What did these places have in common? One answer: in varying degree, undemocratic government' (August 27, 1994). The early mishaps on the road to freedom and democracy raised another aspect crucial to this analysis. Perpetuated by academics, this debate focuses on the mistaken premise that democracy and economic development cannot be achieved simultaneously. These academics tend to promote the idea that democracy is a consequence of development and therefore the promotion of democratic institutions is futile while large segments of the population remain poor. The argument is based on the premise that equality is a basic precondition for democracy and the absence of such a precondition explains the presence of non-democratic governments in TW countries. Thus there is an essential link between industrial capitalism (markets) and democracy (Lipset 1994). That development process is described by Przeworski and Limongi (1997) as:

Modernization consists of a gradual differentiation and specialisation of social structures that culminates in a separation of political structures from other structures and makes democracy possible. The specific causal chains consists of sequences of industrialization, urbanization, education, communication, mobilization, and political incorporation, among innumerable others: a progressive accumulation of social changes that ready a society to proceed to its culmination, democratization (158).

Therefore, sustained economic growth and prosperity are a precondition for the establishment and development of political democracy. Pourgerami (1995) attempts to dispel the incompatibility thesis by suggesting that political democracy and economic development are mutually reinforcing and can be achieved simultaneously (xiii).

While the debate on the incompatibility of democracy with less developed economies continues, it is necessary to enumerate some of the conditions necessary for democracy to survive in TW countries. These are:

the possession by the state of geographical, constitutional and political legitimacy;

consensus regarding rules of the political game and the democratic process;

restraint on the part of the party in power;

democracy is difficult to sustain in very poor countries;

democracy is difficult to sustain in countries in divided societies, and the difficulty of achieving major social and economic transformation in a democratic society (Leftwich, 1996, 339).

Equality is an important pre-condition for democracy and countries lacking it have suffered with the growth of non-democratic government. Efforts to develop greater equality essentially centre around changing the class structure of society. It is presumed that when the state plays an active role in development the emergence of a broad-based class will automatically weaken the power of state elites, enlarge rights and enhance greater public participation in collective decision making (Lipset, 1994). There is an underlying problem in reconciling freedom with equality; excessive freedom undermines equality, while equality restrains freedom (Lipson, 1995).

The debate as to whether political democracy and economic development are compatible or in conflict has arisen because of what I have earlier referred to as the performance of East Asian economies following their adoption of the strong state as a strategy of development. If the historical development of capitalism required restrictions on the role of the state, that premise has now been tested with the concentration of power in a technocratic elite in East Asia. However, the fact that we have variable economic performance in countries having both authoritarian and democratic regimes suggests that one needs to examine a range of intervening factors like institutional structures, the strategies pursued, and the influence of history, culture and religion (Sirowy and Inkeles, 1993; Lipset, 1994).

If a comparison of the two Asias, East and South, reveals a distinct pattern of development brought about by the adoption of state intervention, it becomes necessary to examine the historical evolution of political democracy and its meaning. In commenting on the historical evolution of democracy, Barrington Moore Jr (1966) cites India as a typical example.

That India belongs to two worlds is a familiar platitude that happens to be true. Economically it remains in the pre-industrial age. It has had no industrial revolution in either of the two capitalist variants discussed so far, nor according to the communist one. There has been no bourgeois revolution, no conservative revolution from above, no peasant revolution. But as a political species it does belong to modern world... There is a paradox here but only a superficial one. Political democracy may seem strange in both an Asian setting and one without an industrial revolution until one realizes that the appalling problems facing the Indian government are due to these very facts (314).

Varshney's (1995) answer to this paradox or the Indian enigma relating to democracy and rural poor is: 'Independent India was born agrarian as well as democratic. Democracy preceding an industrial revolution... has led to the empowerment of the rural sector in the polity' (3).

That Indian democracy has evinced such interest in academic circles is no surprise. Among the more recent to evince interest is Lijphart (1996) who offers a consociational interpretation for the Indian paradox, i.e. power sharing. According to Lijphart (1996), the four conditions of power sharing are (1) grand coalition, (2) cultural autonomy for groups, (3) proportionality in representation within a first-past-the-post electoral system, and (4) minority right to veto on rights and autonomy; and India meets all four. Analysts continue to seek answers for the survival of democracy, particularly in a country where access to equal political rights is fundamentally in conflict with an historically entrenched system of social inequality and massive poverty. One explanation for this contradictory situation is the 'complex heterogeniety of India's socio-economic interest groups' (Bardhan, 1988, 214). Hart (1988) isolates the three important elements that have held the democratic framework together. These are the quality of post-independence leadership, the existence of a party with a national following that extends its organization and influence into the countryside and a professional non-political civil service (19).

According to Lipset (1994), India's earlier history as a former British colony, as well as the influence of Hinduism, which according to him has kept itself aloof from political elements, provides a historical and cultural rather than a religious explanation for the sustenance of democratic institutions in India. The fact that both Pakistan and Bangladesh (which were both part of British India before partition) have struggled to maintain democratic institutions raises the relevance of the role of religion in sustaining democratic traditions. 'The reason why India and the Muslim states (Pakistan and Bangladesh) have developed so differently is not hard to find: the tensions in Islam between authoritarian rule and democracy has favoured authoritarianism, largely because in the original Pakistan, before the separation of Bangladesh, it was impossible to build up effective power from below and hence the formal structures of the state became the critical source of power for the society' (Pye, 1985, 318–319).

Huntington (1966) detaches the level of socio-economic development of a country from its level of political development. Although India is seen to be economically backward – it has low levels of per capita income and low levels of literacy, is predominantly rural and has heterogenous language and religious divisions – 'yet in terms of political institutionalization, India was far from backward. Indeed it ranked high not only in comparison with other modernizing countries of Asia, Africa and Latin America, but also in comparison with many much more modern European countries' (84). As long as the Indian National Congress and the Civil Service in India maintain their institutional strength, Huntington feels it is ridiculous to consider India politically underdeveloped. By contrast, the institutional evolution of the civil and military bureaucracies in Pakistan has been imbalanced, i.e., the bureuacracies have always been highly developed than the political parties (85). While the Muslim League, the counterpart of the Indian National Congress, played a significant role in the creation of Pakistan, its actual support base was in minority Muslim areas of India which remained in India after independence.Thus the leaders of the Muslim League in the new state lost their support as well as their cause after the creation of Pakistan. Absence of popular support, domination of politics by landlords and internal bickering have rendered overthrows by civilian and military bureaucracies relatively simple undertakings (Huntington, 1966, 442). While democracy and elections in India and Sri Lanka have enhanced the power of traditional leaders and created intense conflict between the values of representative government and planned economic and social change, the lack of elections in Pakistan in its first 20 years has exempted it from this conflict (Huntington, 1966, 448).

Khilnani (1997) is the latest in this line of writers questioning the durability of democracy in a poor divided country. In his view:

If the initial conditions were unlikely, democracy has had to exist in circumstances that conventional political theories identify as being equally unpropitious: amidst a poor, illiterate and staggeringly diverse citizenry. Not only has it survived, it has succeeded in energizing Indian society in unprecedented ways (9–10).

That historical, cultural and religious influences are likely to have a greater impact on traditional societies in the process of political and economic development is becoming increasingly evident from studies on TW countries. While there are growing reservations on adopting universal categories based on experience of developed political systems, studies continue to adopt criteria such as (1) competitive elections, (2) political parties seeking political support openly, free press, right of assembly, freedom of speech and (3) changes in government based on electoral verdict as requisites to qualify as democratic (Weiner and Ozbuden, 1987). Countries without some or many of these requisites are regarded as quasi-or semi-democracies. In spelling out the criteria for identifying countries that are democratic, the authors clarify that they see 'democracy as a process of governance and as an institutional framework, not as government committed to any particular set of social and economic objectives of a society with particular characteristics' (Weiner and Ozbuden, 1987, 5). In stating their position they are sceptical of the distinction attributed to scholars like Tocqueville and Lipset who distinguish a democratic society from a democratic political system (5).

The term 'democracy' as it is now practised in several countries prompts Collier and Levitsky (1997) to seek conceptual clarification with the growth of 'sub-types involving democracy with adjectives' (431). As the traditional western model of democracy based on competitive politics and periodic elections is inappropriate to TW countries, it is necessary to explore variations. The leaders of newly independent countries, while preoccupied with building the nation state, have displaced traditional associations. Oakerson (1987) questions the over-emphasis on national-level institutions and asks if there is any equivalent in political development to what is simple exchange in economics.

The implicit model of political development as nation-building presumes that national elections, national legislation, and national administration are the central processes that characterise political development. Unanswered in this conception, however, is the character of the political nexus – the sort of relationship among persons out of which a productive political community is constructed. Is the nexus of political development one that is productive in the sense that exchange is productive?

I suggest that productive political relationships follow a pattern of 'reciprocity', and that reciprocal behaviour is the activity that characterises a productive politics. Political development, parallel to economic development, consists of expansion of opportunities for productive reciprocity (Oakerson, 1987, 143).

For Oakerson (1987) the central problem of political development is how to make the intrumentalities of coercion serve the encouragement of reciprocity. Such reciprocity is likely to thrive in a society which believes in trust and an adherence to fairness in social relations. Reciprocity is nurtured in smaller communities and not in large-scale projects. Interestingly, TW countries abound in small communities which are regarded as obstacles for those seeking to build nation-building institutions. They are, however, conducive to reciprocity and therefore generally more productive. Therefore, encouraging the development of local level organizations helps local communities to engage in patterns of reciprocity, 'A multiplicity of primary units may therefore be a necessary condition of the social learning that is relevant to political development' (Oakersen, 1987, 149, also see Evans 1996, Fields, 1995)

Perhaps, suggests Goulet (1989), a new term, 'political participation', can be used in place of democracy, a term that is strongly entrenched within modern industrial capitalism. The term would then be distinguished from that universal model called 'democracy' and it would be possible to develop variations tailored to conditions in different countries. In my view the concept of participation in para-democratic institutions is fairly widespread when economic interests of local communities are concerned. Such local level organizations using democratic participation are quite active, such as, unofficial credit groups (Chiti) and dairy co-operatives in India, Grameen Bank in Bangladesh (Mascarenhas, 1988, 1993) irrigation associations in the Philippines and Taiwan (Korten, 1986) and informal arrangements in fishing villages in Sri Lanka (Ostrom, 1988). While the traditional western model of democracy when applied across TW countries can be regarded as operative in only a few countries, the organizations that do operate with success are the local level organizations with democratic participation referred to above. While it is not an alternative, it could well be the foundation on which political development can be promoted in TW countries (Bagchi, 1992).

Participation is democracy. Representative democracy as now practiced is a very limited form of participation. Participation means a commitment to a more egalitarian society which permits equal access to resources-not only to land-but also to education, health, etc. Where formal power is in the hands of a few and their power is grossly misused, participation means building countervailing power which leads to a healthier democracy (Wignaraja, 1995).

The idea of local-level participation as a foundation for political and economic development has gained further support from recent evidence on social capital (Evans, 1996) and civil society (Hadenius and Uggla, 1996). If organizations at local level are to be successful and not be dominated by local patrons or used by governments to promote patronage, they can become impediments to local participation. To avoid such a likely situation Hadenius and Uggla (1996) suggest that (1) local-level organizations must be governed on genuine democratic principles, (2) they must have the competence to make decisions and (3) they must be independent of government for resources (1631).

If economic development involves an increase in socially productive economic capacity, political development involves the growth of power that is 'equalization of the opportunity for citizens to participate meaningfully and effectively in the shaping of the polity of which they are a part' (Ruttan, 1991, 279). Rudolph and Rudolph (1987) adopt a political economy approach in attempting to understand the role of the state by distinguishing the polity into 'command polity' and 'demand polity'. In the former the state plays a dominant role in development, while in the latter, the state responds to the rising rate of political mobilization and utilizes state capacity to meet political demands. In the former the state is sovereign, while in the latter the voter retains dominance through parties, elections and pressure groups. The authors adopt these categories to analyse Indian political and economic development over a period during which state-sponsored development combined with democratic politics survived owing to stable leadership, the British colonial connection and the dominant influence of Hinduism, which until recently has kept itself aloof from the state (the secular tradition) (Lipset, 1995).

The demand polity tends to respond to public demands in arriving at policies and is oriented towards short-term goals because electoral success is a determining factor. Command polity, on the other hand, is dictated by long-term interest in which the state decides on policies having in view the public interest. The underlying difference between the two types of polity is the demand polity's tendency to respond to immediate demands at the cost of the long-term goals generally preferred by the command polity. In the earlier decades after independence India succeeded to some extent in combining both approaches. The authors sum up the two succinctly:

> Our models of demand and command polity include both political and economic characteristics. The demand polity is characterized

politically by voter sovereignty and the societal direction of the state; the command polity, by state sovereignty and state hegemony (domination or control) over policy and politics. The economic characteristics of the demand model feature shorter-term market or state consumption and welfare expenditure; those of the command model, longer-term investment expenditure in public goods and future benefits (Rudolph and Rudolph, 1987, 213).

Both models have political implications. The demand polity can become ungovernable and the command polity has the capacity to encourage excesses of state authority. What causes more concern, however, is the unequal access to political power in the demand polity, leading to policies that benefit significant supporters of the regime and exclude larger sections of the population. This has led to popular characterization of such states as 'intermediate regimes' which rely on the support of the rich peasantry and the lower middle class to retain power. In return for support such governments adopt a policy of state entrepreneurship that provides access to jobs and scope for small-scale entrepreneurs to supply inputs to public enterprises. The outputs of such public enterprises are provided in the form of cheap inputs like power and water to industry and agriculture. The outputs from agriculture are procured by the state through assured prices and distributed to urban consumers through the public distribution system at subsidised prices (See Table III-2.) The income from agriculture is not taxed, creating in the long run a fiscal management crisis that has to be confronted at some point in the near future (Raj, 1973, Varshney, 1995). This, then, is the perfect model of a responsive demand polity adopting policies of a command polity in order to retain power. While this analysis fits the Indian situation in the pre-1970s perfectly, there has since been considerable change. The unusual phenomenon is that in a country like India, in which over 65 percent of its population is engaged in agriculture and the rural sector enjoys considerable power, there is a constant demand for responsiveness from governments by active participation (Varshney, 1995). This shift from a command to a demand polity impacts considerably on economic performance but at the same time encourages the process of political development. That process of rural political power can be sustained to a point on economic issues, but is curtailed because of cleavages like religion and caste which cut across on a rural-urban or even intra-rural basis (Varshney, 1995, Mascarenhas, 1975).

42

Table III-2   Government Subsidies 1988–89 to 1995–96 (in Rs Crores)

	1988–89	1989–90	1990–91	1991–92	1992–93	1993–94	1994–95	1995–96
A Major subsidies								
Food	6,787	9,032	9,581	9,793	9,414	10,764	11,527	12,128
Indigenous(Urea) fertilizer	2,200	2,476	2,450	2,850	2,800	5,537	5,100	5,377
Imported (Urea) fertilizer	3,000	3,771	3,730	3,500	4,800	3,800	4,075	4,300
Fertilizer subsidy to small and marginal farmers	201	771	659	1,300	996	762	1,166	1,935
	–	–	–	385	–	–	–	–
Export promotion and market development	1,386	2,014	2,742	1,758	818	665	658	16
Sale of decontrolled fertilizer with concession to farmers	–	–	–	–	–	–	528	500
B Debt relief to farmers	–	–	1,502	1,425	1,500	500	341	–
C Other subsidies	945	1,442	1,075	1,035	1,081	1,418	1,064	1,177
Railways	207	233	283	312	353	412	420	418
Mill-made cloth	27	10	10	15	15	16	–	1
Handloom cloth	146	181	185	187	161	174	148	143
Import/Export of sugar	40	–	–	–	–	–	–	100
Edible oils etc.								
Interest subsidies	406	881	379	316	113	113	76	34
Assistance for fertilizer promotion	–	–	–	–	340	517	–	–
Other subsidies	119	137	218	205	99	186	420	481
Total Subsidies	7,732	10,474	12,158	12,253	11,995	12,682	12,932	13,305

Crore: 10 million
Source: *The Hindu*, March 8, 1997.

VI   CONCLUSION

In mapping the journey that TW countries have embarked upon, one cannot but begin by examining the underlying problems and constraints they are faced with. Essentially it is to do with excessive demands caused by growing populations in the context of limited resources. In order to match the two, TW governments need to evolve strategies of how best to manage those resources using the appropriate technology. While the historical experience of the FW is there to learn from, the options open to them are limited.

With better knowledge and research on TW countries now being undertaken, the approach to understanding the problems of TW development has also changed. While the previous focus of governments was largely economic, modelled on the FW, the new emphasis is broader-based with greater emphasis on values of democracy and political development, resource sustainability with environmental concerns and greater public awareness. Such awareness exposes countries to a variety of pressures both domestic and international. What is called for is a move away from general categorization to a finer analysis and the adoption of a different set of criteria to rank countries in some acceptable order of development.

4 State and Market: Alternatives to Development

I INTRODUCTION

The market has been regarded as an efficient mechanism for resource allocation because of the impersonal interaction involved as producers and consumers trade goods and services, the price of which is dictated by factors of demand and supply. This neoclassical concept of the market, the engine of modern capitalism, has not effectively functioned in TW countries and is unlikely to promote types of investment necessary for development (Arndt, 1988). This has led developmental economists to reject the neoclassical reliance on the market in favour of the state having to play a significant role in promoting development. The state has therefore to mobilize resources for capital formation (see Chapter 2).

In line with this thinking, most TW governments have had to adopt a range of policies to promote economic development. In many TW countries this was achieved through economic planning. Governments created the necessary institutions and developed the administrative capability to implement development projects. The early history of state intervention in the TW resulted in excessive bureaucratic control, leading to in unproductive economic behaviour like rent seeking which diverted greater attention to lobbying for protection instead of production. The result of these policies was slow economic growth, benefiting only certain groups with access to political elites (Bhagwati, 1988; 1993; Raj, 1973). Early experience of limited growth led to unintended social consequences like increased urbanization, decline in quality of education, health, housing and other services. The experience of poor economic performance led to a reassessment of the goals of development from solely economic growth to an emphasis on economic growth combined with social values, quality of life and well-being (see Chapter 3). This shift in development objectives was a response to the initial consequences of economic development. Comparisons in performance revealed disparate results between countries: while some showed exceptional growth others, lagged behind.

44

Table IV-1   Performance of East and South Asian Countries

Country	Population (millions mid 1992)	Area (thousands of sq km)	Dollars 1992	GNP per Capital Avg Annual Growth 1980–92	Life Expectancy birth (years) 1992	Adult Literacy Female 1990	Total 1990
South Asia							
Bangladesh	114.4	194	220	1.8	55	78	65
India	883.6	3,288	310	3.1	59	66	52
Nepal	19.9	141	170	2.0	61	87	74
Pakistan	119.3	796	420	3.1	59	79	65
Sri Lanka	17.4	66	540	2.6	72	17	12
East Asia							
South Korea	43.7	99	6,790	8.5	71	7	4
Hong Kong	5.8	1	15,360	5.5	78	–	–
Singapore	2.8	1	15,730	5.3	75	–	–
Taiwan	20.4	36	8,790	7	71	–	–

Source: World Development Report 1994.

The differential economic performance between TW countries highlighted the exceptional performance of some countries identified as the 'newly industrialized economies' (NIEs) and the poor performance of the greater majority which also suffered from excessive international debt, adverse balance of payments problems, increasing unemployment, growing inequalities of income and serious decline in political and administrative capability to confront complex socioeconomic problems. By about the 1970s such variations had fuelled a debate on the reasons for relative success or failure. For some reason, analysts studied relative economic performance in terms of a narrowly focused debate – state versus the market – thus reopening the unfinished debate of the 1950s between the neoclassical and developmental economists. The neoclassicals attributed the extraordinary performance of NIEs to export-oriented open market policies, while poor performance on the part of others was attributed to the adoption of closed, inward-looking import substitution policies. The relative economic performance came to be accepted as a verdict in favour of open market policies adopted by NIEs and has since been promoted as an alternative to overcome the problems of low-performing countries. The question this chapter poses is whether there is sufficient evidence to conclude that NIE performance has been due entirely to open market policies.

Having posed this question, I examine in the next section the reasons for failure of state intervention, and then in the following section 1 consider the factors that contributed to NIE performance. Following that, I look at the structural adjustment policies advocated by the World Bank and its implications for TW development.

II   WHAT ROLE HAS THE STATE PLAYED IN DEVELOPMENT?

In the process of reassessing the shift from economic growth to well-being the state played an even more significant role than that envisaged by the developmental economists. It undertook responsiblity for promoting and developing the infrastructure and for setting up scientific and educational institutions for training qualified manpower, assisted in creating the market by encouraging private enterprises and developed a proper legal and political environment to encourage the market and shape the values and attitudes of its citizens. In other words, it endeavoured to develop the capabilities of its people so as to manipulate their physical, social and cultural environment (Sen, 1984). Thus government actions affected all sections of society from individuals to households and businesses. Such enormous power and authority over decisions in the economy became increasingly strategic as the power of decision making was centralized and located in the hands of a policy elite with limited accountability. Under conditions of limited resources and increasing demand for services and goods, this only served to increase the role of government in the economy and enhanced the influence of decision makers (Grindle and Thomas, 1991).

Such power in the hands of policy elites, which was an unintended outcome of the enhanced role of the state, could, in the context of TW conditions, be counter-productive. I refer to the growing gap between policy elites and the people in terms of level of awareness a product of low levels of education and literacy. The barriers caused by differences in religion, caste, tribe and language combined with poverty create a social gap where access is inequitable. Such inequitable access under conditions of scarcity encourages misuse of power by policy elites who have been given the authority to dispense limited resources in conditions of excessive demand (Bhagwati 1988).

While such reservations associated with the economic role of the state still persist, the initial impetus for state intervention was overwhelming, influenced by the success of the New Deal, the Marshall Plan and Soviet economic planning, with India being seen as the trend-setter. Planning which became the norm was also encouraged by donor agencies for approving projects through responsible state agencies. The academic discussion in developmental economics and political development then taking place in the west advocated planning, central economic management and state building (Grindle and Thomas, 1991).

While all these could be considered general or external factors that influenced the role of the state, the most important view was that the emerging states, short of capital and human resources, could make rapid economic progress if the state were to take primary responsibility for economic development. By doing that, the governments of these countries would be in a position to attract the best educated to work for them and to take responsibility for managing the economy. In the circumstances of economic and social inequality that prevailed in these countries, the state could be seen as the only vehicle to protect the poor from exploitation. Therefore the state took on a major entrepreneurial and regulatory role which was a new and major responsibility for a civil service to handle. In adopting economy-wide planning in 1951, the Indian Planning Commission described the process thus:

> Planning in a democratic set up implies the minimum use of compulsion or coercion for bringing about a realignment of productive forces. The resources available to the public sector have, at this stage, to be utilised for investment along new lines rather than in acquisition of existing productive capacity. Public ownership of the means of production may be necessary in certain cases; public regulation and control in certain others. The private sector has, however, to continue to play an important part in production as well as distribution. Planning under present conditions, thus means, in practice, an economy guided and directed by the state and operated partly through direct state action and partly through private initiative and effort (Rangarajan, 1996, 22).

With the state playing an extensive role in the economy, the government had to create the political and administrative capacity for managing that role. One outcome of such state intervention was an extensive growth of bureaucracy which played, on the one hand, a role of regime maintainance while on the other it worked to promote economic development. That the law and order bureaucracy continues to enjoy prestige after several decades of independence is partly explained by the frequent need in some countries to maintain law and order, particularly in conditions where the legitimacy of some regimes is in question. The concept that power ultimately resides in the people and must flow upwards is unrecognized by most Asian rulers according to Pye (1985, 284). The illusion that power flows downwards has caused some Asian rulers to 'distrust the vaguer ties of civilian hierarchies and to turn to the more disciplined commitments of the military ethic, thereby opting for army rule' (Pye, 1985, 284).

When TW governments needed to create the political and administrative capacity for both allocation of resources and distribution of goods and services, such expansion of government functions (a requirement for development) resulted in growth of public sector employment. An area that has caused concern is the establishment, management and supervision of public enterprises (see Chapter 9).

The strategy of state entrepreneurship gives both politicians and bureaucrats extensive power. Commenting on India, Pye writes:

> The fact that the ideology of the government was 'socialist' in the sense of wanting the state to have a hand in as many activities as possible naturally increased the politician's power. Because businessmen, for example, could do very little without government permits and official contracts, they had to become regular visitors to the offices of the politicians (1985, 313).

While this entrepreneurial role demands highly trained technical manpower, its short supply has in fact resulted in concentration of talent, thus creating an elite with enormous power. In a climate of scarcity such power in the hands of politicians, bureaucrats and technocrats encourages a culture of rewarding certain supporters of the regime.

From the discussion thus far what emerges is that it is not state intervention as such that is being questioned but the distinctive approach to state intervention under specific conditions in different countries. The real issue then to be studied is not merely whether state intervention was responsible for the poor performance of TW countries, but the factors that contributed to the high performance of NIEs which also adopted some type of state intervention. While the above explains why most TW countries have failed to develop on similar lines to the NIEs, it would be grossly unfair to rate the rest as complete failures. Admittedly their performance has been less spectacular while their problems have been equally complex, if not impossible.

III FACTORS CONTRIBUTING TO THE PERFORMANCE
OF NIEs

The countries identified as the high performers of the 1970s, Hong
Kong, Singapore, South Korea and Taiwan, were, because of their common ethnic origin, referred to as the 'Four Dragons' or 'Four Tigers'. Of
these, South Korea and Taiwan in particular have attracted the attention
of academics because both have made remarkable recovery in the three
decades following the ravages of World War II and the Korean War.
Both enjoy high standards of living with per capita income exceeding US
$7000 and an equitable level of income distribution. Their annual
growth rates have averaged eight percent. The Korean economy has
grown from $2 billion in the 1950s to $280 billion in the 1990s. Korea now
has the fourth largest textile industry, the seventh largest steel industry,
the ninth largest auto industry and the third largest semi-conductor
industry (Abegglen, 1995, 121).

In attempts to present East Asia as the dynamic region I observe a
tendency to ignore underlying differences. While both Taiwan and
Korea have had remarkable growth, they have also shown their distinct-
iveness. Taiwan has preferred to avoid the Korean-type 'Chaebol' and
opted for medium-to small-scale enterprise combined with a few large
ones, plus extensive public ownership. A possible reason offered is that
a government largely comprised of mainlanders ruling over Taiwanese
was deliberately preventing the emergence of alternative centres of
power. The power base of the Korean government was more secure
(Abbegglen, 1995, 115). Korea is distinct from the other NIEs, Hong
Kong, Singapore and Taiwan, smaller islands comprised largely of
Chinese émigrés and their descendants. That the Korean economy,
unlike Taiwan, is concentrated in large companies the Chaebols has
prompted Fields (1995) to identify differences in their enterprise organization. The concentration of economic power in fewer companies may
be the underlying cause for the current setbacks the Korean economy is
facing.

The underlying difference in the structure of the South Korean and
Taiwanese economy explains the differential impact of the current Asian
crisis. That is, the crisis seems to have hit South Korea harder than Taiwan. While the East Asian region is economically interlinked a distinguishing factor when assessing the relative impact of the current crisis is
the existence of large business groups like the *Chaebols* in South Korea.
Chaebols are usually controlled by powerful families and linked, like the
Japanese *Kieretsu*, by ties between business, officials and politicians.

Such ties are often used to secure investment funds from banks with the expectation that the recipient would set up plants in politically favourable or sensitive areas. According to official figures 30 odd *chaebols* account for aggregate liabilities of US $255 billion in 1997 resulting in debt-to-equity ratio of 519 per cent (The Dominion, June 10, 1998). Such concentration of economic and financial resources in powerful conglomerates in South Korea is currently cause of concern for any recovery package. According to Columbia University economist Jagdish Bhagwati (1998) South Korea received 'large amounts of investment which produced very high growth rates but their financial structures were ill-tuned to managing this. Enormous external borrowing was funnelled through the banks into untenable investments, mostly real estate' (*Times of India*, January 2, 1998).

Other factors that contributed to the crisis resulting in 8 out of 30 chaebols becoming bankrupt are (1) weak financial system that did not have either an adequate regulatory mechanism or prudent bank practices to cope with the huge amounts of foreign capital (2) the herd mentality of international finance which was evident in the way capital flowed in and fled (3) international obsession with emerging markets which deluded governments into notions of grandeur leading them into indiscriminate investments, and (4) forced and hasty deregulation which almost precipitated the crisis at least in South Korea (Reddy, *The Hindu*, December 27, 1997).

Writing about South Korea Reddy comments that 'selective financial deregulation demanded by Western interests as a price for admission to the Organisation of Economic Cooperation and Development meant that banks borrowed recklessly abroad and financed huge diversification programmes of the South Korean conglomerates. There was always a problem with the country's financial system but sudden deregulation under western pressure without first creating a regulatory apparatus was a recipe for the present disaster' (*The Hindu*, December 27, 1997). A major rescue package of $57 billion offered by the IMF involving major restructuring resulted in layoffs of thousands of workers adding to the 400,000 already unemployed. The South Korean crisis has occurred in time to greet newly elected president Kim Dae Jung who over several years, has suffered persecution for his pro-labour and human rights position at the hands of dictatorial regimes.

Taiwan also a recipient of large investments and regarded like South Korea as a miracle economy has until now weathered the Asian crisis. In a conscious effort to prevent the emergence of large business groups Taiwan encouraged medium and small scale combined with an active public enterprise sector. An important factor for Taiwan's economic stability is the growing regional economy of South China and Taiwan Strait facilitated by language, kinship and origin ties. Such links are lacking in the case of South Korea owing to underlying cultural differences (Abegglen, 1995, 94).

That East Asian economic performance was a product of backwardness and input driven and thus unsustainable without improvements in productivity (Krugman, 1994) is more applicable to South Korea than Taiwan because of the latter's economic link with the mainland. That link provides access to lower cost land and labour with the expansion of the regional economy.

When once it was a case of too many 'nice things' happening at the same time and thus contributing to the Asian miracle (Wade, 1990), it now appears to be a case of too many 'bad things' happening at the same time thus contributing to the Asian crisis. These bad things are (1) slowdown in demand from rich countries for exports from East Asia (2) linkage of their currencies to the United States dollar which boosted exports when the dollar was weak with the opposite effect when the dollar appreciated (3) liquidity of global finance in search of quick returns which utilised the economic liberalisation of East Asia as an attractive investment contributing to a high percentage of mobile capital. Such reliance on mobile foreign finance triggers a rapid outflow of capital at the slightest economic setback (Ghosh, *et al.*, 1998).

In several chapters of this study I have queried the underlying foundations of the East Asian economic performance with its heavy reliance on Japanese capital and technology and US markets for exports. The effects of this crisis, experienced more by the fast growing economies of East and South East Asia more than South Asia, and the differential impact between South Korea and Taiwan is explained above. The underlying foundations of the enormous growth of these economies, and the distinctive pattern of their industrial structure needs further examination (Krugman, 1994, Fields, 1995). In analysing the East Asian miracle I have elsewhere questioned the undue emphasis on economic growth and the neglect of issues of social and political development. What is now apparent is that such success was built on the authoritarian state model based on superexploitation of cheap, non-unionized labour.

Their high levels of economic performance have been influenced by factors like physical proximity to China and Japan and the generous economic and military aid received from the US following the destruction caused by the wars. The potential offered by such opportunities has been utilized to the full by the adoption of appropriate policies developed by a technocracy that enjoyed autonomy in economic policy-making, a vital characteristic of the East Asian developmental state (Fields, 1995).

Analysts have attributed the extraordinary performance of these countries to their adoption of export-oriented open market policies in contrast to the import-substitution closed-economy policies adopted by the low performers. Low performance, according to such analysts, has largely been caused by state intervention. The eventual result was further economic inefficiencies, excessive bureaucratic control and rent seeking. Having arrived at that conclusion, the next logical step for such analysts was to advocate greater market-oriented policies to replace state intervention, referred to as structural adjustment policies.

While the debate in the 1950s on state versus market as alternative models for development remained an academic one between developmental economists and the neoclassicals, that in the 1980s has largely been ideological, led by the World Bank and the IMF and supported by monetarists who are essentially anti-state and pro-market (Kilksberg, 1994). It is now a debate between those who favour state intervention as a strategy of development as against those who believe that the problems of economic development are caused by government failure and that the alternative lies in replacing state with market.

Jagdish Bhagwati (1988), in his analysis of programmes to eliminate poverty, refers to the need for pro-poor bias in preference to directly administered poverty programmes. In his view the lack of growth was caused by poor policies which gave power to politicians, bureaucrats and business who formed an 'iron triangle' in a discouraging culture of 'dont's' i.e. controls, as against those that achieved growth with state policies in an encouraging culture of 'do's'. Comparing different alternatives to overcome poverty, Bhagwati (1988) asserts that growth (indirect route) is possible when proper policies are adopted. The evidence that is emerging from studies of East Asian economies is the important role of the state in their development. In other words, the difference between high-performing and low-performing countries is accounted for by the relative quality of state intervention: one that encourages entrepreneurial behaviour and one which inhibits such behaviour.

Based on the evidence of studies of NIE performance, it is unreasonable to attribute it entirely to market-oriented policies. Such success is a product of a complex array of factors: historical, economic, political and cultural (Amsden, 1989; Wade, 1990; Grabowski, 1994, Fields, 1995); the result according to Wade (1990) of too many nice things happening at the same time. South Korea and Taiwan did adopt import substitution strategies through state intervention in their efforts towards industrialization in the 1960s and gradually moved to export substitution. In rejecting the open market view of South Korean development, Wade (1990) believes that success had more to do with East Asianness or industrial policies or managed trade. This strategy which Wade (1990) likes to describe as the 'governed market model' involves: (1) high levels of productive investment making for fast transfer of new technology into actual production, (2) investing in key industries that would not occur without state intervention, and (3) exposure to foreign competition. The above are a result of a set of policies like incentives and controls that spread risk or governed market processes of resource allocation so as to produce different investment and production outcomes unlikely to occur under either free or simulated market situations (1990, 26–27). The final component of the governed market model according to Wade (1990) is the government private sector political arrangement best described as corporatist-authoritarian which provides market guidance. Government guidance of the market was achieved through:

(1) distributing agricultural land in the early postwar period;
(2) controlling the financial system and making private financial capital subordinate to industrial capital;
(3) maintaining stability in areas that affect long-term investments like exchange rate, interest rate and general price levels;
(4) promoting exports;
(5) promoting technology acquisition and establishing a national technology system;
(6) assisting particular industries (Wade, 1990).

While most TW countries, like the NIEs, adopted import substitution policies, the crucial difference was that in the NIEs government led the market while in other countries governments followed the market, exposing themselves to pressure from vested interests. In so doing the 'governed market emphasises the development virtues of a hard or soft authoritarian state in corporatist relations with the private sector, able to confer enough autonomy on a centralized bureaucracy for it to influence resource allocation in line with long-term national interest' (Wade, 1990, 29).

On the basis of NIE economic performance has emerged a discussion on the hard state and soft state and the issue of distinguishing effective from ineffective state intervention (Myrdal, 1968). Some academics have described the East Asian pattern of tough action by a strong state as purposeful action when compared to the drifter states in Latin America,

South Asia and Africa. When compared to the drifter states, the success of the purposeful states lies in their will to develop, and in 'the salience of achieving of sustained growth among the policy objectives of people who were in a position to take policy decisions' (Dore, 1993, 158). If the hard or authoritarian state is given the credit for the economic performance of NIEs, the negative aspect of that model is reflected in the 'superexploitation' of labour with long working hours, low wages and high rate of industrial accidents. The labour force is generally non-unionized and industrial pollution is widespread. Likewise, there is no place for opposition groups and the media remains under constant surviellance (Jenkins, 1994). Governments which adopt such political systems justify their choice on the grounds that it is essential for economic development (see Chapters 3 and 5).

Grabowski (1994) explains the processes by which a soft state becomes a hard state. They are: (1) displacement of the landed aristrocracy through land reform programmes, (2) experience of major social upheaval like revolutions or wars, and (3) strong government actions brought about by the constant fear of external threat which forces governments to strengthen the economy. Grabowski however rejects the explanations for the hard state and believes the answer lies in the domestic demand for manufactured goods preceded by successful agricultural performance. The failure of other TW countries which relied on import substitution is attributed to the stagnant state of their agriculture.

With the research evidence now available on East Asian economies, one is prompted to question the position adopted by the neoclassicals on the respective contributions of states and markets in East Asian economic performance (Johnson, 1982; Amsden, 1989; Wade, 1990; Grabowski, 1994; Kang, 1995, Fields, 1995). Several countries in the TW adopted either state intervention or free markets or a combination of both, but such programmes did not result in the type of economic performance observed in East Asia. Further analysis has led observers to describe the special relationship between government and business as the developmental state (Johnson, 1982), the disciplined market (Amsden, 1989), or the governed market (Wade, 1990). Essentially the focus of research has been the political and institutional arrangements that bring about synergy in government–business relations, characterized as 'governed interdependence' or more appropriately as synergy or embeddedness (Fields, 1995, Evans, 1996). Therefore, irrespective of the reasoning for successful state intervention by NIEs and the failure of other TW countries, such work certainly confirms that it was not market-oriented policies alone that contributed to economic performance of the NIEs.

The above evidence clearly establishes that the success of the NIEs lay in their ability to develop relations between state and market, rejecting the polarity of either/or and seeking an alternative somewhere between the extremes. The state's active role in promoting development of the infrastructure, education and technology in TW countries establishes that states intervene when markets fail. This was confirmed during the energy crisis of the 1970s, even in the case of the FW (Mascarenhas, 1992, 1996).

That relationship between the state and market is constantly changing and is best understood by adoption of an analytical distinction between state as political authority and state as economic agent (Mascarenhas, 1982, 1992, 1996). The anti-state phenomenon that has surfaced since the mid-1970s, for reasons well justified, fails to recognize that markets cannot function without the state acting as political authority. Dreeze and Sen (1996) term that relationship as one of 'thoroughgoing inter-dependence' (18). They see:

The issue of interdependence, is, indeed, of even greater significance than a history-free analysis might suggest. While markets must be, in this analysis an essential vehicle in realising economic potentials, the long-run influence of active public policy, for example in initiating particular industries and in providing a wide base of public education (as occurred, say, in Japan or South Korea) can be more easily inter-preted and understood in this light (1996, 21).

To understand the relations between government policy and market operations, Dreeze and Sen (1996) consider it important to distinguish between market-excluding and market-complementary government inter-ventions. For them, 'an economic arrangement can be "non-market" in the sense that markets are not allowed to operate freely or even to operate at all. This can be called a "market-excluding" arrangement. Or it can be termed "non-market" in the sense that the state undertakes to provide goods and services that the market does not. Such supplementary operations do not have to prohibit markets and exchanges. This can be called a "market-complementary" arrangement' (1996, 22). An analyt-ical distinction such as this helps to understand the type of intervention when markets cause harm owing either to reasons of omission (not doing) or commission (doing). The distinction between omission and commission helps to understand the role of market and non-market institutions. Dreeze and Sen (1996) suggest more active use of market in industrial production and trade while retaining state intervention in education and health. Accordingly, 'combining the functioning of markets and those of governments can be critically important' (25).

In exercising their role as public authority, governments promote markets and in some cases complement these by acting as an economic agent. If that mix has been successful in the case of NIEs and less successful in the case of other TW countries, the latter's lack of success is attributable to several factors (discussed in this study) but most importantly to a lack of capability. In reexamining that mix, the less successful ones would do well to adopt the analytical distinctions I have adopted in this study. The issues facing TW countries have unfortunately become clouded by events like the collapse of the Soviet Union, the emergence of pro-market governments in the United States and Britain and the influence of right-wing ideologies which have interpreted NIE performance in state-versus-market terms. In that environment TW governments, vulnerable as they are to the dictates of international lending agencies, have succumbed to market-based liberalization which has yet to deliver the promises.

The non-realization of the instant remedy offered by market liberalization has gradually led to the realization that (1) the East Asian miracle was not brought about entirely by market liberalism and (2) that solutions to problems of TW economies do not rest solely on a pendulum swing from state to market. In two papers recently published, Stigler (known to have been associated with the World Bank study *The East Asian Miracle* (1993)) reaffirms his doubts on the over-emphasis placed on markets and underplaying the role of governments in their development. In these papers he adopts a balanced perspective by reiterating that:

(1)   In developing countries where information is incomplete and markets are imperfect governments can fill the gap through effective intervention

(2)   Any such intervention cannot take the form of 'supplanting' the market. Where East Asian governments succeeded was in intervening to make markets function more effectively, by ensuring macroeconomic stability, regulating financial markets, direct investments to ensure resources were deployed in ways that would enhance growth and stability and creating an environment for private investment and ensured political stability (Reddy, *The Hindu*, October 28, 1996, 16).

There is a growing realization that one has to seek a way to get both state and market to work together in both FW and TW. While the research on East Asian economies questions the conclusions drawn by either promoters of the state or market, Friedman, in reviewing this literature, comments:

Instead of considering the numerous complex combinations of disaggregated states and unbundled property that might suit a particular nation, the dominant neoliberal approach offers a static dichotomy of state against market. It is the misconception of ideology that presents false polar choices such as either Statism or New Economic Policies. It is a major contribution of Wu's work to show how politics, property, and state, when conceived in their true multi-dimensionality, permit a far broader array of choices and possibilities (1996, 887).

In rejecting the monetarist explanation of market as the sole reason for NIE economic performance, the extensive literature now available has extended the discussion into several other areas to confirm that development is too complex to credit either state intervention or the market. Several factors, historical, cultural, social and political, are becoming increasingly important in our bid to understand NIE performance. For example, the ability of Japan and the NIEs to produce steel competitively in the absence of raw materials like coal and iron ore but with the emphasis on creative manpower, has caused considerable disquiet among East Asian watchers. A crucial ingredient in creating winners has been the emphasis on education tailored to the demands of the economy. This aspect of NIE performance has also been attributed to 'leapfrogging', where latecomers can take advantage of the latest technology without having to reinvent the process (Dore, 1989). While modern technology provides an opportunity to catch up with the leaders, it however denies newcomers a basic foundation for future innovation. Recent evidence confirms the view that early growth was based on increased inputs and not increased efficiency, raising doubts if such growth can be sustained as inputs like improved education cannot be repeated (Krugman, 1994). In support of such scepticism is the rejection of the 'flying geese' theory in which 'countries are said to follow one another in a developmental trajectory in which latecomers replicate the developmental experience of the countries ahead of them in the formation'. Instead of replicating Japan's developmental experience, the NIEs have been characterized by a shifting hierarchical networks of production linked backwards to Japan's innovation and forward to American markets for exports. In other words, they are dependent on Japanese technology (Bernard and Ravenhill, 1995, 171–172).

Having examined several explanations to explain the reasons for NIE performance, there remains one other, and this is the discipline and respect for authority characteristic of countries influenced by Confucianism. This could be equated with an East Asian version of the Protestant ethic. 'This linkage between the Protestant ethic and the spirit of capitalism is established through the concept of calling. The perception of one's calling as a religious mission motivates individuals to be productive, not only because this will improve their welfare, but more importantly because the fulfillment of their calling is pleasing to God' (Poulson, 1995, 51). Unlike capitalism or socialism, Confucianism is used to 'collectively describe family patterns, educational practices, attitudes toward the state, and other patterns found throughout East Asia' (Rozman, 1991, 13).

South Korea, Taiwan, Hong Kong and Singapore have duplicated the Japanese 'economic miracle' opinion holds, because they share in a regional tradition of diligence, entrepreneurship, striving for education, and (except for Hong Kong) state co-ordination. What all of these arguments have in common is the idea that East Asian social structure and thought differ from patterns found elsewhere and, furthermore, what sets one country in this region apart from the world seems to resemble what sets the entire region apart. Striking similarities shine through amidst the many differences from country to country that also need to be noted (Rozman, 1991, 12).

Religion or social philosophy is a major contributory factor in understanding development and it is difficult to isolate its influence. However, it has been argued that the social, economic and authoritarian influence could be an external influence and not necessarily Confucian (Dong, 1994). Cultural and religious explanations are often used with caution because of their lack of explanatory power. Despite that, Gregor (1995) makes a bold attempt to attribute East Asian success to Confucianism 'in which ruling groups take paternal responsibility for the welfare of the people' (232–235 in Friedman, 1996, 880). There is, however, considerable variation between countries in terms of their Confucian influence on politics, government, business and social life (Darling, 1979; Pye, 1985, Rozman, 1991).

Culture as an influence in economic development cannot be identified as an exclusive factor to explain cross-national variations in economic performance. Evidence from recent research suggests that economic and political institutions are not the only factors in determining differences in levels of economic performance (Granato *et al.*, 1996, 608). Culture as a system of basic common values takes the form of a religion and changes slowly. 'For reasons discussed below, the cultures of all pre-industrialized societies are hostile to social mobility and individual economic accumulation. Thus medieval Christianity and traditional Confucian culture stigmatized profit-making and entrepreneurship. But (as Weber argues) a Protestant version of Christianity played a key role in the rise of capitalism and much later a modernised version of Confucian society encouraged economic growth, through its support of education and achievement' (Granato *et al.*, 1996, 608).

Economists tend to avoid cultural and religious reasons in attempting to explain economic development while at the same time they emphasize the importance of entrepreneurial behaviour. That such entrepreneurial behaviour is found in some societies and not others calls for other explanations in addition to those thus far explored. Social psychologist David McClelland, known for his N-achievement theory, 'assumes that societal values guide parents in rearing their children, which in turn influences their motivational disposition as adults...and *those* who embrace the capitalist virtues of diligence, self-discipline, and independence are likely to rear children with a strong motive to achieve' (Poulson, 1995, 55). While interest in theories of achievement motivation has in the past not excited social scientists, research on East Asian economies influenced by Confucian values has revived interest in such work. Hagen has also focused on family relationships as vital to understanding entrepreneurship. He speaks of social upheaval as being crucial to the emergence of entrepreneurship as it effectively destroys the authoritarian personality linkage in traditional societies and encourages entrepreneurship. He observes such entrepreneurial values in displaced groups who have lost status during a historical upheaval (Hagen, 1968, Poulson, 1995). Those who survive such social or political upheaval show greater readiness to take risks. This is a most plausible explanation for greater risk taken by entrepreneurs displaced by the partition of India in 1947 (Pye, 1985, 218).

At this stage of the argument with the support of the emerging evidence it may suffice to conclude that there is greater prospect for learning from the experience of Japan and the NIEs by examining effective state intervention from ineffective state intervention in the economy as the cause of relative economic performance. The debate has been well summarised by Fields (1995).

The dogged empirical failure of post-colonial late industrializers to live up to these Western theories forced development theorists to acknowledge and reexamine the state. Early calls from developmental economists for state led industrialization to overcome market failure soon gave way, however, to a 'neoclassical resurgence' that documented 'the failures and disasters of regulatory, interventionist states'. This 'neoutilitarian' account of the process of development incorporates a 'public choice' model of the state that sees state officials as rational maximizers creating, capturing, and distributing rents through their intervention in the market. In dialectic fashion, this neoutilatarian vision of the 'predatory' state has been countered by a 'statist counterrevolution' launched by scholars of East Asian development under the rubric of the 'developmental state' (22).

Poor performance of the TW ought not to be seen as a case of government failure as is being presented by the ideologues. Unfortunately, TW countries have been under pressure to adopt structural adjustment on the basis of a premature conclusion that fits the prescription of international lending agencies. Underperforming TW economies in crisis need to rethink their policies and this has to be based on real issues and not on a partial assessment of NIEs.

IV   STRUCTURAL ADJUSTMENT

TW countries shifted their focus during the 1980s from stability and development to improving government efficiency in managing macroeconomic growth in return for access to international sources of capital. This shift in policy is to be examined in the context of the performance of TW countries. Between 1973 and 1980 they experienced average annual growth rate of 5.4 per cent. That growth rate decreased to 3.9 per cent between 1980 and 1987. However, much of the advantage achieved from growth was dissipated owing to:

(1)   indebtedness partly aggravated by the energy crises of the 1970s;
(2)   the long economic recession of the late 1970s and the 1980s;
(3)   excessively high rates of inflation, and
(4)   budget deficits.

As discussed above, most of these countries were unable to achieve development goals they had set themselves. This was largely caused by low levels of government capabilities, adoption of inappropriate policies and the complexity of the problems they faced. Essentially their economies were not productive or healthy enough to pay the debt, and this in turn affected other aspects of their economies. A crucial factor were the energy crises of the 1970s which put increased pressure on the economic performance of TW countries. Some critics, particularly the international lending agencies, attributed the failure to excessive state intervention and advocated a 'minimalist' model and a neoclassical market approach as an alternative. The alternative was advocated on the interpretation given to the success of NICs whose governments according to the World Bank had adopted open market-oriented policies. That interpretation as I have argued in this chapter, is questionable.

The experience of NIEs on which international institutions are promoting a policy of structural adjustment ignores that the conditions in these countries were distinctive, and other nations may be unable to implement similar economic policies because of political constraints.... In ignoring that certain economic policies not only can be isolated and understood but copied as well, we require more comparative empirical analysis and also better theoretical justification. One way of approaching this subject lies in asking how important the Korean and the Taiwanese historical experience were for their subsequent development. In particular, how important was the Japanese legacy of colonisation in shaping or influencing the subsequent development trajectories of Korea and Taiwan (Kang, 1995, 577).

The model promoted by the IMF/World Bank called structural adjustment evaluates development in GNP terms only and not in terms of human well-being. In other words, development should cover basic needs like education, health and housing with economic growth. Owing to ineffective policies and lack of administrative capability for implementation in most TW countries, neither the objective of economic growth nor those of basic needs has been delivered and this has brought them under pressure to adopt structural adjustment.

Structural adjustment involves:

an array of policy measures designed to promote longer term economic recovery, increase economic efficiency, improve resource allocation and enhance the adaptability of developing country economies to changes in the world economy (Grindle and Thomas, 1991).

According to the authors, there were two options facing these countries: either the 'politics as usual' approach or to confront the crisis. The 'politics as usual' approach, where governments respond to political demands of powerful groups, is best described as 'intermediate regimes' (Raj, 1973). The evidence is that many of these countries are unlikely to adopt firm policies as they would then be pursuing regime interest, rather than the national or public interest. The consequences of this approach, combined with the energy crisis and a fair share of natural disasters like droughts and floods, has meant that TW countries, already facing increasing debt repayment to industrialized countries amounting to $140 billion, had been saddled with innumerable inefficient state-owned enterprises, producing a range of poor quality products and were paying subsidies to both the public and private sectors of the economy. All this and several factors resulted in poor economic performance of TW countries (Grindle and Thomas, 1991).

That structural adjustment has been offered as a uniform prescription to solve the problems of ailing TW economies has led Williamson (1994) to name it the 'Washington consensus'. Essentially involves:

(1)   adopting fiscal discipline by eliminating budget deficits reducing public expenditure by redirecting it to productive use;
(2)   broadening the tax base and cutting marginal tax rates;
(3)   liberalizing and deregulating banking and financial institutions thus encouraging market determined rates of interest;
(4)   introducing flexible exchange rates to promote exports and liberalising trade by removing trade restrictions;
(5)   removing all restrictions on foreign private investments;
(6)   privatizing state-owned enterprises;
(7)   deregulating the economy to encourage greater competition, and
(8)   reforming the legal system to ensure property rights (24–26).

Structural adjustment advocated by the World Bank/IMF involves two components; economic stabilization as a short-term strategy and strutural adjustment as a longer-term strategy. The former, intended to be a shock tactic like currency devaluation, is expected to show dramatic results and is therefore easier to implement. The latter, like reducing public expenditure through restructuring, requires greater political will to sustain as results are not visible in the short run. A vital ingredient for promoting the reform is building the political and institutional base. Many countries do not possess the economic and financial institutions to make the transition from state intervention to a market-oriented economy. In democratic countries such as India, powerful vested interests can become a major obstacle to implementing the policies. At the same time, however, other factors like the legal system, political stability, technical and managerial resources and language considerations may encourage greater foreign private investment. If these basic differences are recognized then the effect of structural adjustment will necessarily vary.

Pressure to adopt policies of structural adjustment meant that change was experienced worldwide and the role of the state was reduced from an active one in the 1960s and 1970s to a limited one with the liberalization of the 1980s. The question of the timing of this change needs some consideration. Basically it was a post-cold war adjustment accompanied by the internationalization of the economy and the emergence of the communications and computer technology. Together they assisted in the flow of financial capital across international borders. Another influential factor was the change in attitude towards multinationals who were now more welcome than in earlier decades, when in the context of the cold war, the role of multinationals had been suspect (Moore, 1997). Crucial to all these developments was the shift in ideology, with the neoliberal or monetarist line favouring more open market-oriented economies on the lines of the East Asian economies. Thus globalization of production, changes in the perception of domestic interests, the influence of international financial institutions and ideas played a significant role. The critical triggering effect can be attributed to the recession of the 1980s, the effects of which were felt about the same time as TW governments started realizing the failures of past policies and pressure from significant groups subscribing to neoclassical ideas (Biersteker, 1992).

Reviewing a recent seminar on Indian economic reform organized by the Harvard Institute of International Development, Ravi (*The Hindu*, December 25, 1996) reminded his readers that as Nehru had been influenced by economists from Cambridge University in the 1950s, it was now the turn of the other Cambridge to advise India on economic reform. Summing up papers read at the seminar, he commented that the experience of four decades had not persuaded them that their prescriptions (policies) need to be intermediated through local institutions, local people, and local forces like culture, religion and history, which are unique to each country.

While the dramatic shift in policy in such a large number of countries is plausible, what is surprising is the uniformity of the prescription without consideration being accorded to historical, political, social and economic variations between countries. The fact that the model is derived from homogeneous corporatist authoritarian states like Taiwan and South Korea ignores the fact that many countries lack that element of concentrated political authority to oversee the reform. Some countries have achieved a level of economic and administrative capability to undertake the reform, while others have not. To that extent the package was inappropriate for countries in Latin America and South Asia (Batley, 1994, 489–91).

The reform package suffers from (1) a narrow financial and economic focus, and (2) a failure to recognize the diversity of the countries involved. That these factors have been overlooked becomes evident with the difficulties many countries have faced in implementing them. Recognizing this fact Montgomery and Rondinelli (1989) comment that, 'If international organisations want to implement economic reform policies more effectively, they must take a broader view of the development process and assess more carefully the administrative capacity of governments to make policy changes' (74). Such moderation stands in complete contrast to the evangelical zeal of academics like Jeffrey Sachs, whose prescriptions for economic reforms in India fail to recognize the historical and political context (Ravi, *The Hindu*, December 25, 1996).

Streeton (1993) is critical of the extreme shift in the role of the state to a free market under conditions of inequality. In his concern for the distribution of endowments and resources, he advocates markets that are people-friendly. That option, using prices for economic and social purposes, should be combined with a direct attack on attitudes and institutions. In this process, government can contribute to effective market functioning by:

(1) providing a legal framework, maintaining law and order, including enforcement of contracts, property rights, etc.;
(2) pursuing correct macro-economic policies with respect to exchange rates, interest rates, wages, trade policy, high levels of employment without inflation and economic growth;
(3) encouraging competition through anti-monopoly and restrictive trade practices legislation;
(4) levying a tax on activities it wishes to discourage;
(5) subsidising activities it wishes to encourage;
(6) playing a special role in the development of human resources, research and education;
(7) investing in infrastructure like roads, irrigation and communication;
(8) promoting private sector investment through credit institutions (1993, 1283).

Streeton's model recognizes the compatibility of markets with democracy and the public with the private sector. Support of the alternative model is intended to counter the foothold of international funding agencies assisted by technocrats who lack political and social concern for weaker sections. The natural consequence is the hardship imposed on vulnerable populations in areas such as health, education, housing and employment. Limited evidence of the impact of this swing from state intervention to a market-oriented policy has led to concern in most TW countries.

What is to be sought has been explained by Klicksberg (1994):

These analyses indicate that what is needed is a state that pursues human development as the ultimate goal; that strengthens and increases democracy; that works as a team with private enterprise and civil society towards a national project of productivity, competitiveness and growth; that works in combination with the market that eradicates corruption; that withdraws from sectors where it has no place being; and that uses every possible means to promote and support the organization and development of civil society.This type of state formulates srategic policies, i.e. thinks in the long term (188).

V   CONCLUSION

In the debate on market versus the state as alternative mechanisms for co-ordinating the economy in TW countries, I have raised several issues that confirm, based on more recent research, that the verdict in favour of the market is not as clear-cut as made out by the anti-statists. In what has been an era of anti-state and pro-market writing supported by political elites with a similar persuasion, the growing divergence in economic performance between East Asian countries and other TW countries has been easily attributed to market-oriented policies. To resolve the problems encountered by those TW countries whose economic performance has been less successful, major international lending agencies advocated structural adjustment.

The argument of this study is that economic performance is a narrow basis with which to evaluate a country's performance, and even if it were appropriate, the evidence presented suggests that the success of East Asian economies is attributable to the evolution of appropriate government-business relations. That relationship based on a variety of other historical, cultural, religious and situational factors explains the phenomenon of East Asian success and cannot easily be replicated. Historical, cultural and religious influences, crucial as they are, explain the significance of this comparative study of East and South Asia and are explored in the next and subsequent chapters of this study.

5 Comparative Development: the Two Asias

I INTRODUCTION

Development in this study is viewed in terms of enhancing the political and administrative capability of a country to manipulate the physical, economic and technological resources in the environment, keeping in view fundamental social values such as respect for personal and religious beliefs, protection of property, freedom and fundamental human rights. All of these should contribute to enhancing the capacity of people to participate actively in economic and political development. By enlarging the concept of development, I question the undue emphasis given to economic growth in many of the TW countries at the expense of fundamental societal values. The need to reiterate this position here has arisen because the current tendency for analysts appears to be to offer as a model the success of East Asian economies based primarily on economic growth, overlooking a variety of other factors that contribute to development. In order to highlight this, I have in this chapter analysed the comparative development of the two Asias, East and South, each region adopting completely different paths to development.

Economic liberalization advocated by the World Bank and the IMF and modelled on the success of some East Asian economies assumes uniformity between these sets of countries. I question the approach of this model (Amsden *et al.*, 1996). Important as economic growth is, it ought not to occur at the neglect of fundamental social values. This study, like similar studies in the field (Sen, 1984, Goulet, 1992), emphasizes economic growth with social values. I venture therefore to adopt a comparative perspective to evaluate the achievements of the two Asias, advocating political and social development as an essential complement to economic development. Further, I discuss how different types of political regimes in East and South Asia have contributed towards achieving development.

Admittedly, East Asian economic performance has been remarkable. What is being questioned, however, is whether other countries

67

can be encouraged, as is currently being done, to adopt the policies that analysts assume have contributed to their success. The main thrust is a recommended change from an inward orientation to an outward orientation. A relevant question posed by Bruton (1992) is 'How open?' East Asian economies adopted an outward orientation primarily to attract investment and promote export. Can this be achieved without mere imitation of the west?

In this chapter a brief background to the region is provided by looking into their history, particularly the recent colonial influence of Japan and Britain in East Asia and South Asia respectively; the significance of the role of state intervention; differences in their political and administrative systems and the influence of sociocultural factors like religion, language and region. I also critically analyse the development policies adopted and their outcomes. The aspects covered in this chapter are intended to introduce the two regions. A detailed look at different aspects of policies and the administrative systems for implementation follows in appropriate chapters of the study.

The chapter in section II opens with a comparison of the data on economic performance of the two regions. Section III explores the reasons for the differing performance of the two regions. Section IV attempts different interpretations of their performance, using a different set of criteria to judge performance. In this way I hope to establish the importance of combining economic development with political and social development (see Chapter 3).

II ECONOMIC PERFORMANCE OF THE TWO ASIAS

In Chapter 2 the argument offered was that the TW is distinguished from the FW in terms of levels of economic development and the primary objective of TW countries is to bridge the gap with the FW, in pursuance of which their governments have adopted a range of policies. While it has been convenient to place a large group of countries in this category on the basis of their level of development and label them as TW, it has since become evident that such a grouping does not truly reflect the variety of factors that distinguish countries from one another in terms of resources, history, culture and political and administrative institutions. The effect of these differences between TW countries is to influence the way each country perceives problems and confronts them.

High levels of growth have enabled the East Asian economies to achieve a more equitable distribution of income and therefore a better quality of life (Lim, 1994). Such a level of economic performance has not occurred in South Asia, despite the adoption by governments of policies promoting economic development. In comparison with high-performing East Asian economies, whose performance in the last three decades has been phenomenal, the performance of South Asian economies is less commendable.

Table V-1   Rate of Economic Growth (Percentage)

Country	Average 1978–87	1988	1989	1990	1991	1992	1993	1994	1995
South Asia									
Bangladesh	4.1	3.5	5.0	5.1	4.1	4.8	4.8	4.7	4.7
India	4.5	8.7	7.4	5.9	1.7	4.1	4.2	5.7	6.8
Nepal	3.2	4.3	4.6	6.4	4.1	3.4	7.1	3.0	5.8
Pakistan	6.5	4.8	4.7	5.6	8.1	5.0	0.8	3.8	4.5
Sri Lanka	5.0	2.7	2.3	6.2	4.6	4.3	6.9	5.6	5.4
East Asia									
Hong Kong	8.3	8.0	2.6	3.4	5.1	6.3	6.4	5.4	5.0
South Korea	7.7	11.3	6.4	9.5	9.1	5.1	5.8	8.6	9.0
Singapore	6.9	11.1	9.6	8.8	6.9	6.0	10.1	10.1	8.9
Taiwan	8.7	7.8	8.2	5.4	7.6	6.8	6.3	6.5	6.1

Source: International Monetary Fund, *World Economic Outlook*, Washington, 1996.

III   EXPLAINING THE REASONS FOR EAST ASIAN ECONOMIC PERFORMANCE

Increasing divergence in the economic performance of TW countries has led comparativists to focus their analysis on development strategies which, according to Dore (1992), are 'implicitly defined – as the mixture of forecasts and intentions and assumptions about probable causal sequences held by policy-makers when they take economic decisions' (353). Dore (1992, 353–354) wonders whether policy-makers in TW countries work with a conscious strategy. Much of the analysis of comparative economic performance, he feels, is based on patterns of the past and such analysis has been used to allocate either praise or blame. According to him even the search for patterns is arbitrary:

I suppose, what makes a pattern meaningful is its relevance to valued objects. Much discussion of development is highly ideological. There are sharp divisions between those who believe that good can only come and only good will come, from the unfettering of markets, and those who favour mere structuralists explanations of how economies work, and more interventionist recipes for making them work better (355).

If such analysis is to be useful to policy-makers, then, according to Dore (1992), it should be in a form that helps to explain the difference in patterns between East Asia and Latin America (or South Asia). While conceding that data on economic performance is relevant for comparative analysis of TW economies, such data however cannot be isolated from factors like history, culture, religion, resources, and size of a country, which as initial conditions influence the role that government plays in development.

Studies on East Asia focus on the dramatic turnaround of both Taiwan and South Korea, countries that adopted fairly similar development strategies. Both countries experienced destruction and upheaval as a result of the war. Their geographical proximity to each other and to China and Japan have also influenced their economic performance. Continued hostility with their neighbours, the People's Republic of China and North Korea, encouraged them to adopt a defence strategy that indirectly promoted economic growth, which was acceptable to their supporters on the grounds of national security. As recipients of US military and economic aid within the context of the cold war, both South Korea and Taiwan adopted authoritarian means using the pretext of external threats.

While the discussion thus far is based on results, the question that needs to be answered is the difference in performance and this has been attempted in several studies (Oshima,1993, Amsden,1989, Wade,1990, Fields, 1995, Dreeze and Sen, 1996, Bhagwati, 1993). Adopting the stepwise and backtracking approach, Lim (1994) attempts to explain differences in development performance by (1) estimating the production function of TW countries by identifying the sources of output growth like capital, labour and technical progress, (2) identifying the factors responsible for these sources of growth, and (3) identifying the economic policies needed to bring about these factors and their efficient use (833). According to this analysis, which is supported by other studies, Lim is convinced that 'by far the most important source of output growth in developing countries is increases in capital stock'.

Table V-2   Gross Domestic Investment and Saving as Percentage Shares of
GDP, 1960–90 (%)

	Gross Domestic Investment/ GDP			Gross Domestic Saving/GDP		
	1960–70	*1971–80*	*1981–90*	*1960–70*	*1971–80*	*1981–90*
Newly industrializing economies:						
Hong Kong	21.7	26.5	27.5	20.6	27.5	30.5
Singapore	24.0	41.1	42.0	14.9	30.0	42.3
South Korea	17.6	28.9	30.5	13.7	22.3	31.8
Taiwan	N.A.	30.6	22.6	19.8	32.2	32.9
South Asia:						
Bangladesh	9.9	7.3	11.4	7.8	2.2	2.6
India	17.6	20.8	23.9	15.3	20.5	20.3
Pakistan	16.3	16.4	18.7	8.9	10.1	10.3
Sri Lanka	14.9	19.4	24.8	11.8	13.8	13.3

Source: Adapted from David Lim (1994) 'Explaining the Growth Performance
of Asian Developing Economies', *Economic Development and Cultural Change*,
Vol. 42, p. 836.

Acknowledging that technical progress or efficiency in the use of inputs
is crucial for growth, Lim (1994) concludes that it is where 'East Asia con-
forms to the pattern of the developed world, with the contribution of
technical progress being more significant' (834). As a result of policies
adopted by their governments, the generation of indigenous capital investment through savings and foreign private investment has been considerably higher in East Asia, as compared to the South Asian economies. That
factor, combined with an expansion in education and the implementation
of efficient systems of production, has enabled the East Asian economies
to achieve technical progress and thus move far ahead of South Asian economies. Finally, the adoption of a competitive export-oriented economy
has enabled the achievement of efficiency in capital utilization, a goal
which appears distant to the inward oriented non-competitive South
Asian economies (Lim, 1994; Gary Fields, 1995, World Bank, 1993).

Krugman (1994), attributes the success of the NIEs to three possible
theories:

the occurrence of a major diffusion of world technology which has
resulted in western countries losing the advantage;

a shift in the world centre of economic gravity to the Asian nations of the Western Pacific, and
the greater ease with which economies with fewer civil liberties and more planning can operate.

While less convinced about the first two, Krugman agrees with the third that 'East Asian economic success demonstrates the fallacy of our traditional laissez-faire approach to economic policy, and the growth of these economies shows the effectiveness of sophisticated industrial policies and selective protectionism' (78). While sceptical of dramatic efficiency growth in these countries, Krugman concedes that the level of growth achieved can be attributed to the extraordinary mobilization of resources combined with deferred gratification (1994, 78). Further, he warns that (1994) the use of 'East Asian experience to free markets with the idea of achieving growth represents a hope rather than well founded expectation'.

In questioning the appropriateness of adopting the experience of the East Asian miracle to rescue low performing countries (see Chapter 4), one sees the need to incorporate the historical factor, i.e. the linkage between Japanese colonialism and the growth of East Asian economies like South Korea and Taiwan. The historical factor, that of Japanese colonialism, has been underplayed by the neoclassicals, who prefer to attribute the dramatic economic performance of Taiwan and South Korea to open market policies (Wade, 1990).

III(a)   The Historical Foundation

Explaining the impact of colonial linkages, Darling (1979) distinguishes economic and social policy adopted in the colonies by governments (colonizers) into high-transformative (i.e. action which achieved major alterations) and low-transformative (i.e. policies which caused little or no change) (134). Applying this distinction to Japanese colonization, in Korea and Taiwan, Darling identifies the policies used as high-transformative. A particular focus was the promotion of agricultural development. In Korea and Taiwan the development of mining, forestry and light industry took precedence. During this period the Japanese helped to construct a modern infrastructure, including ports, railroads and communications (138). Wade (1990) cites George Barclay's (1954) conclusion that the Japanese 'transformed Taiwan from a "backward" and neglected land into a thriving region that could regularly export a large share of its agricultural produce. This was a success that would satisfy most of the countries striving for modernization today' (75). Kang (1995), in his review of recent studies explaining East Asian economic performance, also emphasizes the impact of the Japanese legacy of colonialism on Korean and Taiwanese development. He comments that:

> As scholars search for the causes of Korean and Taiwanese economic growth the historical influence of Japan must be considered for even if theories that explain growth using the 1960s as initial conditions are correct, the explanation for why those conditions existed may be unique to the Asian NICs (577).

Friedman (1996), in a review of recent studies on East Asia, reminds us that Taiwanese managers were keen students of the Japanese developmental state: 'Beyond Taiwan lies the real model, Japan' (880). In his review article, Friedman comments that the author has overlooked the fact that 'Taiwan, a colony of Japan from 1895 to 1945, had further international economic advantage from integrating with a fast-rising Japan whose flexible production and protected finances also facilitated catchup in a world of ever more rapidly changing lead market sectors' (882). In other words, to understand East Asia one must, according to Friedman, focus on the Japanese model. Taiwan's excellent educational system, he reminds us, was established by the Japanese during the period of colonization.

III(b)   The Developmental State

The revisionist literature on East Asian economic performance has given new focus to this debate on the role of the state and led to greater interest in bringing the state back into the political economy of development (Evans *et al.*, 1985). Studies on the post-war recovery of Japan emphasized the developmental role of the state, resulting in the recognition that there exist varieties of capitalism other than laissez-faire often promoted by the neo-classical economists (Johnson, 1982, Amsden, 1989, Wade, 1990). While multiple explanations are offered for the East Asian miracle, the linkage between the Japanese influence in the early development of Korea and Taiwan amounts to equating it with the developmental state (Kohli, 1994). While the state played a significant role, other factors have contributied to the extraordinary growth of Korea and Taiwan. One such factor is their proximity to Japan, which in the early 1960s proved ideal for Japan while it sought to export labour-intensive manufacturing processes. That process was eased by the fact, already noted, that both were once colonies of Japan. Apart from physical proximity, both possessed a favourable infrastructure combined with a good educational system inherited from the colonial period (Abegglen, 1994, 112). The Japanese developmental state thus became the natural model for the East Asian states. Amsden clarifies thus:

> The dominance of the Japanese colonial administration in Taiwan's economy mirrored the dominant role of the Meiji government in Japan proper, which distinguished it in important respects from the colonial offices of England and France. The Jiang Jie-Shi forces benefited enormously from their inheritance of Japanese state monopolies, and the whole interventionist approach taken by the Japanese to the development of an occupied territory was not lost to the Guomindang (1995, 79).

Japan's position at the economic centre has led to a dramatic development of new areas linked to South Korea and Taiwan, challenging conventional views of national markets. The development of the East Asian region crosses political boundaries with a rapid pace of development which governments are unable to cope (Abegglen, 1995).

From the evidence presented thus far it is obvious that government played an active role in the initial stages of development in South Korea, Taiwan, Hong Kong and Singapore. Drawing from the experience of Japan, Abegglen (1994) comments that 'an unsurprising conclusion is that growth is most rapid and effective when government plays a directing role in support of a strong private sector – the key, as is often the case, is in the mix and in timing of application of policy' (113).

These facts are undeniable, because the miracle is there for everyone to observe. Is it however an achievement that can be emulated by others while overlooking the variety of non-economic factors essentially unique to the region?

Although I focus largely on the distinctive role of the state and linkages to historical factors (Japanese colonization), it becomes increasingly clear that subsequent policies that were adopted and their success are linked to that historical experience. The following quotation explains it best:

> What accounts for differences in rates of growth of industrial output and productivity among late-industrializing countries is not the degree to which the state has disciplined labor but the degree to which it has been willing and able to discipline capital. The discipline of capital

constitutes a major factor in the success or failure of state intervention in late industrialisation (Amsden, 1992, 61).

An example of conscious policy adopted by Taiwan and South Korea is the subsidizing of industries against export performance targets with penalties incurred if targets are not reached. Such capital investment discipline has been extended to the dissuasion of investment in unproductive investment such as real estate while capital flight is an unfortunate practice prevalent in South Asia. The East Asian model of state intervention that promotes development through the private sector is described as 'embeddedness' (Fields, 1995, Evans, 1996). Derived from the 'new institutionalist' perspective, embeddedness as a critique of economic rationality views 'actions as a fulfilment of duties and obligations deemed socially or politically appropriate, rather than the fulfilment of choice based on individual values, interests, and expectations' (Fields, 1995, 12). Recognizing differences between the 'new institutionalists', the embeddedness approach has been advanced by political scientists and sociologists who adopt the new political economy approach to TW development. While the political economy approach is useful in analysing an economy, in late-industrializing countries the 'dominant role played by the state in capital accumulation and enterprise formation in the early stages of industrialization can permanently shape the internal structure of business enterprises and the institutions of the economy as a whole' (Fields, 1995, 21).

The concept of social embeddedness and synergy advanced to explain the variety of social and economic interactions has prompted calls for 'moving beyond the developmental state' (Clark and Chan, 1994, Moon and Prasad, 1994). It is in this context that Evans (1996) asks 'Can networks which trespass the boundary between public and private divide be repositaries of developmentally valuable social capital rather than instruments of corruption or rent-seeking?' (Evans, 1996, 1120). A closer working relationship between the state and the community helps to develop social capital which acts as a positive factor in societies where social power through pressure groups, media and political parties is not sufficiently developed.

The explanation offered by Amsden (1992) for the absence of rent seeking in Taiwan and South Korea and its occurrence as a feature of import substitution state intervention in South Asia is interesting. In other words the quality of state intervention relies on certain objective conditions that may influence the success or failure of industrialization.

According to Amsden (1992)

> One condition stands out above all others in influencing the process of (capitalist) industrialisation because its influence is intrinisically related to industrialising late – the distribution of income. A more equal income distribution raises the probability of industrial success for a host of reasons related to class struggle and, hence, worker motivation, the expected returns to investments in education, cost – push inflation, the effectiveness of currency devaluations, and other micro and macroeconomic variables. To the extent that more equal income distribution increases the growth of output and productivity, it makes the state more committed to industrialization and willing to impose performance standards on business. In addition, a more equal income distribution makes the state more able to impose performance standards on business (73).

The distribution of income thus establishes the fundamental relationship between the state and business. It also helps to explain the distinction first made by Myrdal (1968) between the soft and hard state. Amsden (1992) regards a relatively equal income distribution as a necessary condition for late industrialization because it empowers the state to discipline business and facilitates the state bureaucracy to monitor the disciplinary process (73). Irrespective of the system of government – democracy or dictatorship – the quality of state intervention rests on the type of income distribution. Where such income distribution is unequal, the wealthy interest groups are likely to overwhelm the authority of the state by virtue of their control over resources (Amsden, 1992, 75). East Asian economies achieved a more equitable income distribution by implementing land reforms and displacing the landed aristocracy. Similar programmes have proved unsuccessful in South Asia, and this explains the enormous power wielded by the rural elite in India and other South Asian countries (Varshney, 1995). While the former undertook the reform under favourable post-war conditions, the latter sought to achieve it through the traditional political process and failed (Mascarenhas,1975; also see Chapter 10).

An internal reordering of the power structure following a period of social upheaval led to distinct transformation in the composition of the policy elite and explains subsequent changes in the political and economic landscape of the East Asian region. While such changes in the agrarian social structure are seen by some as a contributory factor for the emergence of an economic technocracy in East Asia, the existence of an agricultural bourgeoisie is viewed by others as the foundation for a healthy democracy. The economic technocracy in East Asia has been able to formulate and implement policies with limited interference from politicians and interest groups.

Curiously when asked directly to identify the primary cause of development most government and private sector leaders emphasised strong, discretionary government, authoritarian leadership that could act swiftly and decisively, making difficult decisions while riding roughshod over the opposition (Root, 1997, XIV).

The question that comes to mind is: what is the limit of power a democratic country can vest in a technocracy particularly in the context of a globalized and complex economy? Critics of East Asian economic performance equate technocracy with authoritarianism, which some South Asian societies like India are unlikely to trade in return for speedier economic development. In a review of a comparative study of state and development in some TW countries, Friedman (1996) observes that the author is silent on 'political freedom and democracy, key instrumentalities to maintain governmental accountability'. He then goes on to say that 'the issue of the central importance of democracy should be confronted and evaluated... the key issue of democracy versus authoritarianism' (415).

East Asia's one party rule reflects a dearth of democratic institutions. Student idealists, who rally around nationalist and anti-corruption goals, are active if inconsistent force for democracy. Elderly politicians, whose behind the scenes factions are the key to power brokering, operate in an intensely competitive but not democratic environment (Rozman, 1991, 15).

The developmental state relies on a distinct social and cultural foundation that is typical of East Asia. While some attempts at cultural explanation are incorporated in Chapter 4, there is sufficient justification without seeming repetitive to explore its influence on the character of the developmental state. In looking for a variety of explanations to help understand the differences in state intervention, one needs to ask why a strong state that demands discipline, loyalty, responsibility, commitment and identification is endured by citizens in East Asia and not in other TW countries. Clark and Chan (1994) suggest 'bringing society back' into development studies. They say 'Asia presents a valuable context for treating this question because of its great variations in the nexus between state and market. The region contains nations with widely varying economic performance, political regimes, and indigenous cultures. Thus, it should provide a good setting for examining the relationships among state, market, society, and economic performance' (1994, 333) The term 'Confucian ethic' has been offered to explain a range of attributes, values and attitudes in societies influenced by it. Those characteristics are self-denial, frugality, patience, dedication and aptitude for learning.

They are thought to excel in tasks that require unstinting effort over a long period in which gratification or reward is delayed. Persistent devotion to memorization or repetition of a task finally results in a skill becoming well learned. This predisposition prevails whether the skill is mathmatical computation, musical performance, artistic craftsmanship, or applied industrial technology (Rozman, 1991, 27).

In so far as institutions of the state and the market are socially embedded (Clark and Chan, 1994, Fields, 1995, Evans, 1996) and have differential impact on economic performance, it supports my contention that variations in development performance of TW countries have to be seen from different perspectives. The dominant influence of Confucianism on this region is another useful (though partial) explanation to the East Asian developmental state.

IV   SOUTH ASIA: THE PROBLEMS OF DEVELOPMENT

If East Asia emerged as ethnically homogeneous and culturally cohesive with a common language and well defined geographic boundaries all of which are conducive towards the existence of an organic unity (Ranis 1992), South Asia presents a contrasting picture of enormous diversity divided on the basis of language, religion, region, caste and tribe that spreads across political boundaries. Its enormous size and diversity lends itself better to the term 'sub-continent'. Included here are countries that were once under British control but following independence emerged as India, Pakistan, Bangladesh, Sri Lanka, Nepal and Bhutan. Predominantly dependent on agriculture, the region suffers from poverty and underdevelopment and is constantly exposed to the vicissitudes of nature. Its people have survived numerous foreign invasions. It has seen the birth of major religions like Hinduism, Buddhism, Sikhism and Jainism and has become the home of others like Islam, Christianity, Judaism and Zoroastrianism. While such heterogeneity within a democratic political system can contribute to tension, such tension is also present in less heterogeneous states of the region like Pakistan, Bangladesh, Sri Lanka and Nepal. Because of the significant variation in size and the availability of literature, the term 'South Asia' for purposes of this study will generally be equated with India, unless a reference to a specific country is made.

Any evaluation of development policies and their management in South Asia has to be viewed in the context of the tensions arising out of the complex interaction between competing regions, languages, religions, ethnic, tribal, caste and social and economic inequalities. While most countries in the process of becoming independent consider themselves to be nations, South Asia, particularly India, is so diverse that the divisions become accentuated because of the extraordinary level of political mobilization. Such high levels of political mobilization are a product of the national movement for independence and the subsequent democratization following independence. These can be perceived as an obstacle or as healthy participation in the development process. However, governance is affected when goals of economic development conflict with demands of social justice. Typical examples relate to the building of river valley projects and distribution of water from rivers that extend across state boundaries. Thus droughts, famines, political and regional disputes can result in politically explosive situations in such societies, diverting the attention of governments from development to more essential tasks of maintaining political stability. In trying to promote or uphold the legitimate authority of government, even democratic governments often take recourse to the use of civilian and military bureaucracies which are trained in the use of coercive mechanisms. Frequent deployment of such forces for maintaining the peace has given such bureaucracies enormous authority and power and in the process has undermined the value of technical specialists responsible for development. While critics of South Asia are reluctant to condone poor economic performance for reasons explored in this chapter, such factors cannot be overlooked when offered as a contrast to East Asia.

IV(a)   The Historical Foundation

If East Asia's colonial association with Japan has had a positive contribution to its economic performance, the historical experience of South Asia with British colonialism has been less complimentary. When Britain colonized India in the 17th century, India was less developed than Britain. By the time it became independent the gap had widened. The

British, in establishing their rule through a small and efficient bureaucracy and army, remained aloof from the problems of society. Apart from building railways and canals for trade, 'they did almost nothing to promote economic development' (Maddison, 1971, 47). He further comments that:

Nothing was done to break the many traditional obstacles to development which were more severe and persistent in India than anywhere else in the developing world. There were many of these such as the caste system, the fatalistic ascetism, resignation and renunciation of Hindu religion in which people accepted their lot passively, the preference for magic rather than science,…wasteful ceremony and marriage feasts, the joint family system with reduced incentives to work and save, and the low status of women.

An even more important effect of foreign rule on the long run growth potential of the economy was the fact that a large part of its potential savings were siphoned abroad…There can be no denial that there was a substantial outflow which lasted for 190 years. If these funds had been invested in India they could have made a major contribution to raising income levels (46).

The most damaging effect of British colonialism, when contrasted with the Japanese experience, was in the field of agriculture. While significant credit to present-day economic performance of Taiwan and South Korea is attributed to the policy of agricultural modernization carried out under Japanese colonization, the British left India in 1947 when 'food consumption per head of the population declined and so did output per man and it seems perfectly feasible that food consumption and productivity levels were lower in 1947 than they had been two centuries earlier' (Maddison, 1971, 55).

The 'steel frame', according to Darling (1975), 'created and transferred to indigenous control the modernizing governmental structures oriented more toward state-building than nation-building' (171). The influence of British colonialism has some significance for our analysis of the comparative performance of the two Asias. In the case of Taiwan and South Korea, Japan as a colonial power played a significant role in the agrarian transformation of both countries and the high levels of literacy and education. Apart from becoming an outlet for agricultural exports from these countries, Japan introduced modernized rice growing with better varieties and a physical infrastructure far improved from the rice-growing agriculture prevalent in South Asia.

South Asia's association with Britain, although much longer, had a different impact on their economies. While Japan's colonization helped to build the foundation of a rejunevated economy in these countries, British colonialism had a differential impact. 'The British did leave behind a poor and backward country who would have to survive many economic problems before she could make her way in the world. Rationing had been introduced, prices were rising and there were shortages of food in both India and Pakistan. It was to take many years before famine was banished and the British inability to evolve a workable agrarian policy left a legacy of neglect which would take time and energy to overcome' (Royle, 1997, 147). In contrast, it was the excellent service sector established by the British that led to the extraordinary performance of Hong Kong and Singapore. These cities were set up as the headquarters of shipping, financial, trading, and political operations in the region. 'In contrast, British rule in South Asia was exploitative. Unlike the Japanese, the British did little to promote education and rice growing, leaving the population in British India, Burma and Ceylon hostile to capitalistic ways... Consequently a larger part of the differences in growth rates among the three regions was the outcome of the differences in colonial rule' (Oshima, 1987, 94).

The British in India created an agrarian class of zamindars or landlords who acquired enormous power in the rural areas, while its urban counterpart, the Indian bureaucracy, played a significant role in perpetuating the authority and power of this class. Thus the state in South Asia essentially reflected the economic classes that had dominated South Asia over centuries.

IV(b)   The Bureaucratic State

The 'steel frame' (the term to describe the civil service set up under the British) became the instrument of state intervention adopted to promote policies of development. As a generalist administrative service trained to maintain law and order under colonial administration, it extended that role into the area of development through a process of extensive controls for allocation and approvals of programs and projects. As a result, the pre-independence colonial service turned into a powerful bureaucratic state after independence.

The urgency for growth and development in South Asia has been presented in stark figures of extreme poverty and inequality: a rapidly growing population (900 million) of which 70 per cent competes for limited, over-exploited agricultural resources. High levels of illiteracy, inequalities in land holding, combined with caste hierarchy, have resulted in cumulative inequalities. India suffers from several basic problems which have to be understood or taken into account when analysing its approach to policies for development. While most TW countries are subject to a similar variety of constraints and problems (Chapter 2) it is necessary to specify those relevant to issues discussed in this chapter. Briefly they are:

(1) excessive population;
(2) regional, ethnic, language and religious diversity;
(3) a constitutional democracy which is viewed positively by those who advocate a liberal political system, but which can be effectively manipulated by specific groups to their advantage;
(4) a centralized political and administrative system within a federal constitution;
(5) high levels of social and economic inequalities;
(6) a society that prefers incremental to radical change;
(7) a rural-urban divide that is growing;
(8) endowed with a high level of intellectual, scientific and technological humanpower capable of designing and developing sophisticated technology (Lewis, 1995).

The problems faced by South Asian countries in the 1950s were such that it was inevitable that the state should initiate and plan economic development. Education, transportation and communication assumed priority, just as they did in the early stages of development of the FW. Large steel plants of the type necessary for industrialization were set up by governments in both East Asia and South Asia. Considering the size and magnitude of problems inherited with independence, it is not surprising that most countries, including India, deemed state initiative essential in the early stages of development. The private sector was ill-equipped for such major undertakings. Galbraith (1964) comments:

Only individuals with a uniquely simple approach to the problems of economic development, or a peculiarly determined ambition for conservative applause, will make the mistake of generalizing from a market performance in the developed country to what the market can accomplish in the poor country. It is no part of the good fortune of the poor country that this larger state initiative is required. As I stress elsewhere, economic development imposes, generally speaking, the greatest burdens on those governments that are least able to bear them. This is not a happy arrangement of human affairs but unfortunately there is no sign that such affairs were arranged for maximum convenience (65–66).

While state intervention was inevitable for TW countries in their pursuit of development, that strategy varied depending on which sector of the economy the government's focus was directed towards. If the history of development of the FW was looked upon as a guide, then it was natural for that process to begin with agricultural development supported by labour intensive industrialization. In other words, the process was to start with staples and then to manufacturing. Such a process of gradual structural transformation is difficult to replicate in any planned effort. While TW development may have to adopt a more focused approach, there is considerable debate on the advisability of predominantly agricultural economies, as in South Asia, adopting a strategy of industrialization. A plausible explanation for this is the elitist character of society in South Asia (Sen, 1986)

The adoption of a strategy of self reliance in which the state would control the commanding heights encouraged bureaucratic strangulation through regulations which in turn encouraged rent-seeking interest groups whose support then became increasingly vital for the ruling Congress party. Thus emerged the notorious iron triangles that restrained rather than encouraged enterprise (Bhagwati, 1988, 1993). In a democratic society laden with a colonial-type bureaucracy, a strategy of import substitution through state intervention contributed to poor economic growth. Such a strategy may have worked in a technocratic authoritarian system unquestioned by business groups who themselves have been disciplined by the state (Grabowski, 1994). Even then the 'carrot and stick' model of state intervention adopted in East Asia is far more complex and has to be examined and understood in its entirety if it is to be adopted elsewhere. It is the capacity for economic governance that differentiates the successful East Asians from their counterparts, the South Asians. That capacity is not entirely centred on coercion but on competitive collaboration between state and business, otherwise called 'developmental state', 'governed market', 'disciplined market' and 'strategic' capitalism (Amsden, 1992, Wade, 1990, Weiss and Hobson, 1995).

While South Asia allowed its entrenched agrarian class structure to remain intact or possibly enhance its power by introducing democratic institutions ahead of industrialization, the more serious blunder was the retention of vestiges of British colonialism like the administrative class, the legal system, the English language and the English system of education. By retaining them South Asia is possibly better integrated with the west but is also open to both its positive and negative influences. The negative influence, that of the lack of an identity, is expressed in the form of economic nationalism and an ambivalence to anything western. This is exemplified in the openness to western institutions, dress and artifacts, a vestige of colonialism which persisted despite the adoption of a closed economy. Symbolic of this is the rendition of the Christian hymn 'Abide with me' at the ceremony of Beating the Retreat, a re-enactment of the departure of the British and the birth of a new nation, held annually during the Indian Republic Day celebrations (Larsen, 1995).

India's mixed record which includes successes in higher education, science and technology, and failure in the provision of social services, like basic nutrition, primary education and rural literacy and health is attributed to that elitism which goes back into history. The caste system of traditional Hinduism was further accentuated during the British period. According to Maddison (1995)

> English education created a small elite which was more westernised than in any other Asian country, but also more alienated from the mass of the population. Their standards and aspirations were largely British, and after independence they took over the special caste attributes which the British had created for themselves in India (except expatriate status). Independence brought over a takeover, not a revolution, and preserved many of the static elements in the society and the economy. This had some short-run advantages as it led to greater political stability than elsewhere in Asia, but the preservation of caste, social immobility, and excessive respect for bureaucracy were probably harmful to long run growth (306).

The retention of English as the major language of business, even after 50 years of independence, has naturally perpetrated the elite–non-elite divisions in India and become the passport for entry into the public service for a minority English-speaking elite. The English language and the civil service, both inheritances of the colonial model, became the essential ingredients of the post-independence bureaucratic state. As the organizational weapon of state intervention, the power of the bureaucratic state was further enhanced through a system of centralized controls over production, investment and trade, encouraging what became known as 'rent seeking' and an obstacle to development (Bhagwati, 1988, 1993). Considering these historical factors and the emphasis laid on basic industry, science and technology and higher education at the expense of primary education, health and literacy, Bhagwati (1993) comments:

With what we now know about the close relationship between literacy and growth, especially in the context of the Far Eastern economies, though elsewhere too, there seems to be little doubt that India's productivity suffered seriously from both the oppressive framework above and the illiteracy below: the pincer movement killing the prospects for efficency and growth (49).

Table V-3   Rates of Literacy of People aged 15 in 1990

South Asia	41
Bangladesh	33.1
India	40.8
Nepal	20.7
Pakistan	25.6
Sri Lanka	86.1
East Asia	90.5
South Korea	90
Taiwan	91.2

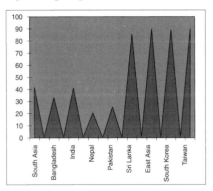

If India suffered as a consequence of encouraging social inequalities and ignored the creation of social opportunities through basic education (Dreeze and Sen, 1996), East Asia was able to achieve growth by reducing socio-economic inequalities and promoting primary education and literacy. By adopting policies for primary education and health, some Indian states like Kerala and West Bengal have shown dramatic regional variations in development performance, thus prompting social scientists to look for explanatory factors (Dreeze and Sen, 1996, Heller, 1996). Both states have had stable governments led by parties of the left or centre-left coalitions which have successfully implemented land reform, generated very high levels of political awareness and participation through unions. Their regimes have been characterized by active government involvement in economic development in co-operation with the private sector. Heller (1996) comments that:

> At this broad level then, state and society in Kerala have reinforced each other in a manner that unambiguously supports the "synergy" hypothesis Evans outlines in the introduction to this special issue. State interventions aimed at providing public goods have built directly on existing social capital resources and have in turn reinforced social capital (1056).

Another explanation offered is Kerala's religious mix of Hindus, Muslims and Christians; the last named are not only in substantial numbers but are known to have been there since the fourth century, followed there by the Jews after the fall of Jerusalem (Sen, 1986, 36). This factor prompts Sen (1986) to suggest the need to incorporate the possible influence of cultural history on development (36).

The 'soft state' phenomenon which explains the absence of social discipline highlights the presence of characteristics in South Asian citizens where the authority of the state is questioned. Expressions of such behaviour include flouting the law, and the application of rules and regulations on particularistic criteria as against its universal application (Blomkvist, 1992). This phenomenon associated with dualism is apparent in India where the influence of Hinduism is dominant. 'Indian culture and philosophy, which abound in contradictions, ignore the canons of logic and the rules of cause and effect, and label and categorize things without going on to seek analytical explanations' (Pye, 1985,133). The dualism arises when one's actions assume an arbitrary nature when influenced by particularistic notions of caste or religion or follow precise rules of conduct and deference to superiors because one is assigned a duty to perform according to his dharma. In the context of caste and one's station in that hierarchy one performs his or her duty strictly according to prescriptions. In the modern context of secular organization, relations between superiors and subordinates are based on unquestioned obedience where one expects rebuke rather than praise. In simple terms, the rules of conduct, obligations and customs are determined by one's dharma. The eternal law of dharma that governs one's life in the Hindu way of life is distinct from the rule of law that governs the modern Indian state (Pye, 1985, 138–139). This, then, is the cause of the underlying dualism.

Indian development has been hindered, according to Derrett, simply because of a want of a true belief in the rule of law amongst the public. and because the profitability of honesty across groups is still being discovered. India's achievement of peaceful co-existence between groups has been through a balance of forces favoured by Hinduism. This mode of resolving conflicts did not require a public spirit because relative status among groups as traditionally determined, and it was the ruler's responsibility to maintain that balance. The price of this Hindu-mediated balance has been an 'immobilisme' and a 'Hindu rate of growth', of around 3 percent for decades (Sudarshan, 1997, 275).

While accepting the fact that religion and culture influence behaviour, it is difficult to establish if Hinduism acts as an obstacle to development. Historically it has had a significant influence over the bureaucratic state by developing elaborate structures, hierarchical gradations, regulations and formal procedures. The system that was created offered those working strictly within the laws of their dharma ample scope to frustrate the system and render ineffectual the machinery for implementing policies. Having analysed power using the above description, Pye (1985) comments: 'Indeed the Hindu personality seems to be most at ease with activities associated with visionary planning and grandiose designs' (144).

V A CRITIQUE OF THE DEVELOPMENT STRATEGY

While the historical foundation for the development of agriculture in South Asia when compared with East Asia was different, its subsequent neglect in favour of industrialization is debatable. East Asian development strategy, was based on agricultural transformation. In South Asia, however, the focus under planned economic development was on industry. Agricultural surplus constitutes the basis for development to occur (Chakravarty, 1986), but India lacked a centralized bureaucracy that could extract the agricutural surplus necessary for growth (Barrington Moore jr, 1966). The British system of rent collection through intermediaries acted as a disincentive for producing agricultural surplus. The resulting lag in agricultural production in South Asia till the 1970s acted as a bottleneck to their development. The contribution of agriculture to economic development lies in producing the inputs and foodstuffs used in the industrial sector. Agricultural surplus contributes to demand in industrial products, export of primary products and assists in balance of payments. In other words, successful industrialization relies on prior success of agriculture (James *et al.*, 1989).

Deriving from the fact that annual income and production in monsoon agriculture is low, Oshima (1987) suggests that a developmental model should start with agricultural productivity. Unless a country is capable of funding food imports through industrial exports, attempts to sustain productivity increases through structural shifts will not be successful without a corresponding increase in agricultural productivity. Alternatively, an industrial strategy in the early stages of growth is difficult in the absence of industrial entrepreneurship, skills and lack of capital (52). Therefore a strategy of development, according to him, should focus on agricultural development and labour-intensive industrialization in the early stages and move gradually to more capital-intensive industrialization. Oshima (1987) feels that attempts at industrialization in some TW countries in South Asia in the early stages of development 'are likely to result in a collection of industries unable to efficiently supply industrial products. The upshot will be an economy growing slowly or even stagnating, as it is forced to rely heavily on government intervention for protection, regulation, subsidies, and foreign loans, and showing wide disparities in family incomes and savings, extensive surplus labour, and social unrest' (70–71).

Given the fact that agriculture in South Asia was virtually stagnant during the period of British rule, it would be expected that these countries would put emphasis in the early stages on agricultural development rather than industrialization. The adoption of a strategy of heavy industry requires considerable resources to stay afloat in conditions of low-capacity utilization and low rate of return. Further, its adoption creates a dualistic economy – one centred around industry and the other around agriculture – which then slows the process of growth. In the 1970s, when India wanted to shift to agriculture and exports, the dualistic economy that had been created had become inflexible and led to overlap (Oshima, 1987, 280–281). The ultimate outcome has been the creation of vested interests in the bureaucracy, the professions, business and the landlords, who by wielding disproportionate power to their numbers have led to the creation of a social and political dualism (Oshima, 1987, 281).

Oshima (1987) asserts that if Nehru had adopted an agricultural strategy followed by labour-intensive industrialization the outcome would probably have been different (286). Such an assertion assumes that the success of East Asia and the failure of South Asia can be attributed directly to the economic strategy adopted. In my view such a narrow explanation for either attributing success or failure of a country's economic policy is flawed. To establish that 'agriculture first and industry later' strategy is the only reason for relative success or failure of the two Asias is too simplistic a conclusion. Firstly, such a judgement fails to recognize the size of these economies. Could the emphasis on agriculture with labour-intensive industrialization have enabled the employment of large urban population in these countries? Secondly, increasing agricultural incomes through increased productivity requires inputs like chemical fertilizers, pesticides and insecticides, irrigation equipment and high-yielding varieties of seeds and – most important – urban demand for the increased agricultural production. For large countries like China and India it seems more reasonable to combine agricultural development with industrialization. In my view it was not the economic strategy adopted that was at fault: rather it was the manner of implementation that has to be questioned.

South Asia's consistently low performance between 1960 and 1980 in comparison to East Asia is squarely placed on the poor policy framework (Bhagwati, 1993, Dreeze and Sen, 1996) that resulted in extensive bureaucratic control over production investment and trade and inward-looking trade and foreign investment policies. While these policies administered through a centralized bureaucracy encouraged rent-seeking iron triangles and hampered growth in the private sector, the public sector, hindered by the lack of clear objectives and policies, poor investment decisions and inefficient management, compounded their problems (Bhagwati, 1993, 46–49). (Discussed in Chapters 8 and 9).

According to Dubey (1994):

> In short, India's development strategy gave a leading role to the state and the public sector and emphasised heavy and basic industry development to the relative neglect of traditional industries; it had a strong import substitution (almost autarkic) bias to the neglect of considerations of comparative advantage and international competitiveness; and it had an interventionist and regulatory character in order to give a social orientation to the activities of the private sector. The 'third way', instead combining the best from other systems, appeared to have combined the worst. The result was a system of 'command capitalism' in contrast to the objective of 'market socialism' (423).

While implementation of the strategy is seen as the cause of poor performance, other related issues were: (1) the balance of payments problems caused by sharp increase in imports; (2) increased demand for goods putting pressure on prices, and (3) the relatively slow growth of employment as a result of the capital-intensive industrial strategy. While these problems were caused by the economic strategy adopted, India had to encounter other problems like wars with China (1962) and Pakistan (1965) which diverted funding for investment towards defence. The crisis on the economic front forced a change in agricultural strategy and a liberalization in trade and industry policy. While the agricultural development strategy remained, the liberalization policy was short-lived. The rural poor excluded from the new agricultural strategy became the focus of a series of poverty amelioration programmes (Dubey, 1994, 422–424).

In the process of adapting to external forces and bringing about changes in policy, the fundamental programme of state-initiated industrialization begun in the Second Five Year Plan remained until mid-1980s. By this stage Indian industry was in a position to produce most industrial goods required for a modern economy, like steel, automobiles, railway and telephone equipment, and defence required industries including aircraft, missiles, satellite communications. This however was an inward-looking strategy which did not encourage Indian goods to be competitive in the international market. By the mid-1980s the bureaucratic controls on the private sector were gradually relaxed, resulting in an increase in industrial production and exports. While the industrial sector was slow to change, the agricultural strategy introduced in the mid-1960s was a success (Dobbs-Higginson,1993, 190–193). There is no doubt that the success of the agricultural strategy, although belated, could to some extent be attributed to the industrial base established in the early stages of development.

In making such evaluations of postwar economic performance the relative historical experience of East Asia and South Asia cannot be completely ignored. India, the largest country of the group, mobilized public support for independence on a reformist agenda led by stalwarts like Gandhi and Nehru, who had differing visions of the future. That India sought to establish itself as a major power in the international arena was reflected in the leading role it played in promoting non-alignment and decolonization. Such a role had to be supported by a strong economy based on industrialization and modern science and technology. The narrow analysis based purely on economic policies adopted by economists neglects the role of a modern nation state like India. In support, it is worth quoting a passage from a highly acclaimed study of India in its fiftieth year of independence.

Rather more expansively, the period of Indian history since 1947 might be seen as the adventure of a political idea: democracy. From this perspective, the history of independent India appears as the third moment in the great democratic experiment launched at the end of the 18th century by the American and French revolutions.... Each of these experiments released immense energies; each raised towering expectations and each has suffered tragic dissappointments. The Indian experiment is still in its early stages, and its outcome may well turn out to be the most significant of them all, partly because of its sheer human scale, and partly because of its location, a substantial bridgehead of effervescent liberty on the Asian continent. Asia is today the most economically dynamic region in the world, but it is also one where vast numbers of people remain politically subjugated. Its leaders have confidently asserted that the idea and practice of democracy is somehow radically inappropriate and intrusive to the more sober cultural manners of their people. The example of India is perhaps the most pointed challenge to these arguments (Khilnani, 1997).

East Asia's adoption of an open economy (export-oriented) with a closed political system contrasts with South Asia's adoption of an open political system with a closed economy. A look at their historical association and experience of colonialism under Japan and Britain will show that such a response is not completely surprising. While such a response appears natural for a country in its early stages of independence, what is surprising is the model of state intervention adopted in South Asia. In open political systems such as that practised in India, the existence of conditions of unequal power has allowed certain groups to influence the political process and support state intervention that has offered them economic benefits. Easy access to the political system has enabled them to acquire increased influence, particularly in India.

In any analysis of the economic performance of TW countries one cannot overlook the impact of geopolitical forces (like the cold war) based on political and military alignments. Countries of East Asia, as members of the western political alliance, were assured of economic support through capital investment. South Asia (excepting Pakistan), being largely non-aligned, was not seen to be receptive to foreign private investment till the end of the cold war. The reluctance on their part to join political alignments and the reservations towards foreign private investment is to be seen from the point of view of their colonial past (see Chapter 2). That reservation has been given expression in the form of indigenous control of important sectors of the economy.

If national independence gained after years of political struggle is to be maintained, then countries not a part of political alignments will need to develop indigenous defence capability, and this can only be developed through a strategy of industrialization. In preserving independence, countries like India have in addition to an industrialization strategy adopted active state intervention and import substitution. Much of the literature on comparative economic performance written in the post-cold war period by economists fails to take into consideration the political and international context which influenced economic policy in TW countries

VI   EXPLAINING DIFFERENCES IN ECONOMIC PERFORMANCE

South Asian countries have inherited from British colonization a political and administrative system which in many respects is regarded as an asset for maintaining stability. However, this can be a liability, because once entrenched it is less likely to provide opportunities for new ideas or institutions to develop. Just as a country which is blessed with abundant resources is referred to as suffering from 'Dutch disease', an overdeveloped administrative system such as many in South Asia can be characterized as suffering from 'bureaucratic disease'. Excessive emphasis on stability and routine at the expense of innovative and enterprising behaviour has become a characteristic of the South Asian bureaucratic state, differing vastly from the enterprizing technocracy of East Asia. While India and Sri Lanka have had democratic governments, Pakistan and Bangladesh have had sustained periods of military dictatorships with periods of elected governments which have not made any significant difference to economic performance. From that, it becomes evident that the factors contributing to the relative economic performance of the two regions have to be beyond just the nature of the political system, to a range of other explanations. However, there is no doubt that the ability of the East Asian economies to discipline capital is the outcome of an authoritarian state. It is not just a case of being authoritarian but having the administrative apparatus to make the appropriate intervention, supported by a social structure that values it and is willing to respond to it positively. Governments and their citizens in South Asian economies have been unable to act with such purpose because society in these countries lacks the unified culture (Ranis, 1992).

In highly politically mobilized societies the absence of social discipline is attributed by some to the 'soft state' (Myrdal, 1968). Blomkvist (1992) describes the soft state as particularistic – i.e. a state whose actions are ordered by other than rules. A state that operates on rules is universalistic (124). This lack of social discipline is a legacy of history, very likely emanating from a period of colonialism culminating in the non-cooperation strategy of the national movement for independence, the introduction of democracy in pre-industrialized societies, the lack of an organised religion, and low levels of literacy and education. Myrdal (1968) warns that 'rapid development will be exceedingly difficult to engender without an increase in social discipline in all strata and even in the villages' (899). Curle's (1970) narration of an interesting episode highlights the differences between China (authoritarian) and India in their efforts to combat intestinal diseases.

> The Chinese built latrines and shot anyone who did not make use of them – a powerful incentive towards hygiene. The Indians, at least in one area of which I shall speak, tried persuasion. A medical officer visited the villages, explained the nature and cause of the illnesses

affecting many of the people, and his men then dug fine latrines. 'Use these', he said. 'When I return in six months I shall find you all much better'. When he came back the latrines, unused, had caved in and the people were as sick as before. Sadly he harangued the villagers on their suicidal folly, ordered the latrines to be redug, and sternly admonished the people to make use of them. But his third visit revealed the same state of affairs – ill people and ignored hygienic facilities. This time he did not bother to make his squad dig out the latrines. He said to the people, 'I have told you what to do, and you have not done it. I shall do no more for you. However, I will leave behind these spades. You know what to do and if you come to your senses you will do it for yourselves'. And they did. Moreover, stimulated by a successful co-operative village effort, they set up an organization which, exercising considerable initiative and energy, planned and executed a number of improvements for the village. It took longer to obtain hygienic conditions in a small area of India than in a large one of China, but the final results were perhaps more important. People who are frightened into doing something do just that one thing; fear engenders neither self-confidence nor initiative (32–33).

The differences in approach to development between East Asian and other TW countries has led commentators to adopt the hard state–soft state distinctions. The above episode illustrates that distinction.

The differences in the pattern of import subsitution industrialization adopted by East Asia and South Asia have been sufficiently explored in this and previous chapters. However, one further explanation may be necessary, i.e. the policy elite. While the decision-makers in East Asia were technocrats from American universities, those in South Asia were generalist bureaucrats supported by academics trained in British or Indian universities. To this must be added the difference in the size of countries and their resource endowments. The lack of natural resources prompted East Asian governments to adopt tough action by a strong state which could not afford the luxury of extended protection. Such pressures were not significant in South Asia. This pressure to prove their economic superiority has to be viewed from the perspective of what Gershenkron calls 'a sense of backwardness' that East Asians may have felt in comparison to western countries (see Dore, 1992).

This upper class to which policy elites belong suffers from what Dore (1992) describes as a weak national bond. They are alienated from ordinary citizens and the legitimacy of policies of the government are seen as not in the public interest. This contrasts with East Asian policy elites who are not alienated from ordinary citizens and who in the Confucian tradition of scholar-bureaucrat are entitled to respect. Development analysts find it difficult to address such cultural traits as 'attitudes to authority, the balance between hedonism in personal life plans, the social cohesion of face-to-face groups, and levels of interpersonal trust. These are loosely connected with the espounded doctrines of professional Confucianists, as individualism is with Christianity' (Dore, 1992, 363). These issues, once central to the modernization debate, are now regarded as unfashionable in the context of the economic language of the universal human being (Dore, 1992, 363).

Therefore, when developmentalists, particularly economists, narrow their analysis to essentially economic strategies to explain differences in the performance of TW countries, they are overlooking a whole range of political, social, religious, historical and cultural characteristics that should be incorporated into studies of development. Hence the usefulness of adopting an interdisciplinary approach is advocated in this study (see Gershenkron, 1988, Goulet,1992, Sen 1983, Hagen 1966, McClleland, 198, Dore, 1989, 1992).

VII   CONCLUSION

In comparing the development performance of East Asia with South Asia, I have in this chapter focused on how the historical foundation has had an impact on the type of state intervention adopted. While the type of state intervention adopted by East Asian governments has been responsible for their success, that success could not have been achieved without the initial foundation of agricultural and industrial modernization undertaken during Japanese colonization followed by successful land reforms. Proximity to Japan (which at that time was undergoing a dramatic economic recovery) acted as a spur and provided a model for South Korea and Taiwan. Added to this was the strong leadership in the form of an authoritarian state supported by a technocracy which adopted a development policy and implemented it efficiently.

South Asia went through a different historical process where British colonialism did not provide a foundation for making an economic breakthrough as in East Asia. Arising from its colonial association, South Asia achieved easier integration with the outside world through the English language and education, its political and administrative institutions and the judicial system. While agriculture was virtually stagnant in the subcontinent, the transportation and communication infrastructure more specifically geared to trade with Britain was well in place. Constitutional democracy, enriched after independence, had its early foundations during the colonial period. The existence of a well-trained civil service provided a stable administrative system but its very strength turned into an obstacle for purposes of development. It encouraged the already entrenched caste hierarchy inherited through centuries, thus perpetuating the elitist-non-elitist distinctions. In a society where religious and cultural influences were not conducive to risk and innovation associated with entrepreneurship, the bureaucratic system of controls over licensing, investment and trade retarded the process of development. The system of rules and regulations that acted as barricades within a society of unequal access provided an opportunity for rent seeking.

Two important caveats to this contrasting conclusion of the two Asias are (1) India's outstanding record in maintaining political stability through the democratic process, and (2) her very size, which deserves a more disaggregated approach for any serious analysis. Both aspects if examined will, it is hoped, offer a more favourable picture than that based on hard macro-analytical data. This study, if not this chapter, is an attempt at broadening the criteria for comparative analysis.

6 Development Policies: Analysis and Implementation

I INTRODUCTION

Third World economies in a period of four to five decades have gone through different phases in their development. Influenced by the experience of post-Second World War recovery of Germany and Japan under the Marshall Plan and by the early thinking of Development Economists, governments of TW countries were led to adopt growth-oriented policies. Thus the first phase of development following World War II resulted in growth without development. Development according to this study (Chapter 3) combines economic growth with well-being, where the emphasis is on enhancing capabilities through the provision of basic services such as education, health, housing, etc. This emphasis on basic development occurring in the mid-1960s, considered the second phase, also recognized the need to change the attitudes and values of these societies from traditional to modern, so that they could acquire the capability to manipulate their physical, economic and social environment.

Both the first and second phases in development policy laid emphasis on the role of the state in promoting development. In the first phase the state focused on mobilizing capital through state intervention; in the second the state undertook a range of socio-economic functions involving considerable resources, as well as developing political and administrative capability. Their experience varied. While some performed well, others performed poorly, incurring considerable international debt after having invested a large amount of public resources without much development. Under pressure for resources, they were led to adopt a new approach, the third phase, referred to as stabilization and structural adjustment. Essentially it involves the withdrawal of the state from major economic activity and increased use of the private sector in development. An outcome of these developments is that the field of development policy and management is divided between contending groups that seek to promote their distinctive ideological positions like state intervention, market liberalism or greater community participation. Experience reveals that all three have useful contributions to make to meet a different set of situations in different TW countries. It is such experience that is recorded in this study.

The study thus far has sought to adopt a broad-based perspective to understand the relative performance of TW countries. In doing so I have questioned the 'state versus market' debate that is used to explain the East Asian miracle. There is growing evidence that one of the factors contributing to better development performance is the quality of policies, a theme that I explore in this chapter. That the link between the formulation of policy and its ultimate implementation is an important problem faced not just by TW countries is an issue that appears to have been overlooked in policy studies associated with developed economies.

The chapter is divided into six sections. Having introduced the theme in section I, I examine the political environment for policy-making in TW countries in section II. The significance of implementation analysis is covered in section III and section IV delves into the importance of distinguishing policies based on technical or social knowledge to assist the process of policy formulation and its implementation. Having made the distinction, in section V, I examine alternative approaches for evaluating policies. The chapter ends with a brief conclusion.

II   THE POLITICAL ENVIRONMENT OF POLICY-MAKING

In the traditional political science/public policy approach to policy-making, a policy is viewed as a formal response by those in political and administrative authority to what is perceived to be a problem. The problem can range from population explosion, declining agricultural and industrial productivity, demand for more education and better health, pressure on improved transportation and better roads, increased power generation or improved telecommunication. These could be considered universal problems encountered by most TW governments, resolution of which must be sought in the context of excessive public demand, insufficient resources, limited information and lack of political and administrative capability (see Chapters 2 and 3). All these factors are characteristic of the TW and have implications for the development and implementation of policies. Accordingly, 'policy is the use of resources by those in authority to achieve preferred ends' (Illchman and Uphoff, 1976, 257).

While markets in industrialized economies play a crucial role in resource allocation, such a role becomes increasingly difficult where such markets are absent and governments, when responding to problems, do not have recourse to market information. Unlike industrialized countries, TW countries suffer from lack of extra-bureaucratic organizations which act as catalysts in particular sectors such as agriculture, industry, health and education and contribute to policy-making. Their development is crucial as such social power can prevent politicians and administrators from using their power arbitrarily (Bhagwati, 1988). The absence of social power in TW countries creates a situation where, under limited resources and excessive demand, access to goods and services is dictated by one's power and influence in the community.

Blomkvist (1992) extends the hard state–soft state distinction and categorizes the FW as universalistic and the TW as particularistic. The universalistic state is one whose actions arc ordered on rules and regulations. A particularistic state is one whose actions are ordered by other considerations, such as political connections, friendship, family or caste affiliations (124). Here the application of rules is governed by personal relationships of politician/administrator to the recipient of public services. The latter is a case of transactional rule-breaking, for pure monetary gain (corruption), for speeding the issue of a license or permit, for political purposes (patronage) or for reasons of social relations like caste or religion (nepotism). It involves either a politician or an administrator, who is in a position of authority, dispensing something of value to a client. In rare cases when an administrator is unwilling to break the rules for legal or moral reasons, politicians may use their power to transfer such officials. In particularistic states in South Asia transfer is a potential weapon of power, often used with great effect. Thus the phenomenon of unequal access under conditions of scarce resources becomes further accentuated in particularistic states under patron–client relationships and is unwittingly encouraged by the democratic process (Blomkvist, 1992, 131–137). 'Thus a state unconstrained by rules, a particularistic or soft state, gives rise to a completely different policy process. With a particularistic state, the significant political struggle will be about implementation, not about policy' (Blomkvist, 1992, 139).

This characteristic of influencing the administration rather than policy formulation is a distinctive feature of Indian politics (Weiner, 1962). Attributed primarily to the politics of scarcity, the form taken by such political pressures on the administration (demand groups) has been seen as reaction to the growing role of the state and its unresponsiveness to public demands (Rudolph and Rudolph, 1987). In the absence of institutions like parties and pressure groups to aggregate interests in India, this particular pattern of public demands emerging in India needs further explanation. One possible explanation is the political process of civil disobedience adopted during the national movement, which has continued after independence (Myrdal, 1968). Another is the introduction of democratic institutions prior to industrialization. Both have influenced this trend and the form in which such demands have been expressed (Varshney, 1995). Such movements are seldom mobilized on a class basis owing to internal divisions based on caste, political factions, regional differences, religion, language and the underlying patron–client relationships (Mascarenhas, 1975). However, they tend to get activated during the political process of elections or inter-state disputes.

The remoteness and inaccessibility of the policy-making process to most individuals under conditions of excess competition and scarce resources is a characteristic of TW political systems and is seen as the reason for placing greater emphasis on outputs of the policy process and less on inputs. If the focus of political activity in industrialized countries is on the input stage, 'in the TW a large portion of individual and collective demand making, the representation of interests, and the emergence and resolution of conflict occurs at the output stage' (Grindle, 1980, 15). From the above analysis of TW political systems and the policy-making process, Grindle (1980) concludes that implementation is the arena where individuals and groups pursue conflicting interests (19).

While the absence of extra-bureaucratic institutions makes governments less accountable and more likely to be arbitrary in the distribution of goods and services, their absence often encourages unrealistic policies for symbolic reasons. Leaders of TW countries who indulge in such ambitious policies which are eventually not implemented have been dubbed 'century skippers' by Gross (1965). Another reason for unrealistic policies, i. e. policies not based on proper analysis, information or implementation implications in TW countries is that those responsible for policy-making are fully aware that detailed work will have to be done at the time when financial clearance has to be obtained from the controlling agency or that field based data will emerge when implementation begins. In other words, unrealistic policies are a product of (1) a bureaucratic system that requires subsequent financial clearance for previously approved policies or projects and (2) the absence of groups that can enhance the capacity of governments in the process of policy-making. On occasions, however, certain groups affected by the policies wake up to the reality or consequences of policies during implementation and either support or oppose such policies. Apparently in many cases it is the implementation process that triggers a realistic assessment of policies.

Montgomery identifies non-decisions as a major weakness of policy-making in TW countries. By this he refers to decisions either deferred or overlooked during the policy-making process which confront the administrator during implementation. Policy-makers need to anticipate a variety of factors that may crop up, bearing in mind that even policies based on considerable analysis are likely to encounter unanticipated consequences. The occurrence of unanticipated factors is, according to Korten (1981), more likely in areas where social, rather than technical knowledge, is the dominant ingredient of policy.

As stated earlier, TW countries tend to encounter a greater share of problems than the FW. To overcome some of the limitations of policy-making and the failures of implementation, Montgomery (1979) suggests the analysis of implementation during the process of policy-making. A deeper analysis of policies at different levels reveals their inter-relation and helps bring up several options to achieve policy objectives, alternative organizational devices to implement the policy and (most important) a variety of mechanisms to motivate users of services. Montgomery (1979) cites instances from irrigation and nutrition programmes in TW countries to highlight how policy decisions that failed to incorporate implementation analysis foreclosed possible technological-organisational-motivational options.

Notwithstanding the complexity of problems related to development, it is important to recognize the differences in capacity for policy-making and implementation between First and Third World nations. Horowitz (1989) questions the existence of a TW policy process and answers his question by identifying the limitations TW countries face in developing policies. They are:

(1)   The legitimacy of TW regimes is in question;
(2)   The policy concerns that predominate in the TW are distinct from those in FW;
(3)   The dominant role played by the state vis-à-vis the society;
(4)   Limited policy-making and implementing capacity when compared with the developed world;
(5)   The channels for participation are less well established and less clearly prescribed;
(6)   The knowledge and the information base essential to policy-making is lacking;
(7)   The demand for services far exceeds the resources available (Horowitz, 1989, 199–200).

In addition to the above, the process of policy-making is further influenced by other aspects such as history, attitudes, values and religion. The following comment illustrates the significance of socio-economic factors in TW policy-making:

> The social heterogeniety of most developing countries is regarded by many political leaders as a problem to be addressed by the policy process, and the measures often adopted touch upon matters, such as religion, that in the West would be regarded as dubious candidates for state intervention. Attitude change and certain cultural practices, little touched by policy in the West and controversial when they are, are very often central targets of policy in countries where such matters are seen as integral to the development process (Horowitz, 1989, 200).

It is also important to recognize differences in the capacity for policy-making between TW countries. The institutions, the resources available, the weight of state power in the society and the capacity of the state to achieve it vary significantly. East Asian economies adopting authoritarian political systems assisted by a technocracy are regarded as 'hard states' likely to develop policies that promote growth and development. Likewise, South Asian countries adopting democratic political systems are regarded as 'soft states' supported by a colonial-type bureaucracy. Their policies are generally a compromise between various groups that bring pressure on politicians and bureaucrats so as to promote vested interests.

Increasing evidence of failure in development, primarily in the areas of social change, has led academics to suggest the adoption of social learning (Sagasti, 1988, Korten 1981). This means that development administrators need to explore the problem in the process of implementation, study data when generated and encourage local-level participation so as to generate knowledge of local conditions. Those responsible for implementation need to reckon with problems at the time of implementation, but it may not always be possible to mobilize enough effort and resources to overcome them. Efforts at problem solving should involve people at the coalface and not be presented 'ready made'.

III   IMPLEMENTATION ANALYSIS

The development experience of TW countries reveals a growing discrepancy between what was planned and what has been achieved. Despite the use of sophisticated analysis and techniques, difficulties have been caused by the inability to anticipate problems encountered in implementation.

While lack of resources, skills and managerial capability are recognized constraints characteristic of TW countries, the social and political uncertainties which are equally significant have been overlooked. To overcome such pitfalls emphasis is now being laid on implementation analysis and 'learning by doing'.

'Implementation analysis requires sensitive application of social theory and the development of refined indicators of performance, but it is not beyond the resources of most governments' (Montgomery, 1979, 4). Therefore, if a government or policy-maker intends to analyse a policy in terms of implementation, Montgomery suggests its disaggregation into first, second and third order decisions – i.e. the level of productive technology, internal organization and public motivation. At each level a distinct discipline or specialized unit is used to improve the quality of analysis varying according to the content of the policy (Montgomery, 1989, 6–10).

As most policies affect some citizens or clients who are the recipients of programmes both the process of policy-making and the process of implementation must incorporate mechanisms to elicit changes in behaviour and attitude. Whether it is agriculture, family planning, health or education, the ultimate success of policies or programmes depends on the response of citizens or recipients of programmes.

The initial policy decision involving a particular technology or its location can often lead to a situation where alternative options at second and third order level are precluded. In order to avoid such a situation Montgomery advocates implementation analysis so that lower-order decisions are incorporated at the time when the initial decision is made. Therefore, when policy involves multi-purpose objectives, it is worth considering implementation problems as a part of the policy-making process. Sensitive application of social theory requires:

(1)   Officials who are responsive to the special values and needs of people without conceding to the pressures of powerful groups who may seek more access or obstruct implementation;

(2)   Political acumen as well as sympathetic understanding of the local environment, i.e. identification of groups supportive and opposed to the change;

(3)   The adoption of a careful balance between central guidance and decentralised operations so as to prevent excesses of local officials;

(4)   The recognition of differences in culture, ideology, nature of political regime, etc., thus suggesting that identical policies due to such sociocultural factors may have to be implemented differently;

(5) A careful analysis of factors such as religion, culture, region, etc. so as to identify them either as a resource or as an obstacle (Grindle, 1980).

IV A FRAMEWORK FOR ANALYSING DIFFERENCES IN POLICIES

In section II of this chapter I adopted a distinction between policies based on scientific knowledge and those based on social knowledge. In the former, analysis entails a rational approach first by defining a problem, then by examining alternatives to resolve the problem, and finally by adopting the best alternative in terms of costs, benefits and likely outcomes. This approach to problem solving is identified with the blueprint approach whereby the human or social element is of limited significance. Unlike scientific knowledge, social knowledge is embedded in a particular social system i. e. governed by complex internal relationships whose observation and measurement is difficult. Problems of this type cannot be understood by dismantling them into components as in the case of scientific knowledge. Social knowledge is based on accumulated social experience and effecting change in this case is a slow process.

A further step in this direction in implementation analysis lies in the classification of policies using the content–context distinction (Grindle, 1980). The content refers to the actual policies and programmes developed by governments to achieve development objectives and context is its actual implementation i.e. the organization. When implementation of a policy is considered a variety of environmental aspects must be studied in addition to quality or type of policy and resources.

Thus the context of a policy brings into play a variety of political and administrative aspects of implementation not considered in the content of policies. The content of policies becomes important because some policies are more difficult than others to implement. Grindle (1980) adopts a framework which helps to identify different dimensions of complexity/difficulty in implementation.

The success or failure of programmes does not rest entirely on the response of recipients of the programmes but on a variety of other implementation factors. For example, some programmes involve considerable integration of a variety of agencies operating at the field level. The greater the number of agencies involved in policy implementation, the greater the chances of conflict. This leads to difficulties at the site of implementation, depending on whether the programme is concentrated in one area or dispersed both geographically and organizationally. The more dispersed it is, the more difficult the execution of the programme. Development policies can lead to conflict between beneficiaries of policies and those who do not benefit and yet have to bear the costs. Certain areas of development policy such as family planning (seen as insensitive to religious tradition) or building a multi-purpose river valley project (which inundates large tracts of land to benefit downstream farmers) or land reforms which alter traditional economic and social relations in rural areas, can cause discontent which may be expressed in the form of demand groups. i. e. sporadic outbursts of anger arising out of frustration (Rudolph and Rudolph 1987). Issues such as these need to be handled either by public entrepreneurs (Mascarenhas,1982) or by integrative generalists (Gross, 1965) who can resolve conflict, mobilize support and build institutions. Do TW countries possess such public entrepreneurs to handle implementation problems? In such situations there is a thin line that separates an administrator from an active politician and such administrators are resented by politicians.

These are issues that need to be examined and explored while development policy is being formulated.

V   ALTERNATIVE APPROACHES

The uncertainty and complexity of TW development has to be understood in the context of limitations faced by TW policy-makers. Of the several that need to be reiterated are (1) imprecise goals and objectives, (2) lack of appropriate or adequate data, (3) lack of understanding of social and cultural factors, (4) absence of incentives for changing behaviour, (5) excessive political intervention in the implementation of projects and (6) low levels of administrative capacity. While these limitations may be overlooked by overzealous promoters of centralized planning and systems, their outcome in terms of programme failure can be compounded if persisted with. Having identified such limitations, Rondinelli (1982–83) calls for a more realistic approach to development planning and management by viewing 'social problem solving as an incremental process of social interaction, trial and error, successive approximation, and social learning' (63).

When there is uncertainty about the outcome, alternative approaches to implementation of programmes have to be considered. It is helpful to have access to a form of analysis that can predict success or failure. The following three alternatives are suggested: pre-testing of policies, scope for pilot projects and selective implementation. Of these, pilot projects can help predict the likely problems of implementation. However the well-known Community Development Project at Etawah in Uttar Pradesh, India, initiated as a pilot project before the introduction of the community development programme in 1952, failed to produce any results of use as underlying principles of community development were not adhered to at the implementation stage (Hart, 1971).

A problem with pilot projects is that the extraordinary political and administrative support afforded at the pilot stage is not always forthcoming when the programme is actually implemented. As in the case of Etawah, Project Poshak, an integrated health nutrition scheme based on a 'take home' approach suffered similarly due to lack of political and administrative support. During the transition from a pilot project to an operational stage, project administration was confronted by a myriad of problems that were political and managerial in nature. Designed and administered to reflect a real-world situation, the project was not extended despite being regarded a success (Pyle, 1980). The decision of the state government to return to onsite feeding was based not on cost or efficiency, but on personalities, bureaucratic practices, publicity and political realities.

Based on a study of Project Poshak, Pyle (1980) distinguishes flexible planning from unspecified planning. In the case of the former, while the objectives are fixed, the means to achieve it are amenable to change. In the case of unspecified planning, the objectives themselves are left vague. According to Pyle, Poshak suffered from the latter i.e. the original agreement did not specify how the 'take home' concept would be extended once the pilot study had been completed.

This shows that while pilot projects are useful to test a new idea or technique, they appear to flounder when faced with the reality of the political process. Was Poshak a demonstration, a pilot or a research project? (Rondinelli, 1993). Evidence shows that it included elements of all three. Strangely, the state government had not made any financial commitments to the project. Such low concern shown by the government could be attributed to the importance given to curative medicine as against preventive medicine reflecting the reality that the likely beneficiaries of preventive medicine have limited political voice.

While pilot projects are widely adopted, the prospect for adopting pretesting or a demonstration project has greater scope when a new type of food, drug or new type of seed or new equipment is being introduced. For example, demonstration farms are commonly used in agriculture. When large amounts of resources are spent on a programme, it is advisable for governments to adopt selective implementation and extend the programme following the observation of results. To avoid possible objections on political or ethical grounds Montgomery suggests caution when governments adopt an experimental approach (Montgomery, 1974, 221). Development depends on the response of people to various policies, an area which I think needs greater focus. The focus of the first phase was on growth. While that focus during the second phase shifted to the provision of basic needs and the improvement of the quality of life, the success of such policies depended on effective implementation and impact on society. However, the crucial element the implementation of policies, depended on the development of administration (see Chapter 7). As implementation of the first and second phases had suffered owing to the absence of effective administrative capability, the TW came under pressure to adopt the third phase – structural adjustment. Poor performance and the success of NIEs prompted the IMF/World Bank to advocate an open, export-oriented, competitive market model with a reduction in the role of the state.

The response of the IMF/World Bank was to prescribe a uniform package which turned out to be inappropriate for countries in Latin America and South Asia. This program of economic stabilisation and structural adjustment suffers from a narrow financial and economic focus and an intrinsic failure to recognise the diversity of these countries. That these factors have been overlooked has become evident with the difficulties that so many countries have experienced in implementing them. Recognising this fact, Montgomery and Rondinelli (1989) comment that 'if international organizations want to implement economic reform policies more effectively, they must take a broader view of the development process and assess more carefully the administrative capacity of governments to make policy changes' (1989, 74). These should involve:

(1)   decisions relating to the allocation of resources for economic growth
(2)   policies for social equity
(3)   international transactions for capital and technology and
(4)   public sector administration (Montgomery and Rondinelli, 1989).

V   CONCLUSION

Differential performance among a group of countries identified as undeveloped decades ago has resulted in a re-categorization of these countries into several different groups. Evidence of relative performance, relating particularly to those which adopted economic restructuring, has led to a refinement of the category known as TW. Some have been successful in implementation, while others have performed indifferently. As a result, a growing divergence has now appeared between countries based on relative prosperity and relative poverty (Grindle and Thomas, 1991).

In viewing this divergence as a product of differing policies adopted by different TW countries, I emphasize the importance of recognizing, firstly, the resources and constraints; secondly, the political and administrative capacities for developing policies and implementing them, and, thirdly, the significance of historical, cultural and religious factors that influence TW development policies. Therefore the greater the impact of non-economic factors the greater the need to recognize the differences between scientific and social knowledge in the content of policies. If the content of policies seems to veer towards social knowledge it is likely that the policy issue is embedded in social institutions and this then suggests that a different approach should be adopted, governed primarily by local factors. If this distinction is made to assist policy formulation it is appropriate to adopt the Decision orders framework of Montgomery (1979) and the Content/Context distinction of Grindle (1980) to examine implementation issues.

7 Developing Capability for Managing Development

I INTRODUCTION

Development, as I have discussed in earlier chapters of this study, has to be a planned process of economic and social change undertaken through the apparatus of the state in the absence of the market. Constraints on resources in the TW have led the state to play a more active role compared with its role during the period of capitalist development when the market was a driving force. Initially academics, particularly economists and policy-makers, believed that appropriate policies with investment were important for development. Then it dawned on them that the development of the First World had come about through the capacity of institutions and through individual skills (Esman, 1991). So it was realized that, irrespective of the economic strategy adopted, attempts to promote development require the capacity to manage development by creating an effective political and administrative system. That recognition by academics in the 1960s led to the emergence of Development Administration as distinct from traditional Public Administration as a field of study. Development Administration 'refers to organised efforts to carry out programs or projects thought by those involved to serve development objectives' (Riggs, 1971, 73).

Early writings on development categorized countries into two groups: the developed as the First World (FW) and the underdeveloped as the Third World (TW). No recognition was given, however, in these categorizations, to the fact that countries belonging to the TW in economic terms had had their own distinctive history of political and administrative development. While the type of political and administrative system inherited from their colonial past would doubtless have made a significant contribution to extending the legitimacy of new regimes, it did however pose an obstacle in terms of economic development under a system of state intervention (La Palombara 1971).

Focusing on integrating the role of political and administrative systems in the development of TW countries highlights the need to integrate two segments: the constitutional system (institutions of governance) with the administrative system (organization and management of government activities). The relationship between the two segments is unclear, since TW countries have been through different colonial experiences. The relative difference between countries in the relationship between the political system and the administrative system rests on the nature of civil society, which Morgan (1996) describes as 'the corpus of social arrangements defining state-society relations and public-private domains of relative autonomy' (228). In TW countries a civil society to mediate the relationship is yet to evolve. While the emphasis in South Korea and Taiwan has been on developmental outcomes, resulting in the emergence of a technocracy, countries like India have focused on representation and political responsiveness with less concern for development outcomes. Both sets of countries, as discussed in this chapter, have worked towards integrating the constitutional and the administrative segments through the process of reform.

In comparing the two regions with relation to their capacity for achieving development, one can adopt Drucker's (1985) description that East Asia has a technocracy which was trained to do the right things, while South Asia has a bureaucracy trained to do things right. The former is capable of adopting a responsive/adaptive analytical approach while the latter is more likely to adopt a reactive/ control approach. The former is more suitable to managing change whereas the latter is more appropriate to maintaing stability (Gawthrop, 1983). In this chapter I focus on the political and administrative system for managing development by adopting, in the next section, a diagnostic approach to understand administrative systems in relation to the development function. In section III I explore the concept of balanced development by distinguishing the development of administration from the administration of development. In section IV I discuss two alternative approaches to identify distinctive administrative demands. In section V I consider the outcome of different strategies to promote administrative capability such as institution building, administrative reform and governance. I conclude by tracing the evolution from bureaucratic administration to development administration, and from there to development management and finally the emergence of governance.

II   A DIAGNOSIS

In their quest for development TW countries have had to face excessive demand for services with limited resources at hand. Efforts to utilize such resources for development have not produced the desired results.

Here I focus on management and administrative capability for development in the two Asias.

The concept of development adopted in this study places emphasis on both aspects: the political and the administrative. Insulation from political interference permits the technocracy in East Asia to do 'the right things'. A crucial factor in the high performance of East Asian economies is the extensive legislative and policy-making power vested in the bureaucracy, insulating it from a legislature (political) (World Bank, 1993, 70) which in most cases did not exist. The bureaucracy appears to have played an influential role in both the land reforms (1948–52) and the economic reforms (1958–60) which transformed the economy of Taiwan. Indeed, the influence and power wielded by a group of technocrats was such that their recommendations became national policy and were effectively carried out. While the role of technocrats was important, credit must also be given to the competence of middle-level bureaucrats who worked out the details of policies and administered them on a day-to-day basis (Ho, 1995, 52–53). As a result the technocracy in East Asia acquired enormous power without corresponding political accountability.

By contrast, such power in South Asia was concentrated in the political leadership which was reluctant to enlist the support and skills of its bureaucracies. This difference between East and South Asia in the role of the administrative system in development can be traced to the type of administrative system that both sets of countries inherited from their colonial past (Darling, 1979, Kohli, 1994). While South Asia promoted the apolitical civil service based on the British model, the East Asian economies were influenced first by the Japanese developmental state and later by the United States. A plausible explanation for this unified view of development (insulated from political interference) is the adoption of non-democratic systems of government by separated elites (that is, not dependent on powerful indigenous sources of power) following the postwar political realignment of forces. The process was facilitated by the elimination of the rural aristrocracy through the successful implementation of land reforms, social upheavals and the perceived threat of invasion. All these factors combined to allow a narrow political elite to govern without any political and constitutional constraints. The authoritarian regime politically excluded the popular sector, abolished elections, prohibited strikes, restricted the organisation of labour unions and violated basic human rights. 'Efficiency, rationality, and social stability replaced democracy as the basis on which the regime laid claim to legitimacy' (Im, 1986–87, 239–240). With South Korea's historical experience such a transition to 'bureaucratic authoritarianism' in 1971 was achieved without much difficulty (Im, 1986–87).

In the context of different historical and cultural circumstances, most countries in South Asia (except Pakistan during periods of military rule) sought to adopt a balanced concept of development in which both the political and administrative elements were to operate in an open political system. Elective political institutions operating from central government, state and local levels combined with high levels of pre- and post-independence political mobilization, meant that governments in South Asia found themselves constantly responding (demand groups) to public pressures. Such response had to take into consideration constitutional constraints, regional demands of language, ethnic and religious pressures, communal harmony between religious groups and the need to adapt to the demands of disadvantaged socio-economic groups which had received constitutional rights to education and jobs. All these conflicting demands had to be reconciled within a political environment of frequent elections, volatile demand groups, highly organized trade unions and an active media aptly described as a fractured democracy.

Five decades of independence in India have not eased the underlying conflicts of communalism, nationalism and democracy. Nor has the relationship between the political (legislative) and the administrative been rendered smoother. An apolitical neutral civil service modelled on the British system has struggled to operate in a highly political environment. If exposure to political interference in the functioning of the public service is endemic, the public service on its part has retained its pre-independence elitist attitude and with it all the negative values associated with it. The term 'bureaucratic state' is I feel, an apt description. The difficulties have been compounded owing to an underlying conflict between the pressure of re-election in a democracy and the inability to obtain the necessary commitment from a bureacratic elite which originates from a different social background to that of elected politicians. In such a climate of divergence of purpose any form of state intervention merely allows greater scope for vested interests and further undermines development objectives.

The alternative systems, the technocratic and the political (or democratic) are embedded in their respective historical, social, cultural and religious backgrounds. In other words, the technocratic model which is instrumental in the performance of East Asian development is unlikely to succeed in South Asia, while the reverse is possibly true. More important is the presence or absence of politics in the calculus of development administrators in their approach to a problem. These calculations are likely to be less of a constraint in the East Asian 'technocratic state' than in the case of the South Asian 'democratic state.' In the case of the latter political support becomes vital and can be conflictual, depending upon the political forces.

TW governments often find it difficult to separate the traditional role of public administration (law and order) from its developmental role. The two become indistinguishable, particularly in democratic countries, when a development programme creates divisions between groups – those who benefit and those who pay the cost of the programme. Such conflict of interests emerging as political issues can arise out of a major irrigation project that benefits downstream farmers but inundates larger areas for the dam. In democratic societies, those incurring costs of such projects are more easily mobilized as demand groups and such demands cannot be easily overlooked. When such development programmes due to conflict turn into law and order issues, then the development administrator has to give way to the law-and-order bureaucracy. Such situations can arise during implementation of land reforms, programs of population control or demolition of unauthorized dwellings in urban areas. (Blomkvist, 1993)

The terms 'soft state' and 'hard state' inducted into the development literature fail to incorporate such broader political and social contexts. Though democratization can be taken to its limits – i.e. highly politically mobilized South Asian countries (demand groups) – the alternative, often witnessed in East Asia, is the other extreme. The significant political groups that exist or emerge in democratic societies as a result of development programmes must be recognized as a part of the process of development which demands a distinctive type of administrator described as 'integrative generalists' (Gross, 1965) who can mobilize support and resources, handle conflict and build institutions. Such integrative generalists are difficult to develop in TW countries currently governed by bureaucracies whose concern is 'doing things right' with an elaborate set of rules and regulations – a system that breeds rent seekers rather than innovative entrepreneurs (Bhagwati, 1988).

Until a level of development is achieved it is evident that the arm of the bureaucracy which exercises power and authority is likely to enjoy dominance over the arm involved in development activities. Riggs (1971) feels that excessive power in the hands of the bureaucracy is detrimental to development but thinks that a decline in the power of traditional bureaucracy can happen only if a country adopts a balanced approach, i.e. both political and administrative development. Our analysis of both East Asia and South Asia reveals lack of balance between the political and the administrative system. Riggs (1971) comments that:

> In other words, our administrative principles may prove helpful in bringing about some improvement in administrative performance in balanced polities. By contrast, they may further undermine administrative performance in unbalanced polities. In these systems priority needs to be given to efforts to achieve balance, either by strengthening the constitutive system or the bureaucracy, depending on which of these key institutions is relatively less powerful (82).

Administrative systems in TW countries, unlike that of the FW, are closely interrelated with the political, social and cultural factors, and their functioning must be understood in the context of the larger society. It is a case of modern bureaucratic organizations being superimposed on traditional social systems. Their functioning therefore needs to be understood in the context of the conflict of cultures. Riggs (1964) advocates a two-way linkage between society and administration: the ecological approach, adopting structural–functional analysis. Accordingly, TW administrative systems are functionally diffuse and decisions are influenced by societal values. Therefore societies which are in the process of moving from traditional to modern are in the transitional phase and such societies can be analysed as prismatic i.e. societies that are going through the process of change. To understand the behaviour of officials in such societies, he adopts Parsons' 'pattern variables' (Riggs, 1964). Prismatic behaviour which reflects values of both traditional and modern society (overlap) is caused by the lack of political development, i.e. absence of social power (pressure groups, extra bureuacratic organizations) where officials tend to be arbitrary (i.e. permissive) or exercise authority by over-emphasizing rules and procedures.

While societal influence has a bearing on the behaviour of officials in TW bureaucracy, such countries suffer from lopsidedness – i.e. they suffer from overbureaucracy (excessive rules and regulation) and a simultaneous dearth of skills in project planning, project estimates and project management. Over-bureaucratized administrations expect too many reports from field agencies (over-evaluation) but suffer from a shortage of personnel with the appropriate skills for evaluation (under-evaluation) (Kapp, 1960). While such an assessment of TW administrative systems reflected conditions in the 1960s, it would be no surprise if such conditions persisted in bureaucracies with the culture of 'doing things right'.

Both centralized planning and state intervention possibly encourage, if not accentuate, such non-performing bureaucratic systems. Experience of such systems has prompted some specialists to advocate an open, flexible and broad-based issue approach to development administration. The demands of development require a range of analytical, integrative and leadership skills united in a problem-solving environment called 'policy guidance cluster' (Gross, 1970).

III A FRAMEWORK FOR IDENTIFYING PROBLEMS RELATING TO DEVELOPMENT OF ADMINISTRATIVE CAPABILITY

While societal influences on administrative systems should warn policy-makers against blind imitation or replication, the question posed is whether organizations can be created by external stimulus before a society has generated the prerequisites for development. The question becomes relevant with the enormous prospects for what Esman (1980) calls 'enclave development', by which he refers to projects such as an oil refinery or other types of process technology where contextual factors like culture, skills, etc. have minimal effect. This type of industrial capital has increasingly moved from industrialized economies to low-wage economies (non-unionized) with the new international division of labour – i.e. the feasibility of world market-oriented manufacturing in peripheral countries. This shift in capital has been helped by the revolution in transportation, computer and communication technologies as well as the increase in industrial wages in industrialized countries. This dimension to industrial development has not been sufficiently explored by analysts of East Asian economies (see Chapter 8).

Contextual factors are more likely to affect equity-promoting programmes such as nutrition, agricultural practices and family planning where development administrators have to account for diverse needs, capabilities, preferences, values and attitudes. In such socially embedded rural development programmes it is necessary for the ideas to be tested and experimented in the field. In such cases, a universal technology is replaced by an approach requiring joint exploration and learning in a mutual learning environment where data and information generated by the participants act as the basis of new learning. Therefore we need to recognize the two parallel tracts: modern technology which is universal and a creative approach adapted to local situation called social transformation (Esman, 1980, Korten, 1981, Friedman, 1987).

Just as institutions that have been successful in one context cannot easily be replicated in another, similarly governments have to examine the relative effectiveness of alternative types of organization to carry out development activities. It is becoming evident that institutional perform- ance can vary across sectors than among countries. The difference in performance between sectors is determined by the extent of 'specificity' and 'competition'. Specificity refers to the ease or clarity in developing objectives, methods of achieving them and their impact. Competition refers to other than the external market surrogates, such as clients and controlling agencies, that bring pressure on institutional performance (Israel, 1987). Development programmes intended to transform the traditional sector in TW countries generally fall into the 'low specificity' and low competition end of the spectrum and thus lack the incentives for performance (Israel, 1987, 4–5). As small operators working under local conditions, their success depends on responding to village experi- ence, introducing 'routinization' to meet local level needs, the willing- ness to learn from mistakes and the adoption of a practice of learning with people and building new knowledge and institutional capacity through action, as opposed to uniform centrally planned and directed programmes (Mascarenhas, 1993, 476, Korten, 1980). The recognition of distinctive characteristics as contributing to relative success of rural development programmes has encouraged comparative analysis (Jain, 1994, Grindle, 1997).

Grindle (1997) explores the varying performance of organizations operating under similar conditions, focusing on the successful ones. Goulet (1992) describes these as 'microsuccesses' in an environment of 'macrofailure'. In the case of successful organizations studied, Grindle (1997) found that positive organizational cultures, such as mission, performance-oriented managerial style, and autonomy in personnel matters differentiated those that performed relatively well from those that did not (482). While organizational culture is regarded as an import- ant explanation for successful organizations, the contextual problems I have focused on in this chapter continue to be a major problem for management of development. Such contextual factors like rigid civil ser- vice rules and regulations applied uniformly and centralized, attitude of public sector unions, political interference in appointments, preval- ence of corruption together affect the behaviour of people in public organizations. If a culture of organizational performance is to be encour- aged, such environmental and contextual factors need to be changed (Grindle, 1997, 490–491). East Asian countries have overcome some- what similar constraints by creating neutral competence based on universalistic, rather than particularistic, methods for conducting government business.

To develop such organizations, 'development administration literature makes a distinction between development of administration and administration of development' (Riggs, 1971). Analytically the former refers to enhancing the capacity of the administration (organization) and the latter has to do with the actual implementation of programmes and projects of development. The two are not distinct. Therefore the definition of development administration is 'organized efforts to implement programmes and projects thought by policy-makers to serve development objectives' (Riggs. 1971). By making the distinction between the development of administration (developing the managerial capability) and the administration of development (the capability for implementing projects) a country is developing the capacity to change the environment. If a country is not able to achieve a programme of immunization or a family planning target, it can be due either to lack of system capacity (shortage of paramedics) or due to the lack of urgency and need felt in the environment for adopting the programmes. Riggs distinguishes this into content and context; the question here is: are they separable? Not easily, as this is a case of circular causations – i.e. are organizations the cause or consequence of development? This is an example of the chicken-egg problem all over again. In other words, it is difficult to treat the development process sequentially.

What is important is for the system to constantly adapt to changes in the environment as the environment constantly responds to outputs from the system. Development as a cause or consequence of organization renders the distinction between development of administration and the administration of development increasingly difficult. The former enhances the internal process of the system to cope with increasing demands from the environment, resulting in system differentiation; that is, the number of organizations increases to meet new demands.

The changes in the environment give people in such societies greater discretion in their choice of response, i.e. in influencing the environment. Therefore the process of development involving policies and programmes results in increased capacity of TW countries. Riggs (1971) is of the opinion that the principles or ideas that govern the functioning of administrative systems in the FW are not appropriate in dealing with the problems of the TW. Therefore, he emphasizes improving the context – i.e. political, economic and social – to face the challenges in the administration of development. To manipulate the physical environment he considers the interrelated existence of a balanced polity, a salaried bureaucracy and organizations as essential to development: the existence of one facilitates the development of the other.

The administration of development (the environment) which is the object of change can be effectively achieved by governments with the enhanced administrative capacity. Therefore the physical, human and cultural environment can be changed through a variety of development programmes. Shortage of personnel with skills is an environmental problem which can be overcome by setting up programmes and projects to train personnel and educate them in order to change their attitudes. These are not constraints on the administrative system.

By initiating programmes and policies of development a country is essentially enhancing its capacity – increasing discretion reflected in the levels of differentiation. The more developed a society is, invariably it has created organizations to influence the environment. Therefore development can be defined as the capacity or the ability of human systems to manipulate the human, physical and cultural environment. (See Chapter 6.)

IV   ALTERNATIVE STRATEGIES TO ACHIEVE ADMINISTRATIVE CAPABILITY

If a country needs to develop its administration in order to manage development, it can adopt a range of approaches to assess its needs, taking into consideration the demands of development. While the development of administration and the administration of development are conceptually distinguished, governments are concerned with strengthening their managerial capabilities to undertake development tasks and to manage ongoing development programmes. In this study I have emphasized that the difference between East Asia and South Asia is their capacity to manage development. Esman (1991) reiterates that:

> What most distinguishes advanced societies and their governments is not their "culture," nor their natural endowments, not the availability of capital, nor the rationality of their public policies, but precisely the capacities of their institutions and the skills of individuals, including those of management (20).

To enhance such managerial capacity for development I examine some approaches in this chapter. These include the performance, structure, environment model developed by Gross (1969) and the country profile approach advocated by La Palombara (1971).

Gross (1969), in his performance (objectives) structure environment model, focuses on the essential linkages between a country's or organization's objectives, the relevant structure to implement those objectives and the impact that such organizations (structures) have on the environment. It involves a stepwise analytical process requiring an assessment of how planned objectives or performance indicators are to be achieved. That involves (a) resources, both financial and material, (b) skilled personnel, and (c) available technology. All three must be matched to the level of performance expected. In addition, what is needed is a structure that links the resources and technology to achieve the desired purpose. Such analysis can be adopted either at a micro or macro level but begins with identifying objectives or indicators of performance.

Gross's model adopts a definition of 'organizations as man – resources systems performing activities through a process of interaction among its parts and in relationship to its environment.' The organization establishes interaction through linkages for acquiring inputs and for exporting outputs. Such input–output linkages are not easily established in TW countries because existing imbalances inhibit their development. To identify the appropriate sources for establishing linkages it is helpful to adopt a systems approach.

By adopting such an interrelated systems approach, TW countries can identify areas which they need to focus on. There might perhaps be a shortage of personnel with skills such as economic analysis, project analysis and evaluation, technology assessment and cost-benefit analysis. At the next level, when implementation of programmes is considered, policy-makers need to examine if the objectives can be achieved through existing organizations or if new organizations need to be created. If new organizations are deemed necessary, this may entail organizational reform, extensive training and in some cases institution-building. When examining implementation, it is necessary to explore the type of device to adopt market or non-market, whether centralized or decentralized, departmental or non-departmental.

La Palombara (1971) adopts profile analysis to identify the constraints and obstacles. According to this approach, administrative capability is to do with the need of a country (or its political system) to produce new behaviour. That goal or objective is dependent on the type of administrative system, or whether the existing system can resolve it, on its power structure and on the values of that society. Do they facilitate or impede such administrative capability?

If the existing values of the society and its administrative and political structure are to be analysed then they are to be examined in terms of what La Palombara (1971) categorizes as crises of legitimacy, participation, penetration and distribution. To resolve these a country needs increased production of unavailable goods and services, the equitable distribution of such goods and services and greater public participation. Achieving these basic objectives becomes difficult if a country continues to search for political identity, integration and legitimacy. Most TW countries have had to invest considerable resources into holding the nation together: a crisis of legitimacy becomes a primary concern in comparison to increasing production of unavailable goods and services and their equitable distribution.

Identification of the crisis is the next step. Once the crisis is identified, it is necessary to (a) develop a profile of a country's physical, organizational and human resources (b) map out its transport and communication facilities (c) to extend government authority (i.e. penetration) and (d) to achieve greater balance of power between politicians, bureaucracy and non-political elites. The profile must understand and recognize existing values of society, traditions and religion.

Thus a profile of a country's resources is matched in relation to the type of crisis in order to identify whether a resource is a strength or an obstacle. For example, the South Asian bureaucracy we have previously referred to was a resource for penetration but has proved to be an obstacle for development. Traditional values fostered by Confucianism are a strength in East Asia, while Islam, Hinduism and Buddhism can be an obstacle in South Asia. Whether an obstacle or a strength, a resource has to be analysed in the context of the crisis that is specific to the country being analysed.

The profile then becomes the basis for developing a set of strategies such as a balance between politicians and the bureaucracy (i.e. harmonization of relations). In La Palombara's view the bureaucracy in Japan is viewed as the guardian of society. In developing alternative strategies it becomes evident that the quality of human resources – content of human minds – rests on an educational strategy which emphasizes compassion, intellectuality and predisposition to empiricism. Emphasis on human resources has been the foundation for a successful development strategy in East Asia. Whatever strategy a country develops, it must build on existing values and institutions.

In this section of the chapter, I have compared the organizational approach of Gross (1967) with the broader societal approach advocated by La Palombara (1971). Research focusing on administrative capability for development is an indication of the concern among academics of the performance of TW governments. In response to such concerns donor agencies and policy-makers have moved to institution-building, administrative reform and issues of governance which are discussed in the next section of this chapter.

V ALTERNATIVE STRATEGIES FOR THE DEVELOPMENT OF ADMINISTRATION

It took policy-makers, donor agencies and academics a considerable time to realize that technology and material resources on the scale invested in Europe under the Marshall Plan would be insufficient to bring about development in the TW. Such expectations based on narrow economic analysis of the experience of industrialized economies failed to consider the absence of the political and administrative infrastructure necessary for industrialization. Its absence became even more glaring in the areas of health, education and rural development where traditional social values came into direct conflict with new demands like programmes of population control, improved sanitation and drainage and systems of education. To address these problems three strategies are examined: institution-building (source for new skills), administrative reform (changing existing organization), and governance (developing political institutions).

V(1)   Institution Building

In recognizing the significance of institutions that help to sustain development programmes and projects, it helps to revert to the distinction made earlier in the chapter between enclave development and non-enclave (contextual) development. In the latter factors like culture, religion, values and attitudes to social change are vital. Programmes of social change provide opportunities for social transformation but the decisions to adopt them remain those of the individual. To help that process we need institutions – public, private and non-governmental (Korten 1981, Esman, 1987, Israel, 1987). An institution is an 'organization which incorporates, fosters and protects normative relationships and action patterns and performs functions and services which are valued in the environment' (Esman, 1972).

Selznick (1957), who introduced the term 'institution' to distinguish it from organizations (i.e. as imbued with values), did not visualize its particular relevance to TW situations and therefore did not draw our attention to it. However, subsequent evidence of lack of sustainability of planned social change has directed the attention of developmentalists to the significance of institutions as mechanisms for sustaining change. Institutions as mechanisms of social change are to be distinguished from institution-building, which is the creation of new organizations for promoting change. While the distinction I make in this chapter is confined to its use in the development management literature, without bringing in the 'new institutionalists' (March and Olson, 1989, Arkadie, 1991).

Early discussion of the institution-building model was initiated by the Inter-University Consortium involving four American universities. Their emphasis is on protecting initiatives on social change by creating formal organizations on the basis of variables like leadership, doctrine, programme, resources and structure. The organization enters into transactions with the environment and establishes enabling linkages for resources, functional linkages for inputs and outputs, normative linkages for formal support and informal support through diffused linkages (Esman, 1972).

Such support through formal organizations becomes necessary because:

Social change involves the introduction of a new technology which demands adaptation by recipients;
It may require change in attitude and values, from ones you are accustomed to, to ones you are not so familiar with – that is, known to the unknown;
Such change is induced or planned and not something that individuals take initiative for, and it tends to upset the internal balance of social relations or power relations (Esman, 1972).

These factors, therefore, suggest that change needs to be introduced with a strategy which can anticipate various forces that are likely to promote or hinder change. Secondly, those introducing change ought to adopt an institutional rather than instrumental perspective. That is, has the value of change been made known to the recipients of the programme? Failure to inform and to establish linkages by programme administrators allows opponents of change the opportunity to muster opposition. Interests representing groups bearing the costs of change are likely to mobilize forces against the introduction of change. Such planned change needs to be based on social rather than technical knowledge; it should be integrated with the local environment; it should be acceptable to the local community and should acquire the capacity to sustain itself and influence the larger environment. Essentially, it is a case of compatibility between new organizations and the socio-economic environment. According to Root (1996), 'It suggests that being able to craft and adopt new institutions is as important as the ability to formulate new policies. The introduction of new organizations, new rules, and new procedures, however, is not reflected in calculations of total factor productivity growth. As a result, institutional change is systematically underestimated' (16). Therefore, institutions play a broader-based role than organizations. Institutions influence the environment by producing outputs (new doctors, new devices) which are likely to have a basic influence on the values and attitudes of those affected. The term 'institution' conveys the fact it is imbued with certain values, that it is permanent and that its activity has an influence over other organizations in that environment.

Institutionalization, as a process in organizations as described above, is to be distinguished from the prospect that certain types of bureaucracies can emerge into institutions and become obstacles in the process of economic development. It is such bureaucracies that we examine in the next part of this section. The following description of institution building as 'programmes of sustainable, constructive change in organizations which are designed to make them better at doing what they already do, and more efficient, or which are designed to change the character of institutions by modifying their goals and strategies, cultures, ways of functioning, management styles and so on' (Blunt and Collins, 1994, 115), fits both meanings – i.e. creating new institutions or drastic reform of existing institutions.

V(2)   Administrative Reform

Institutionalizing for development purposes (innovation, social change) is different from institutionalized bureaucracies (Bjur and Caiden, 1984). In the case of the latter, the organization tends to be valued by its members. The organization (bureaucracy) achieves this through the process of becoming autonomous. Therefore authors identify such bureaucracies by their age and their persistent nature. Generally, they are less responsive, lack public accountability, tend to overemphasize rules and regulations and suffer from a poor public image. Administrative reform is viewed here in terms of political responsiveness and public accountability. It also takes into consideration efforts to improve performance through a variety of efficiency measures. While earlier efforts towards the latter objective were more instrumental with limited results, more recent efforts to improve efficiency have been incorporated into overall economic reform with some success. Root (1996) comments that:

> The East Asian experience challenges an assumption-institutions are given and are not subject to change – that has profoundly shaped the development field. The transformation of key institutions responsible for the formulation and implementation of policy is central to the success of East Asia's high performers. Corrupt bureaucracies were reformed, a dialogue between the public and private was initiated, and single party governments developed firm foundations for democratic practice. All of these suggest the need to go beyond matching policies to institutions; rather institutional innovation must become part of the development agenda (1996, 16).

A review of the consistent failure of administrative reform in TW countries led (Bjur and Caiden, 1978) to the development of this distinction between instrumental and institutionalized bureaucracies. Apart from the characteristics described earlier, the latter are committed to a mission, have strong leadership (elitist) and are generally 'anti-politicians' in attitude. Issues of succession are generally decided from within. Reform of such institutionalized bureaucracies requires a political rather than a managerial approach. Therefore, the strategy advocated must pose a threat to its survival by raising questions on the legitimacy of its mission, its values and its status, thus making it vulnerable. Such strategies adopted through external pressures such as public action groups can be effective. Institutional bureaucracies generally assume the power to decide on succession. According to Bjur and Caiden (1984), questioning the legitimacy of institutionalized bureaucracies is the key to administrative reform.

While a distinction between instrumental and institutionalised bureaucracies is useful in developing a strategy of administrative reform, one cannot overlook the desire of some organizations to seek autonomy from political and bureaucratic meddling, which can be a frequent occurrence in the TW. A selective strategy is important in any reform of the administrative system. It is also essential to avoid the blind search for economy and efficiency on the lines of market-oriented private sector organizations. The danger of efficiency scrutinies is that in their need to promote economy reformers are inclined to overlook the need for reliability. Similarly, the application of principles of economy and efficiency needs to be varied in the case of emergency services such as hospitals, ambulance and fire services, educational institutions, airport control operations and mental health services. It is necessary in such cases to have some amount of duplication (redundancy) to ensure reliability and safety.

In making a trade-off between economy and reliability, Weick (1995) applies a useful test, i.e. whether there is scope for trial and error learning in such organizations. Secondly, when there is a case for requisite variety and such variety being generally complex is beyond human capacity for problem solving. In such cases, the only method by which one reduces the chances of system failure is to reduce the gap between system complexity and human complexity (147).

The Development Administration movement of the 1960s and 1970s, having recognized the absence of administrative capability for development, advocated institution-building and administrative reform as specific strategies to develop the administrative capability for the management of development. However their impact has been minimal in most TW countries. Recognition of the lacuna and efforts to overcome them seemed insufficient when confronted by the serious problems caused by ineffective policies of an earlier era. Critics (the new political economists) attributed the blame for inappropriate policies to the state, which they felt was not equipped for the task. In their view TW countries ought to adopt more market-oriented policies that would promote the private sector and encourage more foreign private investment in the development of infrastructure such as power generation and communication, once considered unattractive to the private sector. This shift in policies is discussed earlier in this study (see Chapter 4). Here I briefly examine the administrative implications of structural adjustment.

As in earlier phases of development, a major obstacle to implementing structural adjustment policies is the lack of political and administrative capability. On the basis of their study of implementation of structural adjustment, Montgomery and Rondinelli (1989) conclude that assessing administrative capacity is a complicated task. Most TW countries adopt Western models which fail to reflect the cultural, legal and political realities of TW countries in which they are applied. In their view, 'the processes by which governments adapt and change policies and guide development activities toward new goals may be thought of as the essence of development administration' (1989, 77).

According to Montgomery and Rondinelli (1989), countries that have been successful in managing economic reforms have adopted an effective guidance system to channel activities of public and private organizations in specific policy arenas. The characteristics of development administration displayed by these countries include:

(1) The state at least initially took a strong role in guiding public and private activities in three or four of the major policy arenas;
(2) The state showed strong political leadership and enjoyed long periods of political stability;
(3) Political leaders were flexible, pragmatic and responsive to economic conditions;
(4) The political leadership was able to create strong public or private institutions to carry out development policies, and
(5) The formulation and implemention of policies in all four arenas – economic growth, social equity, international transactions and public sector management – by their governments.

'Development administration is the purposive centre of these policy arenas' (Montgomery and Rondinelli, 1989, 89). In highlighting this, the authors shift their focus from government's role as primary actor in earlier discussions to a role of providing central guidance to several public and private actors contributing to economic and social change. This shift is described by Evans (1996) as 'synergy' or 'complementarity'. Countries that were unsuccessful in achieving reform are those that have failed to adopt the above strategies. The focus in these countries has taken a different form and is called 'governance'. The difference is that the reform agenda has moved from narrow economic and financial issues to political issues of democratisation, human rights and effective political and administrative systems.

V(3) Governance

Governance, now used by the World Bank to focus on managerial and administrative issues (i.e. a technical strategy for improving performance), has been advocated to meet the failure of adjustment policies in Africa. 'Good governance on this account came to be equated with "sound development management"' (Jayal, 1997, 407). In questioning the World Bank's narrow approach to the term 'governance', I offer instead a liberal interpretation of the term. After decades of support to authoritarian regimes in TW countries, such urgency for governance strikes a strange note. Is it a reflection of changes currently taking place, like the emergence of neo-liberalisation in the west, the rise of pro-democracy movements, the end of the cold war and the early success of structural adjustment policies? (Leftwitch, 1994).

Governance is to be viewed from three levels. From a systematic point of view, governance is wider than government (which refers to formal structures). Primarily governance refers to a system of political and socio-economic relations and rules by which the productive and distributive life of a society is governed. The second level refers to the state's enjoyment of legitimacy and authority derived from a democratic mandate and built on the liberal notion of a clear separation of legislative, executive and judicial function.

At the third level good governance refers to an efficient, independent, accountable and open public service. This includes accountability for action and legal rules and framework for development, information and transparency. Critics of the third interpretation largely preferred by the World Bank point to the fact that it fails to recognize that governance is a function of state capacity which, in turn, is a function of politics (Leftwitch, 1994). 'The governance perspective offers an alternative viewpoint of economic development in which institutional arrangements directly influence the productive capacity of an economy' (Root, 1996, 150). The World Bank, widely known for promoting the concept of governance, refers to 'the manner in which power is exercised in the management of a country's economic and social resources for development' (Root, 1996, 181).

The definition centres around the strategic interaction between government officials and citizens and is a reflection of their accountability, transparency and predictability. With its emphasis on implementation capability, the focus of governance has less to do with political institutions and more to do with the bureaucracy and its interaction with citizens. By adopting this position on governance international institutions, such as the World Bank, can offer the East Asian miracle as a model without having to defend their record on democracy. Likewise, by narrowing the definition of governance they can overlook the democratic record of some TW countries, where the democratic process itself has been responsible for poor economic performance. In promoting bureaucratic institutions more than political institutions the proponents of governance would prefer to limit the scope for politicians to respond to pressures from particular groups. They prefer the growth of community or private organizations that mediate between people and the government. This old-style pluralism, more popularly known as 'civil society', is being promoted as a substitute to democratic institutions which are less representative, at least in TW countries (Williams and Young, 1994). In adopting this managerialist perspective 'governance is presented as if it were an autonomous administrative capacity, detached from the turbulent world of politics and the structure and purpose of the state' (Leftwich, 1994, 364).

Like the partial analysis adopted to credit the success of East Asian economies to market-oriented policies (Chapter 4), the recent attempts to attribute that success entirely to an apolitical technocracy autonomous from the political system is in the same light an attempt to overlook the role of the 'developmental state' (Chapter 5). It betrays underlying contradictions (Jayal, 1997). In this study, my approach is to view the synergy or complementarity of both the political and administrative system (developmental or bureaucratic state) and the market as vital to TW development. An effective balance between the two, one that can arrive at appropriate policies and implement them, will ultimately account for success or failure of development. The chapters thus far clarify how some countries have succeeded and others have not, because the type of state intervention and its implementation have differed. The learning process ought to be free from particular bias and should recognize particular historical and cultural circumstances which are not easily replicable.

VI CONCLUSION

A feature of TW countries is their limited administrative capability to achieve development objectives. In hoping to promote such capability, governments of TW countries and academics have examined the problems they face. In diagnosing the problem I have focused on the differences between the East Asian technocracy and the South Asian bureaucracy and studied their respective impact on development. I differentiate them on the basis that while the former has trained to 'do the right things' and the latter to 'do things right': the East Asian technocracy enjoys is given freedom from political interference while the South Asian bureaucracy, which works within a democratic system, has to respond constantly to political dictates.

In order to understand the complexity of administration for development a distinction is made between the development of administration and the administration of development. While the two are not easily distinguishable, it helps to focus on how a country can create an organization to implement actual policies. To help in that process I have explored several different analytical schemes to identify areas where such capability is lacking and then examined various strategies like institution-building, administrative reform and governance to overcome them.

8 Technology and Industrialization: a Strategy for Development

I INTRODUCTION

A general distinction between the TW and the FW is the identification of the former with a predominantly agricultural economy and of the latter with industrialization. However, over a period of time much change has taken place, rendering such categorization less relevant and leading us to search for greater refinement in our analysis. The current pace of economic and technical change has led some analysts to forecast that both China and India will join the United States and Japan as the most powerful economies in the world. Notwithstanding this prediction, one has to accept the fact that industrialized economies have greater capability to use science and technology to manipulate their physical and social environment. Apart from possessing lesser capability to use science and technology for development, TW countries tend to be more prone to environmental pressures. Meanwhile the gap between and within countries is growing.

In pursuit of industrialization, TW countries sought technology from the FW in the form of capital investment. This dependence of the periphery on the centre for technology for industrialization then led to the development of a range of development strategies. As discussed in earlier chapters of this study, the state had to adopt an active entrepreneurial role because the private sector had not reached a sufficient stage of development. In seeking to promote industrialization through state entrepreneurship the TW was faced with obstacles. The first was the lack of capability to make policy choices on the type of industrial strategy. The second related to the reluctance of the centre to sell the technology it had developed to the periphery. Finally, the technology developed in the FW tended to be capital-intensive and thus inappropriate to the needs of the TW, which is essentially labour-intensive.

In adopting technology for development it is necessary to emphasize the contrasts between FW and TW development. The TW faces greater handicaps. 'Furthermore these differences in the speed and character of industrial development were to a considerable extent the result of

128

application of institutional instruments for which there was little or no counterpart in an established industrial country. In addition, the intellectual climate within which industrialization proceeded, its "spirit" or "ideology" differed considerably among advanced and backward countries' (Gershenkron, 1988, 112–113).

While the above obstacles were regarded initially as a setback to the development objectives of the TW, they appeared to have been gradually overcome. It must be admitted that the TW itself caused some difficulties for itself by adopting policies that sought to protect its independence and with it, its indigenous private sector, promoting what I have described as economic nationalism. 'For some decades after independence, statist and nationalist economic policies were pursued and legitimized in part on the grounds that private business was (largely) alien, and could not therefore be expected to pursue national priorities' (Moore, 1997, 332). Within the TW political context, state entrepreneurship was seen as the obvious option leading to a policy of industrialization resulting in limited growth.

The dramatic shift that took place in the early 1970s with the introduction of the 'gas station model' was seen as a significant development. This involved a shift in the international division of labour by relocating production to the periphery. The centre undertook this for a variety of economic reasons:

Prospects for enclave development where level of skill was irrelevant;
Availability of cheap labour due to international competition;
Political stability of the region;
Development of transportation and communication technologies, and
Globalization and internationalization of economies.

With these changes in the international economy and the revolution in transportation and communication technology, traditional distinctions between labour-intensive and capital-intensive technology, appropriate technology, proximity of industry to the sources of raw material, transport outlets and markets became increasingly irrelevant. Taking 'coals to Newcastle' is no longer appropriate when the cost of carrying a tonne of coal or iron ore in bulk carriers 30,000 miles is the same as carrying it 30 miles from mine to the plant by traditional modes like road or rail (Dore, 1989).

Having posed this phenomenal transformation in technology which has occurred in recent decades, I examine in the rest of this chapter the role of technology and industrialization in the development of East and South Asia. In section II I explore the changing nature of technology and how it has influenced industrial development strategies adopted by TW countries. In section III I discuss the institutional foundations on which different countries based their industrial strategies focusing on alternative approaches to achieve development. In section IV I compare the industrial development policies adopted by these countries. The development of technology is discussed in section V and the issue of technology transfer is examined in section VI.

II   CHANGING TECHNOLOGY

In stating that TW countries over a period of time have shown different levels of performance, thus belying broad categorization into 'developed' and 'underdeveloped', I recognize the variation that exists between countries and between industries. Such variation ought to be understood in the context of specific obstacles faced by each country or even a specific industry. Developments in technology and their impact on the process of industrialization have to be studied to help us understand the role of government in the development process. It is in this context that Amsden (1997) calls for 'bringing production back in – understanding Government's economic role in late industrialization'. In making a case for emphasizing production, Amsden comments that:

> Instead, development economists writing two centuries after Adam Smith have focused overwhelmingly on the constraint of the market rather than on the division of labor. Markets have been interpreted almost exclusively in terms of exchange rather than production, as in 'new institutionalism,' according to which growth is retarded by high transaction costs (why not high production costs); or international trade studies which emphasize the importance of relative exchange prices between domestic and foreign sales, ignoring how a capacity to produce tradeables for sale in any market arises (1997, 470).

A look back at the historical process of development of countries shows that it centred on the process of industrialization which began with the industrial revolution. Countries that followed sought to catch up with the ones which had already industrialized. Late industrialization, which involves policies and processes adopted by TW countries, continues in the same historical tradition but with a difference (Gershenkron, 1988).

When compared with early industrialization there is a distinct shift in the development of technology. For example, the United States, Germany and Japan sent engineers to Britain to observe the development of a particular product. On their return the process was to be replicated (Bhatt, 1980). This concept of reverse or backward engineering was also done by importing a machine, opening it up and learning the process. This equates to 'learning by doing' (Mascarenhas, 1982). When the industrialization process began in England it relied entirely on inventions. Countries like Germany and the United States, which followed, adopted innovation. In the case of TW countries, the basis is one of learning (Amsden, 1989). While adopting the learning model as a strategy of late industrialization (from an agrarian or raw material base), countries like South Korea and Taiwan have been able to achieve higher growth rates because 'the institutions on which late industrialization is based have been managed differently' (Amsden, 1989, 4). However, scientific advancement has had a significant effect on the industrialization of TW countries. Transformation in industrial and manufacturing technology from an emphasis on material inputs to creative human effort has placed the East Asian economies in the race towards industrialization. While the East Asian miracle has raised a number of questions casting doubt on traditional notions of industrial development, the very changes in technological frontiers have forced a rethink on industrial strategies (see Chapter 2).

I agree with Amsden (1989, 7) that there is a greater scientific content as industrialization has progressed but her argument that such technology has, as a result, become easier to transfer, is debatable (Mascarenhas, 1982, Dore, 1989). Technology is now far more complex; designs and specifications are more intricate (they have to be transferred from one mind to another mind), and thus the whole process of technology absorption is a more difficult process (Dore, 1989). 'The politics of modernization is now much more complex and unyielding than in previous decades, while at the same time social and cultural conditions are far less favourable. Modern technology makes more demands on society than its forerunners and societal needs are more urgent and more difficult to fulfil than ever before' (Montgomery, 1974).

Other factors that need to be considered in understanding the change that has taken place in the international movement of capital and technology include the distinction between 'early comers' and 'latecomers'. In some cases the latecomers are at an advantage because they can adopt the latest technology, particularly when the pace of obsolescence in the case of process-based technology is faster than in other types of technology. It is a case of avoiding the reinvention of the wheel all over again. Similarly, the time gap between basic research and its operationalization into a product has also changed. For example, while the movement from semi-conductivity technology to transistors took 40 years, only five years have elapsed from the developmental to the commercial stage in the case of biotechnology (Dore, 1989).

The nature of technology has thus undergone a dramatic shift, raising doubts about the development process. However, it may seem hasty to conclude that the dramatic changes are a widespread phenomenon. The reality is that these changes have been confined to one specific region centred around Japan, its former colonies (South Korea and Taiwan) and the two city states of Hong Kong and Singapore. From there the move to other Southeast Asian economies has been gradual. From this we conclude, firstly, that it is not a universal phenomenon applicable to all TW countries; secondly, that it centres around the phenomenal performance of the post-war Japanese economy, and finally that the economic pressures on the manufacturing sector are geared to meet consumer demands in industrialized economies. Together these have led to the international movement of capital and this process has been assisted by advances in communication and transportation technology.

An illustration to support my misgivings on the universality of technology transformation is provided by Bernard and Ravenhill (1995) who have disputed the 'flying geese' theory of countries following one another in a developmental trajectory. What we observe as the industrial dynamism of the East Asian region is not the replication of the Japanese developmental experience; rather it is 'shifting hierarchical networks of production linked both backward to Japanese innovation and forward to American markets for export of finished goods' (Bernard and Ravenhill, 1995, 172). One can aptly describe East Asia (minus Japan) as 'technologyless' industrialization, because their development is dependent on technology developed elsewhere.

The East Asian (Taiwan and South Korea) strategy for industrialization was based on establishing manufacturing facilities for products at the low end of technology, based on locked-in production hierarchies which derive components and other inputs on an 'original equipment manufacturing' (OEM) basis. It thus exploited low costs production so as to maintain export competitiveness. This approach 'transnationalizes their firms differently from the way it is done by companies coming out of industrial contexts...while these countries have moved into sophisticated products through accumulation of production skills but it does not diminish their structural dependence on Japanese technology' (Bernard and Ravenhill, 1995, 192–94).

Contrast this with a country like India, which has not achieved the same level of growth and industrialization as East Asia but which possesses high levels of scientific 'knowledge' comparable to that of advanced countries (Amsden, 1997, 470). The Minister of Industries, Mr Maran, is reported as saying 'we may have missed the industrial revolution, but we are not lagging behind in the information revolution...the London Underground is run on software developed in India..., there are more software companies in Bangalore than in Boston' (*The Hindu*, July 11, 1997). Another long term observer of India, John P. Lewis, comments:

> The modern professional and intellectual elites have a large quotient of scientific, technological, and managerial sophistication. The numbers of such people are not only large because the population is large; they are abundant relative to the present endowments of other developing countries. India already possesses large cadres of distinguished scientific and medical researchers, engineers, public administrators, economists and other social scientists (1995, 299).

Although critics question the priority placed by India on science, technology and industry ahead of agriculture in its development strategy, that that policy was instrumental in laying a foundation for the development of technology is now an established fact (Mascarenhas, 1982).

III   THE INSTITUTIONAL FOUNDATIONS

Given the dramatic transformation in the international movement of technology and capital, one cannot overlook the fact that any efforts to capitalize on this depend on the foundations laid in each country. 'No country reached eminence in any major sectors of development without itself contributing to the technology required' (Montgomery, 1974, 152). If a country needs to lay the foundations for development of technology it is necessary to identify some of the impediments. Montgomery (1974) lists some of the impediments. They are :

(1)   Classes necessary for industrialisation are underpopulated;
(2)   Skilled labour is scarce;
(3)   Entrepreneurs prefer to speculate, and
(4)   Existing agrarian social structure discourages innovation.

An underlying dilemma for countries having once experienced colonial domination is their desire to acquire technology from other countries without undermining their economic and political independence. Every society possesses a technology of its own and awareness of the limitations of its traditional technology leads it to establish contact with the outside world (Hayashi, 1990). If a country is to seize the opportunities offered by technology, it must have the confidence to borrow technology without losing its own identity. Japan's early experience with foreign technology has been described by Dore (1989) as 'teeth-gritting humility'. Friedrich List, a contemporary of Adam Smith and an advocate of state intervention, while recognizing the importance of borrowing skills, manpower and technology from advanced nations for the purpose of creating national economic power, was quite unconcerned about creating any dependency (Tickner, 1987). Not surprisingly, List enjoys a larger following than Adam Smith in East Asia (Fallows, 1994).

Unlike East Asian economies which resolved this underlying conflict by realizing the importance of foreign technology to development, the Indian response, largely deriving from Gandhian influence, has been ambivalent. That ambivalence persists even to this day, reflecting simultaneously the Gandhian concept of self-reliance and Nehru's concept of science and technology which transcended national boundaries (Bhatt, 1980). According to Tickner (1987) the development policies adopted by India were closer to the Listian concept of building productive capacity and national power than to the Gandhian version of self-reliance (167).

For countries with a colonial past and the experience of exporting primary goods as raw material, the desire for self-reliance assumes political overtones. In earlier chapters of this study, I have referred to this as economic nationalism and examined its influence on policies, particularly those of South Asian countries (excepting Pakistan) in their dealings with western sources of capital. A desire to maintain independence from western political and military alliances has led India to seek technological collaboration from the former Soviet bloc and to adopt state capitalism to avoid undue interference from multinationals in domestic economic policy-making. Economic analysts narrow their vision to the type of economic strategy adopted (heavy and basic industry import substitution) but fail to understand the political compulsions faced by large TW countries like India. In the context of the cold war the construction of the Bokaro Steel Plant was embroiled in controversy involving both the United States and the Soviet Union (Bhatt, 1980). In the late 1960s, the refusal of western oil companies to refine crude imported on favourable terms from the Soviet Union resulted in India seeking to develop its own indigenous refining capability. In the mid-1970s, a public sector undertaking interested in acquiring vacuum-blowing technology to produce lamp-making machinery failed in its attempts to acquire it through Philips (which had a dominant market in India) and ultimately had to acquire it from a Hungarian firm. Similar obstacles were faced by India when wanting to produce milk powder from buffalo milk. Opposition came from dominant milk-producing countries using FAO/WHO and multinationals afraid of losing a major milk market (Mascarenhas, 1982, 1988). These are a few of the many impediments faced by TW countries in their efforts to acquire technology from advanced countries.

Similar constraints were faced by Taiwanese and South Korean firms in their transactions for technology with Japanese companies. While the cases relating to India were a mix of political and commercial reasons, those relating to the East Asian situation were primarily commercial. It was a case of reluctance to transfer technology to potential rivals. When the technology transfer is built into the production process, this quite often demands a dependency relationship and is not seen as mutually beneficial.

While the historical, ideological and socio-cultural influences are significant, the primary objective of any policy for technology development is the reduction of dependence, otherwise defined as self-reliance. In their search for a strategy of self-reliance TW governments would like to enjoy an element of autonomy in their choice of technology and in how best to use that technology. That rests on the ability to translate such decisions into action in the form of goods and services, i.e. steel, machine tools, fertilizers, etc.

Seeking autonomy in the choice of technology and decision making involves the capacity of governments to arrive at priorities – i.e. a development strategy. When once the priorities are clarified, the next step lies in translating them into action in the form of investment in capital. To do that a country needs to develop expertise in locating the source of capital and acquiring it at least cost (Roemer, 1981).

In the context of the current world economy, a strategy of selective dissociation and not one of complete dissociation is advocated if a country wants to move towards greater self-reliance in industrial development (Hveem, 1983). If such a strategy of development is to be successful it is important that the country acquires the skills and capability to generate independently the critical elements of technical knowledge required for a particular product or process – i.e. the capability to develop the required designs for a particular process or product including the standards and specifications for various components to be manufactured, as well as the assembly of such components. In order to achieve that, it needs trained people, appropriate information, and the required facilities in plant and machinery for manufacture, including engineering and managerial capabilities. There should also be sufficient availability of raw materials without recourse to outside sources. The last-named is becoming less significant with the evidence of countries like Japan, South Korea and Taiwan, which have been in a position to produce steel more efficiently than western industrialised economies, without indigenous sources of coal and iron ore.

Therefore, in the context of an industrial development strategy, a country must identify different types of dependence which are then considered as targets of policy (Roemer, 1981). These are (1) dependence on a single market for exports, (2) technological dependence where a country relies on buying it from outside, (3) managerial and entrepreneurial dependence, and (4) limited economic flexibility because of a narrow economic base. Any strategy for industrial development must address these issues. Therefore, in the context of the types of dependence identified, Roemer (1981) examines types of industrial strategies to cope with. Accordingly, the strategies discussed are: import substitution, further processing of primary products, diversification of exports, adopting basic and heavy industry and small-scale labour-intensive strategy.

Of these, import substitution, export substitution and basic industry strategy have been widely adopted by TW countries to promote industrialization. Large economies like India have adopted import substitution with basic industry, while East Asian countries like South Korea and Taiwan first adopted import substitution and gradually moved to export substitution. While endorsing the basic industry-cum-import substitution model for large countries, Roemer (1981) warns against the inefficiencies associated with continued protection to domestic producers granted under political pressure. By adopting a range of industrial strategies, countries gradually move from an imitative stage where they buy or borrow due to lack of skills and then move to a phase of indigenous industrialization trying to use local endowments like skills and materials and finally to internationalization of technology through the acceptance of multinationals or competitive exports.

The current wave of structural adjustment and the globalization of the economy clearly suggests that unwittingly most TW countries have adopted export substitution strategies and are not too enthusiastic about import substitution. Does this phase of donor-dictated policies suggest that industrial policies adopted by TW countries to achieve self-reliance have either failed or are irrelevant in the changing economic context?

By describing the shift in industrial strategy as 'donor-dictated', it becomes necessary to clarify the specific use of the term. It is necessary in the context of my earlier assertion of political and economic autonomy (economic nationalism) to explain the reversal from an inward-to an outward-oriented open economy. Countries in South Asia, like most of the TW, incurred high levels of debt, their economic performance was unsatisfactory, they suffered setbacks due to the energy crisis of the 1970s and they were affected by the breakup of the Soviet Union. Together these factors contributed to a shift in economic policy, and were precipitated by pressure from the World Bank which came to the financial aid of these countries. It must be remembered that these inward-looking closed economies like India were politically open and were the scene of an ongoing debate on the type of industrial development strategy.

In the sixties, many inside and as well as outside the Government of India began to wonder whether much of the detailed economic decision making that government functionaries had been doing directly – for example, allocating imports, choosing investments, and setting inputs and output prices, could not better be left to various markets that were allowed to adjust themselves competitively within an environment set by broad commercial, monetary, and fiscal policies and framed by government regulation designed to permit as much freedom to transactors as was consistent with the avoidance of creating an unreasonable exercise of market power (Lewis, 1995, 28).

While the debate in the background has been ongoing, the shift to more market-oriented policies in the 1980s, although recognizable, is not necessarily a policy of moving away from state intervention. In advocating an outward-looking, market-oriented export strategy, the donors fail to consider the crucial role played by state intervention in the case of East Asian economies (Chapter 4). The real difference between the East and South Asian economies is that between state intervention in a closed polity as against state intervention in an open polity. In the latter, state intervention import substitution becomes a haven for bureaucratic stranglehold with enormous opportunity for rent seekers (Bhagwati, 1988, 1993). State intervention import substitution in a closed polity encourages the development of disciplined entrepreneurial capitalism which has been responsible for the economic performance of East Asia (Amsden, 1989, Wade, 1990). That discipline declined with liberalization and partial democratization at least in South Korea leading to questionable investment dealings between banks and large conglomerates.

Another distinction that helps to explain the difference in industrial development strategies of East and South Asia is that while the former achieved equality within a closed polity, the latter perpetuated inequalities within an open polity. Evidence of East Asian economies shows that there is a positive relationship between equality and economic growth. Under conditions of income equalities governments are in a better position to formulate and implement industrial policies. According to Amsden (1997):

> The fundamental reason for this is simple: assuming peoples' political opinions and policy choices are primarily a function of their absolute and relative income levels, then the more homogeneous incomes are in a society, the less political conflict and anti-social behavior there will be. An absence of anti-social behaviour suggests a better chance than otherwise for rational policy making (475).

The influence of distribution of income on policy formulation, according to Amsden (1997), has a bearing on all aspects of production. They are: (a) government support to firms is influenced by their size or ownership; (b) state-owned enterprises appear more prevalent in countries with relatively unequal income distribution on the justification that they best serve the public interest; (c) reluctance to allocate subsidies to create big firms is characteristic of countries with unequal income, and (d) countries with large populations and high levels of poverty are reluctant to encourage modernization for fear of job losses. Amsden believes that income distribution has greater impact on policy implementation. In conditions of income equality there is greater discipline, which helps the adoption of conditionality of performance in return for subsidies and assistance. If income distribution reflects on the concentration of resources, the assumption is that performance standards are difficult to establish under conditions where alternative investment opportunities for resources are available and resource concentration creates inequalities. Amsden further comments that 'the relationship between income distribution and production is intimate and multidimensional. To ignore the connection between them is to miss a crucial element in how latecomers have grown' (1997, 476).

IV COMPARING INDUSTRIAL DEVELOPMENT POLICIES

A comparison of the industrial development policy of East Asian and South Asian countries reveals that both groups of countries began with import substitution strategies of consumer durables by adopting protectionist measures to aid the process. East Asian countries phased out the protection so that new industries could become competitive and export, and thus support further phases of import substitution industrialization in intermediate and capital goods as well as consumer durables. South Asian countries began with heavy and basic industry and in the case of consumer durables extended protection for too long without becoming competitive in world markets. India, to which this applies more than to any other country, has a very large domestic market which tends to discourage any pressure to export.

While countries that industrialized late adopted state intervention to promote industrialization, the difference in outcomes according to Amsden (1989) rested on the varying manner in which 'the institutions on which late industrialization' were managed (4). The institutions that contribute to the success of late industrialisation are an interventionist state, large diversified business groups, an abundant supply of competent salaried managers, and an abundant supply of low-cost, well-educated labour. Of these the salaried engineer played a critical role in the industrialization of South Korea (Amsden, 1989, 6).

Like South Korea, Taiwan relied on state intervention to initiate, facilitate and support programmes for technological development and economic advancement. Simon (1995) identifies five major components that constituted the strategy for technological development adopted by Taiwan. They were:

(1) To provide incentives for firms to adopt new ideas and innovations, attractive financial and tax policies were introduced.
(2) To facilitate the diffusion of existing technology the government combined economic policy instruments with financial incentives. This was supported by setting up the Institute of Information Industry as a state-sponsored institution.
(3) To improve the process of importing technology and its utilization, the government reduced taxes on technology imports and eliminated administrative bottlenecks.
(4) To build a skilled workforce, investment in education was increased with an emphasis on engineering and science education.
(5) Taiwan's literacy rate of 90 per cent is one of the highest in the world.

In contrast to the industrial development strategy of East Asia, the South Asian countries adopted state intervention import substitution and implemented it through bureaucratic controls. The objectives of the industrial strategy were the reduction of dependence and the enhancement of national power and prestige through the adoption of import substitution and involved investment in basic and heavy industry such as arms, atomic energy, iron and steel, engineering, chemicals, and communication. The concept of self-reliance centred around the production of requirements within the country and reliance on imports for products it was unable to produce at home. The industrialization policy clearly enunciated in the planning documents was a cornerstone of economic independence. Most of the basic and heavy industries established were set up under public ownership because the private sector was not equipped for the task. This also signified the importance the government attached to these industries. In economic terms the performance of these industries has been less than successful. However, this is difficult to assess when one considers the multiple objectives they were set up to achieve.

The industrial strategy centred on a system of industrial-cum-trade licensing administered through bureaucrats and resulted in 'the stifling of private initiative, the diversion of resources into unproductive rent-seeking activities stimulated by controls, and costly bottlenecks reflecting artificial rigidities... illustrative of the unnecessary economic costs imposed by this control-infested system' (Bhagwati, 1993. 56). India's adoption of a strong state-owned sector with restrictive entry to domestic and foreign private sector eventually resulted in an inability to promote a level of industrialization expected of a large country endowed with natural resources and a sophisticated institutional structure for the development of science, technology and higher education (Mascarenhas, 1982).

Liberalization of the Indian economy since 1990 has revealed the poor level of technology in the communication and industrial spheres, largely the responsibility of the public sector. The enormous difficulties faced, particularly in the infrastructure, are best illustrated by the efforts of public entrepreneurs like Sam Pitroda (1993). Pitroda – an expatriate Indian and successful telecommunications technologist living in the United States, keen on assisting in the promotion of the telecommunication technology in India – sought entry with considerable difficulty. His experience highlights the tensions between levels of development promoted by communitarian and statist models of self-reliance. For him, 'Telecommunications was as critical and fundamental to nation-building as water, agriculture, health, and housing, and without it, India's democracy could founder' (Pitroda, 1993, 68). This statement essentially reconciles the differing views of independent India's leaders, Gandhi and Nehru.

That modern technology and rural development are reconcilable and can become a reality has been demonstrated by Pitroda by developing rural telephone exchanges that meet the local demand and withstand local conditions. By 1993, Telecom in India was installing 25 rural exchanges every day. By 1995, 100,000 villages were expected to have telephone services. It was hoped that, by the turn of the century or very shortly after, almost all of India's 600,000 villages would be connected. 'Once in place, the village telephone ... becomes an instrument of social change, fundamental to the process of democratization' (Pitroda, 1993, 78).

Indian achievements in industrial and technological development appear uneven or lopsided. India has made great strides in defence, space, electronic and computer technology and has a sophisticated science and technology system which produces trained personnel. However, at the same time it suffers from high levels of illiteracy with little attention paid to primary and secondary education. The result is an uneven quality of education, a lacuna recently recognized by leading commentators (Dreeze and Sen, 1996, Bhagwati, 1993). The internationally known science journal *Nature* (1984) described the Indian science and technology scene as 'excellence in the midst of poverty' (581). A perceptive analysis of education policy in India identifies the folly of shifting from basic to general education in the 1960s with the intention of giving emphasis on science and technology geared towards the 'Green Revolution' (Kumar, 1996). By contrast the concerted effort made by East Asian countries in the area of education has resulted in great strides towards development.

I have on several occasions in this study commented on the Indian strategy of self-reliance adopting the basic and heavy industry strategy. Using this strategy, India established an industrial foundation that is capable of producing basic metals, such as iron and steel, machine tools and industrial machinery, computers and communication satellites. This industrial strategy continued to be a drain on resources and the slackening of controls in the late 1980s showed dramatic results in growth (eight per cent, and exports went up by 20 per cent).

An active state sector based on regulation is essentially a product of India's traditional distrust of business. Business is viewed as primarily motivated by profit and thus cannot be relied upon for industrialization of the economy. India, according to one critic, appears to have combined the worst from other systems. In its early stages of implementation such a strategy of industrialization was faced by increased imports and increased demand for wage goods and pressures on prices. Relative neglect of agriculture and slow growth in employment are now seen as a result of the capital-intensive nature of industry, exacerbated by external factors such as war with Pakistan in 1965 and 1971 and the energy crisis of the 1970s (Dubey, 1994).

V   TECHNOLOGY AND DEVELOPMENT

Advocates of self-reliance have been classified into statist and communitarian. Communitarians advocate a radical reorientation of the strategies of development, using local resources and indigenous technology and focusing on rural and agricultural development. Statists place emphasis on the nation state as fundamental to the implementation of a self-reliant strategy of development. With self-reliance as a strategy, the state becomes an appropriate institution to effectively achieve favourable terms from the centre to the periphery.

A self-reliant strategy envisages a regime of tariffs and subsidies to promote indigenous industry, and this is a task the state needs to undertake. The clash between the communitarian focus on small scale rural-based development and the statist focus on large-scale development has, in the case of India, caused tension. This tension originated with the national movement led by two people, Gandhi and Nehru, with quite distinct ideas regarding India's future development. The former represented the communitarian viewpoint while the latter promoted the statist viewpoint. Although the statist prevailed over the communitarian, the continued influence of the latter surfaces intermittently, revealing the underlying inconsistency which is a cause of the lopsidedness that I commented on earlier (Tickner, 1987).

Of the TW countries, India probably fits the concept of selective dissociation or self-reliant strategy more completely than others. That strategy is a product of internal debate between the closed indigenous model advocated by Gandhi and the open science and technology model advocated by Nehru. The latter model has enjoyed support with a set of science and technology institutions contributing to India's industrial base and capable of producing complete systems of design, process and manufacturing supported by a strong knowledge base (Hveem, 1983, Mascarenhas, 1982).

Both Hveem (1983) and Bhatt (1980) question the direction of India's industrial development strategy in terms of its linkages with the domestic and traditional sectors of the economy. Hveem describes it as a 'blurred xerox copy' (Hveem, 1983, 298–299), while Bhatt (1980) questions the excessive emphasis given to foreign technology at the expense of indigenous developments. In support of his criticism he cites the lack of support for developments like biogas plant, baby food, bamboo tube well, protein food extract, Swaraj tractor and design and construction of Bokaro Steel plant (Bhatt, 1980, Hveem 1983, Mascarenhas, 1982).

The failure to promote indigenous industry and the continued reliance on foreign technology is partly explained by the system that was created. This eventuated into a replica of western industrial technology, and encouraged the 'quick fix' or 'ready on the shelf' approach to development. Indigenous development of technology has thus been indirectly discouraged. It becomes necessary then to recognize the significance of 'technology as a relationship to social carriers'. In other words, linkages must be built to help the development of local technology, and for this a policy of selective dissociation is needed. Therefore:

> the socio-political and cultural context of technology, then is decisive as to its impact. And it is in the ability to achieve appropriate linkages among these that successful development depends. In most cases, establishing such linkages will require measures of selective dissociation (Hveem, 1983, 304).

Bhatt (1980) advocates a broad-based institutional strategy to help this process.

Here it is worthwhile to explain the inconsistency one may observe in my analysis of economic nationalism (economic and political autonomy or independence) and the overlooking of indigenous technology in favour of ready-made technology. In Chapter 3 I comment on the costs a country pays for not totally detaching itself from the erstwhile colonial system. In my view economic nationalism constitutes one facet and internationalism the other. While economic nationalism is a negative device to protect against external dependence, internationalism is an elitist response aimed at maintaining historical linkages with the west. Both facets have proved expensive. While one protected inefficiencies and vested enormous power in the hands of bureaucrats, the other created an imitative elite which compensated for economic nationalism by rejecting indigenous research and development, earning the description 'blurred xerox copy' (Hveem, 1983, Bhatt, 1980). This inner contradiction between inwardness and outwardness has to do with India's duality and is a product of a historical past. While the need to cling to tradition and reject western technology is ever present in the Indian mind, the concept was further reinforced by Gandhi's stance and his warning in 1909 that 'should India ever resolve to imitate England, it will be the ruin of the nation' (Ekins and Max-Neef, 1991, 5). Although this position has proved untenable in an interdependent world, it continues to reappear in Indian discourse and explains underlying contradictions, typified by the rendering of the hymn 'Abide by me' that conclude the annual Republic day celebrations held in New Delhi (Larsen, 1995).

This contradiction or conflict between traditional values and modern technology is a universal problem. While many TW countries recognize the importance of new technology to confront the problems of health, nutrition and agricultural productivity, they lack the prerequisites needed by the technology. Attempts to change social values and traditions to meet the needs of technology often lead to conflict which can be minimized by a 'national consensus which is a matter of political leadership and of cultural legitimacy' (Hayashi, 1990, 51)

> Today's developing countries have not had so dramatic and innocent an encounter with modern technologies. They have been using technologies far more refined and sophisticated than those that so shocked the Japanese more than a century ago, but what they have been using and enjoying have not always been suitable for the purposes of their development. Developing countries often lack a national consensus as to the purpose and priorities of development, and their expectations are frequently too great. Finally the way in which technology has been used has possibly not always been wise (Hayashi, 1990, 51).

Bhatt (1980) is concerned with the effect of living standards of the west on the elite of the TW which renders it imitative, alienating it from its own people. To overcome this imitative elite problem (particularly in South Asia) Bhatt promotes an isolation-cum-contact model. However, such interaction with sources of science and technology only, and not with the culture of the west, is impossible in South Asia, where the influence of English and the developments in communication technology are ever-present. Comparing the relationship between professionals and peasants in Latin America and Japan, Dore (1992) remarks that while the Japanese professional is more at ease with local peasants than with professionals from other countries, the Latin American professional feels more comfortable with his American counterpart than with a local peasant. He attributes this distinction to a strong or weak national bond as against an occupational bond. The elite of South Asia fall into the latter category. A sense of identity can be restored only through education and a sense of pride in achievement. If and when this occurs, the brightest scientists and engineers of these countries will have moved away to opportunities offered elsewhere.

That sense of nationhood or pride that is characteristic of East Asians as distinct from other national groups has been mentioned by Dore in another context. He distinguishes confident nationalism from insecure nationalism. While the rejection of indigenous developments like a bamboo tube well and biogas plants can be blamed on an imitative elite, the expectation that a country of India's size and resources should isolate itself from international interaction reveals the other element – insecure nationalism.

Such discussion of promoting indigenous technology followed the 'small is beautiful' trend of the late 1960s and 1970s when the terms 'intermediate technology' and 'appropriate technology' were debated in international forums and backyard furnaces and barefoot doctors symbolised China's cultural revolution. Prior to this, a generation of economists had debated labour-intensive and capital-intensive technology as appropriate to a country's endowments of labour or capital. In that vein Dore (1989) poured scorn on alternative development strategies and expressed apprehension at the 'day when some ingenious blacksmith in Bihar (India) would produce a genuine TW alternative to the bicycle' (1673). Such expressions of dread are not far-fetched, particularly when one hears of a national institute of management investing considerable resources researching improvements to the bullock cart, while the nation is simultaneously investing resources in space technology. This co-existence of two ages was depicted in a photograph in a newspaper showing a man carrying a computer placed in a basket on his head. To understand such underlying inconsistencies in traditional societies one needs to adopt divergent rationality (Ekins and Max-Neef, 1991).

In critiquing those visions of alternative technologies as a wasteful debate, I recognize what I call 'marginal adaptations to local conditions'. For example, automatic watches designed by Citizen for Japanese physical movements had to be adapted to the physical movements of Indians. Technology is universal in that it does not have national boundaries, but it has to be adapted to local conditions like climate, soil, water, skills, etc. (Mascarenhas, 1982, Pitroda, 1993). An interesting case of adaptation to local conditions relating to the distinction between TW and FW based on climate was highlighted in the recent campaign for mass immunization against polio undertaken as a part of the technology missions in

India. For the vaccine to retain its potency, it needs to be stored below a certain temperature.

Thus the vaccine has to be transported across the nation, packed in ice or what is referred to as 'cold chain'. How do you know whether a vaccine given to a child is potent or powerless? This problem has been solved elegantly. An enterprising group decided to add a coloured compound to the vaccine solution as an indicator. If the vaccine is potent, the solution in the vial displays a particular colour. When it is not kept cold and its potency is lost, the colour changes, thus letting the health worker know that this vaccine vial needs to be thrown out. The indicator itself is benign and does not affect the properties of the vaccine in any way – truly an ingenious solution to the problem (Balasubramaniam, 1996).

There is considerable evidence to suggest that imported technology requires the involvement of local engineers for its effective development (Mascarenhas, 1982).

In regard to the technological self-reliance of a country, native engineers should ultimately play the most important role in R&D. Foreign engineers and technologists can and should play only a supplementary role. This is an essential finding of our project on the Japanese experience. This is because in spite of the diachronic, trans-cultural nature of technology, it cannot function independently of the society and culture in which it is expected to function. Only members of that society can make the best use of a technology. In other words, only native engineers can adapt a foreign technology to their country's climate and history, can intermediate, stabilize, disseminate, and finally root it firmly in their country (Hayashi, 1990, 53).

Confident nationalism displays the ability or confidence to learn and master a technology and yet remain practical enough to realize that that technology must be learnt from others even if they are foreigners. In confining his comments to the Japanese, Dore (1989) states:

> The nation has devoted a large share of its best brains into learning from others. The teeth-gritting humility which this has required should not be underestimated. In this effort governments play a crucial role. In countries with strong nationalism it accepts the status of a pupil when it is necessary, invites the foreign firms which have something to

teach into joint ventures, and it knows how to be satisfied with the best bargain possible. Behind that strategy must lie a certain confidence – a confidence, in the first place, that one's officials will actually exercise surviellance over foreign interests and not get into bed with them, and a confidence, second, that in the end one will be able to catch up, that one's intellectual resources are capable of doing the job and that one's state of backwardness is only a temporary condition, product of the accident of history. Inevitably, that confidence comes more easily to nations with a long history of regional military power..., the peoples of the Confucian cultural sphere have an advantage over those of South Asia, and those of South Asia over those of sub-Saharan Africa (1674).

VI   TECHNOLOGY TRANSFER PROCESS

In adopting Dore's (1992) distinction between confident nationalism and insecure nationalism I have observed how countries with the former characteristics adopted a policy of selective dissociation while countries with the latter adopted complete dissociation. The two approaches in many ways sum up the strategy of industrialization through technology adopted by both East and South Asia. Complete dissociation overlooks the prospect of a desire to explore the black box, because decision makers have decided to close down the access for knowledge of technology. A model of selective dissociation recognizes on the one hand a desire to be independent of foreign sources of technology but encourages the desire to explore the black box.

Dore (1992) speaks of a cultural trait, which, in effect, is the 'inability to tolerate black boxes without wanting to take them apart – the sort of drive for intellectual mastery that makes a man or woman uncomfortable to have to use machines whose workings they do not understand – and even more uncomfortable if the only people who do understand and can repair the machine are foreigners' (364–365).

Therefore a technology transfer policy that focuses on the regulatory process in terms of meeting certain conditions, such as the rate of indigenization and royalty payments, fails to recognize the fundamental basis of true technology transfer. As technology transfer involves the interaction of people generally from two different countries, the process should recognize history, culture, work practices and the national priorities of the two parties. Further, it should recognize the differences between countries and between transferers, be they Swiss, German,

French, American or Japanese. Each has a different approach to technology transfer and differences exist between firms and between types of technology. Similarly, there are differences in approach of the recipients of technology and this is a significant factor (Mascarenhas, 1982).

Amsden(1989) laid stress on the role of the salaried engineer in the late industrialization of South Korea, likening it to gatekeepers of foreign technology transfers (9). While equal importance was given to educating engineers and technologists in South Asia, their role in development was secondary to the administrator. Most engineers in South Asian countries are products of universities with limited emphasis on practical problem-solving skills. This is compounded by a cultural failing widespread among educated middle-class South Asians – a failure to recognize the dignity of labour. Their role is seen by them to be a 'white collar' one, i.e. essentially responsible for paper work, while lower-level staff are left to supervise shop floor activities. This problem surfaced when young university-qualified engineers found it difficult to learn from non-university-trained technicians sent by the collaborating firm (Mascarenhas, 1982).

The irrelevance of university education to the real-life situation is generally recognized by young Japanese engineers who regard 18 months on the job is a more effective learning method (Dore, 1992). If a university degree is not combined with a desire to learn on the job, then that may help to explain why collaboration agreements in South Asia are continually renewed. Obviously the learning process is not taking place during the period of collaboration. This attitude to learning the technology from collaborators is sometimes reinforced by the regulatory process which does not place sufficient emphasis on learning the technology, by the attitude of young engineers towards collaborating technicians, and a system of education that does not encourage exploring the 'black box'. Together they have contributed to the poor showing of Indian industry in technology transfer for development (Mascarenhas, 1982).

Dore's (1992) comment is highly relevant:

Technology transfer is not a simple all or nothing process. When a new plant is bought, and the embodied technological knowledge with it, it is one thing to learn to run the plant efficiently in normal operation. It is a significantly different thing to be able fully to repair and maintain the plant with one's own indigenous resources. It is yet another thing to understand enough about the plant, and about the scientific principles that underlie its design, to be able to reproduce it, and another thing again to be able to reproduce it with significant modification derived from the experience of running it. All that learning takes place faster in countries with a higher density of people who suffer from the 'intolerance of black boxes' syndrome (365).

In real terms it amounts to 'getting knowledge which is only in some foreigners' heads into the heads of one's own nationals' (Dore, 1989, 1673). That process is much more complicated than when technology was learnt through what used to be called 'patent literature' backward engineering (Mascarenhas, 1982). Whatever the qualitative nature of the change, considerable government involvement is necessary, and with it a strong desire to learn. That value has to be inculcated at all stages of learning, both within society and through the educational system. The pressure to do so becomes increasingly significant for countries that are more dependent on creative humanpower than material resources.

When countries or firms interact in the development and transfer of technology, it may be necessary to use alternative sources and methods. Following liberalization, foreign private investment or alliances are now seen as attractive and are encouraged even by countries like India. While that option was effectively utilized by East Asian governments in the 1960s, India with its closed model viewed it with suspicion, preferring instead selective collaboration through licensing of technology. The two other options available to TW countries are joint ventures or turnkey projects. A major problem for TW countries, particularly in the early stages of development, is their limited capability to make decisions on options which can result in their becoming victims of imposition.

East Asian countries adopted turnkey plants, capital importation, licensing and joint ventures to acquire and develop technological competencies. Their success in steel, automobiles and consumer electronics is evidence of their ability to learn and develop such competencies (Ungson *et al.*, 1997, 134), Between 1962 and 1993, the Korean government approved 8,766 cases of technology transfer, of which over 50 per cent was from Japan and the United States. Korea's pattern of technology acquisition and development is regarded as appropriate to recognized methods of technology transfer. Its success is attributed to:

(1) continuous inflow of technology through formal and informal mechanisms;
(2) development of trained workers willing to learn;
(3) increase in R&D investment particularly in the private sector;
(4) the entrepreneurial spirit generated through equity participation of multinationals;

(5)   Government's role in directing *chaebols* and selectively allocating resources to them to achieve growth (Ungson *et al.*, 1997, 137–138).

Technology transfer is more than just the establishment of a plant for the manufacture of a particular product. It is the laying of a foundation for creating a technological society which demands a careful approach to all aspects involving the transfer process and the creation of an environment for learning the technology through the absorption, adaptation and development of new designs. That modernizing behaviour cannot occur if a country engages a foreign collaborator to establish a manufacturing plant on a turnkey basis. In the 1970s a German machine tool manufacturer was engaged by a country in the Middle East to set up a plant for the manufacture of machine tools on a turnkey basis. On completion of the project UNIDO recommended that a third party be asked to certify that the German firm had met its contractual obligations. While undertaking the assignment, the third party noted with surprise that not a single engineer from the host country had been involved until the plant was ready for commissioning. The technology had been transferred in a physical sense only and certainly not in the sense Dore (1989) is talking about. Therefore, it is important for TW countries to examine carefully the different approaches to technology transfer, taking into consideration the type of technology, indigenous capability for absorbing the technology, and the specific firm or country from which the technology is to be acquired. All three, plus the basic industrial strategy (discussed above), contribute to effective technology transfer.

A fundamental aspect of the technology transfer process is the acquisition of modernizing behaviour (Montgomery, 1974). That modernizing behaviour can also be learnt in the process of adapting to the demands of a new organization has been demonstrated by India's 'White Revolution' – the story of dairy development. For example, villagers soon learnt to queue up punctually at a dairy co-operative to have their milk samples tested for fat content prior to its transportion to urban milk-processing plants. Likewise they learnt to use artificial insemination to improve cattle breeds with the help of vaccinators. This willingness to have their cattle vaccinated against foot and mouth disease is another example of modernizing behaviour (Mascarenhas, 1988).

To illustrate the lack of modernizing behaviour, here is an example from the Indians of the Grand Canyon who received a tractor to help with ploughing. They dismantled and transported it on mules back to their fields lower down the mountains with great effort, but it ended up as a heap of rust once winter set in. This is just one example of several that are noted of the experience with technology but common in TW countries (Duestch, 1971).

Several recorded cases of mishaps typify the absence of an underlying culture or what is otherwise referred to as social carriers – the need to create an industrial culture or industrial discipline that can adapt to the demands of technology. In other words the regulatory approach that has been in operation in South Asia over emphasises the restrictions on entry so that indigenous industry is protected but fails to emphasise the development of technology which is the engineering orientation like indigenisation of equipment, product and systems development. This then explains the continuous dependence on technology suppliers (Mascarenhas, 1982).

VII CONCLUSION

Late comers to industrialization have adopted various strategies for developing or/and acquiring technology for development. Their experience has varied, influenced by historical, social, political and economic circumstances. One of these is the limited institutional capability TW countries possess in the development of policies for industrialization. In that context they are dependent on technology and capital on the FW which produces most of the new technology that is required by the TW. In wanting to acquire the technology the TW is constantly made aware of its long history of colonialism which naturally complicates renewal of that relationship, although in a different context. Some East Asian countries with a different historical experience have found the problems of industrialization less difficult.

In five decades (1945–95) the TW has undergone considerable changes. The East Asian experience dispels some of the misconceptions often debated in development economics. While continuous questioning is a healthy trend, there is no doubt that most TW countries have had to evolve some industrial strategy to overcome different types of dependence. In this both East Asia and South Asia adopted a strategy of import-substitution industrialization with completely different outcomes. From our analysis two important differences are noteworthy. The first is the distinctive institutional framework within which it was implemented. While East Asia adopted an open economy with a closed political system, South Asia adopted a closed economy with an open political system. The latter also used its bureaucratic structure to regulate and control the process of industrial licensing and resource allocation. The second and more important factor in the formulation and implementation of policy for industrialization was the nature of income distribution. Greater income equalities favoured the East Asian countries, while income inequalities were distinctly unfavourable to South Asia in both policy formulation and implementation.

That East Asia was more successful than South Asia in the area of industrial development, despite the latter's sophisticated science and technology infrastructure and high-level manpower, has to be understood in the context of the policies adopted. An underlying inconsistency is detectable here as the very same economic nationalism which promoted self-reliance was unable to encourage promising indigenous developments. The modern scientific infrastructure that emerged therein was an imitative model of the west quite unrelated to the needs of a TW country. As a result we witness continued dependence on outside technology with very few efforts to develop indigenous technology. On the other hand, South Asia has made significant strides in developing capacity in several industrial sectors, including communication and space technology. Its impact however on basic industrialization of the economy has been limited and needs to be examined in the context of the values and attitudes of the policy elite in South Asia.

9 Public Enterprise and Development

I INTRODUCTION

When used as a strategy of industrialization, state intervention involves the setting-up of public enterprises as instruments of development. Public enterprises are established by government and produce goods and services that are sold on the market for a price, fee or charge and are distinct from other types of public goods (Mascarenhas, 1982a). In the absence of a private sector in TW countries and the consequent inability to raise capital or attract entrepreneurs and managerial skills, governments set up public enterprises. As TW countries sought to promote economic development through rapid industrialization, the state became the natural source for mobilizing the resources for such investment. It is in such a context that public enterprise as a strategy of development is to be viewed, not from the narrow financial and economic perspective that currently dominates thinking (Mascarenhas, 1996).

In analysing public enterprise as a strategy of development, I highlight firstly the change in the role of the state in the economy from one of active involvement to one of gradual reduction. Secondly I view public enterprise as a product of the existing political and administrative system in which existing policy-making skills are used to make complex decisions of a technical nature. Finally, I advocate that public enterprises ought to be evaluated adopting a broad-based multi-purpose objective. In other words, I adopt a developmental perspective to understand the role of public enterprises in TW development.

The chapter is structured on the following lines. In section II, I develop some basic distinctions to clarify confusion in terminology and offer alternative frameworks to explain the conditions under which a country is likely to favour public enterprise as a development strategy. In section III, I examine the variety of reasons or motives for a country to establish public enterprises. Section IV looks at some of the problems, both decisional and operational, associated with putting that strategy into action. Section V argues the need for the creation of different types of organizations to blend conflicting demands of business and public accountability. Section VI examines the political and operational factors which are crucial to the performance of individual enterprises. In section

VII, I critique different approaches to understand public enterprises and sum up the issues in the concluding section of the chapter.

II THE CONCEPT OF PUBLIC ENTERPRISE

Public enterprise is distinguished from the public sector because it offers goods and services on the market like the private sector, the consumption of which is based on a price, a rate or a charge. While public enterprises are often included in the public sector, their products are distinct from public goods. In effect they are goods and services provided by the state to all its citizens, irrespective of their capacity to pay. They are called 'public goods' because it is technically infeasible to exclude consumers and such goods cannot be packaged and marketed to individual customers at a specific price. Such goods range from fresh air to open roads and police protection. While such a broad distinction is sufficient for our purpose – to distinguish them from public enterprises – it is necessary to note the scope for imposing restrictions on the use of public goods through tolls and the existence of merit goods like health and education provided by the state in the public interest and by the private sector (Mascarenhas, 1982a).

Governments are differentiated from firms and firmlike institutions in developing countries above all by the fact that they produce the collective or public goods that the private sector characteristically cannot produce in optimal quantities. In most cases public goods have two properties. First, if the good goes to anyone in that area or group, it goes to everyone in that area or group. Second it is largely nonrivalrous, in that additional consumers can enjoy the good without substantially diminishing the consumption of those who are already consuming the good. Defence, pollution control, and law and order are classical examples of public goods that have these properties (Mancur Olson, 1995, 99).

If public enterprise, like its private sector counterpart, produces goods and services which are sold for a price, how then can one justify the role of the state as entrepreneur? A universal justification offered by economists is the market failure argument. In addition to public goods, governments adopt public ownership in case of natural monopolies to protect the public from exploitation by monopoly operators. Alternatively public enterprises may possess externalities which a private operator is not likely to account for. Elimination of these market failure arguments leaves us with the task of developing a set of altern- ative arguments to explain the reasons for a country's adoption of public enterprises.

The state is called upon to play the entrepreneurial role in TW coun- tries because of the absence of an effective market. Thus public enter- prises are distinguished from other types of goods and services provided by the state and possess the following characteristics:

(1) They are wholly or partly owned and controlled by government;
(2) Their products are sold on the market for a fee, price or charge;
(3) They are owned and operated by government because govern- ments regard them as essential;
(4) They have certain characteristics that governments consider to be important to the state and therefore to be retained under its control;
(5) The private sector may consider it uneconomical to invest in such areas.

If these are general economic reasons why governments in the TW adopt public enterprises as a strategy of industrial development, there are also situational factors that explain why some countries, and not others, resort to public enterprises. If there are variations between coun- tries, how does one distinguish them from others? This issue is addressed in the next section of this chapter.

III   A PREDICTIVE FRAMEWORK

In exploring the likely variation between countries in their adoption of public enterprises as a development strategy, I examine four possible explanations. They are: (1) type of industrial development strategy, (2) stage of development, (3) regime characteristics, and (4) a contingent or positive public enterprise strategy.

III (1)   Type of Industrial Development Strategy

In Chapter 8 I discussed alternative industrial development strategies which countries may adopt to achieve economic self-reliance. Two main strategies seem to have engaged the attention of policy elites: the export substitution strategy and the import substitution strategy. While the

former encourages foreign direct private investment by offering incentives, the latter opts for a selective import of foreign technology with
encouragement to the indigenous private sector. However, where import
substitution strategy is combined with a basic industry strategy, most
TW governments are likely to establish public enterprises and to adopt
various mechanisms of collaboration to acquire capital and technology
(Mascarenhas, 1982b, Roemer, 1981).

For example, in the case of a country adopting a basic industry strategy
the reasons for the state taking the initiative could be:

(1)   Such basic industries like steel, power generation, telecommunica-
       tion, etc. are considered crucial for the foundation of an economy
       and therefore strategic for the state to control;
(2)   It involves extensive capital investment and is not generally avail-
       able in the private sector;
(3)   Such investments (which involve a long gestation period to provide
       returns) do not attract the private sector investment even if capital
       is available.

III (2)   Stages of Development

Sherwood (1971), in his analysis of public enterprises, uses Riggs's (1964)
framework of prismatic society to identify which countries are likely to
adopt a public enterprise strategy of development. Using Riggs's (1964)
analytical scheme based on the level of functional differentiation where
countries are placed on a continuum from 'fused' to 'diffracted', Sherwood views institutional capacity in terms of the needs and operational
aspects to determine the likely group of countries on that continuum that
may adopt public enterprises. In his view, countries at both ends of the
continuum, the fused and the diffracted, are unlikely to adopt public
enterprise for different reasons. Those at the fused end lack sufficient
institutional capacity to make decisions and for operational reasons are
not in a position to set up public enterprises. Countries which are sufficiently diffracted as to possess the institutional capacity to adopt a range
of alternative strategies, including a developed private sector, adopt
public enterprise as a last resort.

Countries that fall between the fused and the diffracted, which Riggs
terms 'prismatic' – i.e. countries in the transitional phase of development
(from traditional to modern) – are likely to adopt public enterprises as a
strategy of development. In TW countries that are moving from a traditional to a modern economy one observes public enterprises operating

under a variety of circumstances. This group of countries being sufficiently large in number and spread across the two ends of the continuum provides a firm basis for the evolutionary role of the state alluded to above.

III (3)   Political Character of Regimes

While the extent of public enterprises in TW countries can be explained by using the industrial development strategy and the level of institutional development, there is no doubt that historical and political factors also play a significant role in decisions by governments to adopt public enterprises. Sherwood (1971) recognizes public enterprises as a potential source of power for the regime. For example, Malaysia adopted public enterprise in its 'Bhumiputra' (children of the soil) policy favouring indigenous Malays so as to alter existing power alignments. The Indonesian public enterprise Petromana (petroleum complex) has been known for its political influence and has been used by the regime for a variety of political purposes. In earlier chapters I have referred to regime interests and economic nationalism as factors influencing the attitudes of TW governments to foreign private enterprise. On occasion public enterprise has become a vehicle for such policies. The Indian government's investment in oil and natural gas exploration and refining was prompted by the refusal of Western oil companies to refine crude imported on favourable conditions from the Soviet Union. (Mascarenhas, 1996).

TW countries in which the lower middle class and the rich peasantry exercised a major influence on the survival of elected governments and where public enterprise was used to gain the support of such groups have been characterized as 'intermediate regimes' (Raj, 1973). Public enterprises offered opportunities for the indigenous private sector (as opposed to foreign private enterprise) to provide supplies to large public enterprises, as well as to utilize its outputs like water, power, transport, telecommunication, steel, fertilizers, etc. at subsidised prices. In Taiwan, where support from groups was not necessary, the government used its fertilizer monopoly as barter for rice, pricing its fertilizer well above the comparable rate paid by farmers in other countries (Evans *et al.*, 1985). Public enterprises (in intermediate regimes) were also used to provide jobs for the newly educated middle class who had received their education in government supported educational institutions. It appears then that public enterprises were set up basically to promote the political interests of governments being set up in regions that lacked the basic infrastructure or being used to provide employment for supporters. The result was that political objectives overshadowed the economic object-ives which are used to evaluate their performance.

III (4)   Positive or Contingent Approach to Public Enterprises

During the 1980s debate focusing on the appropriate role of the state in the economy, many countries adopted the 'commanding heights' approach. In certain demarcated areas such as military hardware, air-craft manufacture, mining, oil exploration, etc. regarded as vital to the economy, the state played a dominant role by setting up enterprises under public ownership. For example, the military which controlled power in Taiwan ran its own production facilities, supplied with basic inputs by state enterprises (Amsden, 1985, 99). In 1952, 57 per cent of manufactured output was accounted for by public corporations. Under pressure from USAID, 100 per cent equity in four public corporations was transferred as compensation for land taken from landlords during the earlier land reform programme. Although public ownership had dropped to 20 per cent by the 1980s, government continued to dominate fields such as steel, shipbuilding, heavy machinery, petroleum, synthetics, fertilizers and semiconductors. Banking was virtually state-owned, while other lending institutions remained under strict state supervision. 'Thus, if the government in Taiwan does not quite "control the commanding heights" it goes a long way toward doing so' (Amsden, 1985, 91–92).

The contingent approach is one where the private sector is not equip-ped or interested in the development stages of an enterprise involving large investments. In such cases the state played the role of entrepren-eur and transferred them to the private sector once these enterprises were operational. In Taiwan the government set up new upstream indus-tries and either handed them to the private sector or ran them as public enterprises (Wade, 1990, 76). The problem with that approach is that only successful enterprises are likely to be divested, leaving the unsuc-cessful ventures to remain as public enterprises to be financed from tax-es. Both the positive and the contingent approach, in addition to the others discussed, help to explain variations between countries in their use of public enterprises as a developmental strategy.

While the above framework helps us to understand the type of strategy countries are likely to adopt, there are some specific reasons that explain the justification for public enterprises in TW countries. They are:

(1)   to develop the market by initial mobilization of capital;
(2)   as a device for collaboration for acquiring technology;

(3)   for reasons of national security and to prevent concentration of power in the private sector;

(4)   use of their outputs as inputs for other public enterprises such as telephones for telecommunication and railway stock for railways;

(5)   use of their surplus as a source of funds for further development;

(6)   to rescue declining firms in the private sector, and

(7)   finally, for political reasons by locating enterprises in politically sensitive areas and providing jobs for supporters.

Public enterprises in the TW are as we have seen products of the political and administrative system prevalent in the early stages of development of newly independent countries suspicious of private capital. That the decision to establish public enterprises has been influenced in part by political reasoning rather than pure economic analysis suggests that they usually begin their operations with an inherent disadvantage. The expectation in establishing a range of public enterprises is that it will result in development, and create a market (private sector) (Sherwood, 1971). In evaluating their performance, I advocate a broad-based perspective. Further I consider it worthwhile to study the political and adminstrative system that was instrumental in creating them and the policy and operational environment within which they were expected to function. In all fairness these constraints must be incorporated into any meaningful understanding of their contribution to development (Mascarenhas, 1972, 1974, 1982b, 1996).

IV   POLITICAL AND ADMINISTRATIVE SYSTEM FOR POLICY-MAKING

In proposing the idea that public enterprises are business ventures involved in the production of goods and services using complex technology, it is worthwhile to examine how a private sector entrepreneur makes an investment decision. Assuming as an objective is the maximization of returns on investment, the entrepreneur would adopt a careful analysis covering the market for the product, the necessary technology to produce it and the material, human and financial resources necessary to produce it, and would combine all these factors through proper organization and management to achieve the desired objective: profit. In such a case the end result has to be evaluated in terms of rate of return on investment, disregarding the imponderables that can affect any business venture.

This approach appears rational enough for any reasonable entrepreneur to adopt. However, it is less likely to be adopted in the case of a public enterprise for several reasons. To begin with, the establishment of a public enterprise is a political process with objectives that are both economic and political, such as security, employment generation and regional development. Further, in the absence of qualified manpower in the early stages of development technical decisions are made by civil servants, resulting in such decisions being less than optimum. An analysis of decisions taken during the process of setting up public enterprises in India reveals that:

(1) Public enterprises were set up to produce a product for which there was no market or that capacity was far in excess of current demand;

(2) Lack of foresight in planning an enterprise has led to the duplication of facilities at increased cost, a situation that could have been avoided if capacity expansion had been built into the original plan;

(3) Choice of poor technology has resulted in inefficiency and higher costs in operations;

(4) The raw materials available were not of the quality specified under existing technology;

(5) The absence of proper project evaluation and analysis led to inaccurate cost estimates impacting on subsequent financial performance;

(6) Poor contractual arrangements and ineffective project management, etc. resulted in delays and cost escalations.

To avoid mishaps, it is necessary to improve capacity for policy-making, elsewhere termed as 'policy efficiency' (Mascarenhas, 1982a). While not exclusive to the TW, such mishaps assume greater and more unfortunate consequences in the TW with significant financial costs and declining morale caused by constant criticism levelled against the management.

In my view the initial policy decision involving the establishment of a public enterprise is crucial as it contributes to its success or its failure. I do not suggest here that such failure can be completely eliminated or that it is completely absent in the private sector. However, its occurrence in the TW is likely to be greater because of the political and administrative context in which such decisions are made. Whether public or private, it is imperative that any business or other decision goes through a systematic process, involving different aspects such as the product mix, location, type of technology, resource availabilty, and the possible market for the product. Once its feasibility is established, the project should go through a detailed project report and be entrusted to project management for its implementation. As success or failure affects the operations of other enterprises, both in the public and private sector, and performance is closely related to the policy-making process, I consider it especially important that the policy-making process be improved.

V ORGANIZATION AND MANAGEMENT OF PUBLIC ENTERPRISES

If public enterprises have to be useful devices to promote development it is necessary to create the appropriate organization and the political conditions for their effective performance. Two important requisites for a successful business operation are long-term stability and short-term flexibility. Stability in the long term involves continuous growth, managerial continuity and the capacity to accumulate resources for future investment. Flexibility in day-to-day operations involves giving managers the freedom to procure materials, to hire and fire personnel, to plan operations, to deal with clients and to fix prices. Both stability and flexibility are important for business success.

To provide for both long-term stability and operational flexibility an enterprise needs both directive autonomy and procedural autonomy. Directive autonomy is freedom from political controls with access to long-term funds so as to avoid the uncertainities of annual budget allocation. Commitment of long-term funds enables the enterprise's board to make long-term capital investment decisions and to enter into long-term contracts with its top management. Procedural autonomy is freedom from bureaucratic controls, particularly from bureaucratic procedures like financial approvals that apply to traditional departments. The above are crucial requirements for operating in a market environment, where high-level expertise is required to operate complex technology. In such conditions, enterprises need to create a climate which can attract expertise and provide an environment for them to function. In order to provide such directive and procedural autonomy a different type of organization and environment is necessary (MacMahon, 1961).

It is acknowledged that the requirements spelt out are difficult to achieve without some changes to existing systems of government management. Procedural autonomy is possible to achieve within existing departmental systems of management by introducing modifications, such as separate budgets, revolving funds, the creation of distinct personnel systems and the modifying of rules and regulations. Directive autonomy requires the creation of quasi-governmental organizations by statute or general enactment, to be managed by independent boards of directors, provided with separate funds and freedom from detailed government procedural controls. In other words, the autonomy required to manage a public enterprise can be created by modifying existing departments or creating public corporations or/and government companies. While the bestowing of quasi-government status provides a basic form of organization that provides the minimum level of autonomy laid out in the statute (ascribed), the real substance rests on achieved autonomy. What is crucial here is that the autonomy provided ensures successful performance and that it remains reconcilable with public control and accountability (Mascarenhas, 1972). Here the conflicting demands of control and accountability to protect the public interest and managerial autonomy to operate as a business enterprise can cause problems. There is no strict formula that establishes the suitability of a form of organization for a specific type of enterprise, just as there is no guarantee that a specific form will result in greater independence. There are a variety of factors in addition to form of organization that contribute to the success of an enterprise and that, in a nutshell, rests on its capacity to retain its independence from the constraints imposed by government.

V (a)   Departmental Public Enterprise

Most TW countries were able to operate and manage public enterprises like telecommunications, postal services, railway systems, road transport and electricity undertakings by adopting the departmental form of organization with modifications. An example in case is Indian Railways, one of the largest railway networks in the world, which has an independent budget, a separate personnel system and a board that runs the enterprise. The operational demands of such enterprises are met by what I have discussed as procedural autonomy. However, the real issue for such undertakings is the prospect of being embroiled in political debates that occur when such enterprises have to seek funding through the annual appropriations process. The uncertainties of annual appropriations, while normal for traditional government activities, interferes with long-range planning for investment and freedom in arriving at pricing and other financial policies. The other constraint that departmental undertakings face are the procedural requirements of prior approvals from controlling agencies when certain financial and other decisions are made. (Mascarenhas, 1982a). However, such modifications are not sufficient to justify their use for operating a majority of public enterprises.

V (b)   The Public Corporation

The public corporation has been widely used for a range of public enterprises which have been set up to undertake developmental activities, such as multi-purpose river valley projects, development banks, transport and communication undertakings. The use of this form of organization provides an independent statutory status tailored to the needs of specific enterprises where the respective powers of the board, which is responsible for managing the enterprise, and government are spelt out. It provides for both procedural and directive autonomy, coupled with an independent legal and financial status that should provide a sound foundation for successful operations. With public enterprises now operating in a variety of businesses, and sometimes in competition with the private sector, the government company offers an alternative mechanism for achieving development.

V (c)   The Government Company

The creation of government companies to operate public enterprises, particularly for manufacturing activities, was intended to provide conditions similar to the private sector, without undermining the public interest. Government companies operate within the private sector under the Companies Acts where the powers and responsibilities are clarified in the articles of association and the memorandum of association. These articles can be modified with ease without having to seek special approvals as in the case of public corporations.

Government companies have been widely adopted in TW countries to manage public enterprises. They operate within a common legal framework which provides greater flexibility by bringing about necessary changes to meet the demands of an operational nature. However, this very same flexibility can become an opportunity for excessive government and political interference under a weak management or when its performance is questionable.

While all three forms of organization are widely used, there is no formula to help decide which particular form will be suitable for a particular type of enterprise. There is no guarantee that a specific form will result in greater independence. There are a variety of factors in addition to form of organization that contribute to the success of a public enterprise.

Accordingly, if the decisions for initial establishment of the enterprise and the organization for managing it are seen as appropriate, the next crucial component is the political and administrative environment within which managers operate. Managers of public enterprises do not always enjoy complete independence. They are often required to respond to political demands, regional and local pressures, directives from officials in the various ministries, and demands of political accountability through parliamentary committees and audit reports. As public enterprises have grown in number and in the extent of investment, the number of specialized agencies for evaluation and monitoring have also increased.

If the decision to set up a public enterprise is based on inefficient policy decisions, it is more likely that that public enterprise will perform poorly. Poor performance brings pressure on the enterprise to seek subventions and thus attract public attention and become a cause of concern for the government. While government is likely to accede to such requests for assistance, it does so on condition that it meets a set of prudential controls. As the number of such prudential controls increase and restrict the enterprise's autonomy, there is likely to be a further decline in performance. That cycle is unlikely to be broken unless the machinery for making the initial decision is improved or the initial problems that affected performance set right. If the cause of poor performance is basic such as wrong product mix, poor location, raw material deficiency or inappropriate technology, common policy problems faced by TW countries owing to lack of skills and expertise or the very political nature of public policymaking, the latter option is less likely.

Therefore all three aspects – the initial decision, the form of organization and the political and administrative environment – become crucial ingredients for public enterprises because they are placed in the awkward position of having to achieve the best of both worlds – i.e. function like a business enterprise, while at the same time be publicly accountable to various political and administrative agencies. This ability to operate independently of the political and administrative environment is referred to as 'enterprise autonomy'. However, the reality is different.

While arriving at an optimum relationship between ownership and managerial autonomy is a difficult task, the emphasis on autonomy is essential because:

(1)   They are business operations that are publicly owned;
(2)   Their public nature brings them into continous interaction with several different agencies which exercise authority over them and to which they remain accountable;
(3)   They are primarily established to undertake the goals and objectives of government;

(4) They inherit all aspects associated with the decision making process that results in their establishment.

In such a context, the dynamics of the relationship of the enterprise with the enabling system (several agencies responsible for its establishment, continued support and evaluation) is central to understanding the problems of managing public enterprises. For that relationship to be favourable, the three ingredients should be positive. Any deficiencies here will render that relationship unfavourable. This conclusion is based on studies of successful public enterprises like Hindustan Machine Tools and the National Dairy Development Board in India (Mascarenhas, 1982b, 1988).

While successful enterprises can be used as a basis for analysing and improving the decison framework of public enterprises, unfortunately unwise decisions or actions persist. The origin of many can be traced to a poor initial decision compounded along the way by the attempt to achieve a variety of socio-economic objectives. Several, such as the creation of employment, promotion of regional development, encouragement of indigenous industry and research, can and do have an adverse impact on public enterprise performance. Efforts on the part of governments and analysts to develop a comprehensive approach to incorporate these into performance evaluation have yet to be made (Mascarenhas, 1974).

Thus no consideration is given to the enterprise's efforts to achieve socio-economic objectives when the need for additional funding surfaces. Instead, the enterprise is subjected to prudential controls and perhaps even to the control of new agencies created for the purpose. In the absence of an enterprise culture, the counterpart bureaucracy takes control, thus perpetuating the cycle of declining performance.

As the performance of public enterprises is a concern for governments of TW countries, it is essential that they:

(1) examine carefully the type of policies first initiated by governments which are quite often the cause of poor performance;
(2) initiate measures to set right the problems caused by ineffective policies;
(3) lay greater emphasis on enhancing the capability of policy-makers i. e. policy efficiency;
(4) provide an appropriate political and administrative environment for effective functioning.

My emphasis on the importance of policy efficiency as a prerequisite to operational efficiency is echoed by Hying-Ki Kim (1988), who calls this process the creation of a synergism. Kim advocates the drafting of a new institutional framework for decision making, similar to the efforts of the Korean government in recent years (Hying-Ki Kim, 1988, 212–225).

VI MEASURING PERFORMANCE

If the discussion thus far suggests that public enterprise in the TW has been adopted as a development strategy to achieve a range of objectives, then in my view it is necessary to adopt a broader-based integrated approach to performance measurement in preference to the narrow efficiency approach based on a rate of return basis. Critics fail to recognize that public enterprises are distinct from and not comparable with the private sector, whose objectives are precise and clearly measurable (Mascarenhas, 1974). Both private and public enterprises prefer precise measures of performance, and what better measure than the bottom line? The problem is that the bottom line is not always a true measure of performance.

The financial indicators used to measure enterprise performance do not reflect the true health of an enterprise as reflected in growth, quality of internal organization, the state of productive machinery, quality of staff, morale of the organization and level of industrial discipline. The use of financial indicators like value of shares based on profits as a guideline overlooks a crucial factor in the long-term health of an enterprise. In the case of public enterprises, which are required to undertake a variety of socio-economic objectives, such objectives cannot be measured in purely financial terms. Included in this category is the role played by public enterprises in providing housing, transport, schools and hospitals, all of which are social amenities which public enterprises are required to provide to their employees.

Taking these factors into consideration, I adopt a systems approach to measurement in which I develop a three-tier framework of objectives (unit, sectoral and national) for evaluation of public enterprises. In this three-tier scheme the increase in production is accounted as a contribution to sectoral objectives at the second level. Achieving self-reliance or import substitution at the first tier is deemed a contribution to national objectives (Mascarenhas, 1974). In doing so I separate responsibilities of government from those of enterprise managers and set up clearer measures of performance for each enterprise. While this approach may not meet the standards of measurement on private sector lines advocated by economists, it does avoid the fuzziness that can arise when one talks in terms of the public interest. Further, it fits in with the social indicators approach that gained momentum during the 'great society' programs of Lyndon Johnson in the United States (Gross, 1965).

VII AN AGENDA FOR REFORM

The poor performance of public enterprises in which TW countries have invested considerable resources over the years is a cause of major concern. Apart from being victims of inefficient policies, public enterprises are expected to undertake multiple objectives under adverse conditions. I have advocated two possible options. The first is to improve the process of policy-making so that decisions on setting a public enterprise are made on proper economic and technical analysis. The other is to adopt a broader-based approach to measuring their performance. In doing so, I question the rate of return approach often adopted to compare the cost of capital, which does not truly reflect conditions that led to the creation of the enterprise.

Despite the current wave favouring privatization, I have, on the evidence of both successful and unsuccessful enterprises, advocated changing the operating environment. Where offered as an alternative, privatization conveys a view that ownership provides an incentive. This is so in small-scale operations. However, in the case of large organizations, it is the operating environment that really matters. Privatization as advocated suffers from ideological overtones equated with free enterprise and democracy (Dinavo, 1995). In many TW countries there are several enterprises which ought not to be under public ownership as they are not fulfilling any public purpose. In such cases they should be disbanded or divested.

In advocating privatization in TW countries, one has to take into consideration existing limitations. A primary limitation is the lack of a private sector capable of managing complex industrial enterprises. Even if such capabilities are present in some countries (notably India), the political obstacles such as opposition from vested interests have to be surmounted. The World Bank (1995), which advocates privatization of state-owned enterprises, recognizes the obstacles in its path.

India probably has the largest public enterprise sector (245 undertakings at the central government level) with a record of indifferent performance. Even with a private sector capable of operating such enterprises, the government has been reluctant to move along the privatization path. In 1992 the government had sought partial divestment of up to 20 per cent of shares in 31 public sector undertakings in energy, fertilizers, machine tools, petro-chemicals and the electricals industry which were operating on commercial lines, similar to the private sector. Such partial divestment was easy to undertake because most of these were in the industrial sector, where the private sector has had considerable investment and experience, and because they had been established as government companies. The first such exercise in 1991–92 resulted in a loss to the exchequer of $30 million, earning the criticism of the Public Accounts Committee of Parliament (Maheshwari, 1995). While privatization has not been wholeheartedly promoted by the government in India, there have however been efforts to reform existing enterprises.

VII   CONCLUSION

In this chapter I have examined the problems of managing public enterprise in TW countries. An underlying problem for any analysis of public enterprise in TW countries is the criteria that government should adopt to decide whether an enterprise is to be under public ownership. In the early stages of development, when the state is the only entrepreneur, the public enterprise sector tends to be quite extensive and varies between countries. To provide a perspective I have attempted four different frameworks to predict the likely prospects for a country to resort to public enterprise.

With the emergence of a market, i.e. a private sector, governments in TW countries have less need to set up public enterprise. The reality is that public enterprise as a strategy of development fails to create a private sector because of underlying policy contradictions. The policy contradictions enter into our analysis of public enterprise at the stage of their establishment, as the absence of capability results in inefficient decisions. Such inefficient decisions result in public enterprises being unable to meet expectations. The other aspect that I have posed is the interrelationship between a public enterprise and small private entrepreneurs who thrive on the former as suppliers of inputs and recipients of outputs at subsidized prices. While this interrelationship perpetuates the growth and continued existence of public enterprise, it indirectly transfers its inefficiencies on to the private sector where the two co-exist.

If the initial policy decision is inefficient then all other factors associated with the management of public enterprises, like independent organization, managerial autonomy, control and accountability, become increasingly less relevant. The fact that they are unlikely to perform as expected because of a poor decision further undermines the operating independence of the enterprise, because any request for subventions is likely to be conditional to prudent practices. In other words, a poorly performing public enterprise is likely to be saddled with increasing controls. In order to understand that process I adopt inter-organizational analysis using the power-dependence framework. According to my analysis effective independence rests on achieved autonomy and that can only be possible if basic conditions for successful performance are met in the form of an efficient policy decision. From a complex set of interrelationships and the broad nature of objectives set out, I advocate a different approach to performance evaluation. It is from that perspective that I favour changing the political and administrative environment of public enterprises and advocate privatization in case of public enterprises that ought not to be in public ownership.

10 Strategies for the Development and Management of Agriculture

I INTRODUCTION

In Chapter 1, I described the TW as burdened by excessive population, predominantly agricultural economies, limited resources and limited exposure to institutions of the modern economy. To remedy such circumstances, it follows then that governments of TW countries need to develop policies which can effectively control population and increase agricultural productivity. Historically, countries generate surplus from increased agricultural productivity, thus providing a foundation for structural transformation of the economy (Johnson, 1997). Under given resource conditions, the underlying differences in economic development between countries are then determined by the quality of policies. This in my view is fundamental to the extraordinary performance of East Asia when compared with South Asia. In previous chapters of this study I have emphasized several aspects, such as differences in historical experience, impact of culture and religion, type of political and administrative system, etc., all of which influence the manner in which governments develop policies and implement them.

In establishing a relationship between policy and the role of agriculture in development, I have incorporated the influence of regime characteristics to highlight the likely policies that TW governments may adopt. In Chapter 5 I have noted the importance of agricultural modernization of South Korea and Taiwan under Japanese colonialism and subsequent efforts to promote equity and efficiency through a programme of land reform. This fortuitous legacy of Japanese colonialism was not available to countries of South Asia, whose historical experience was of a very different nature (Moore Jr, 1966) and cast a marked influence on the direction of post-independence agricultural strategies. Analysts who have attributed the current economic performance of NIEs to those strategies have looked at India and questioned the basic and heavy industry strategy adopted by that country, citing it as the possible reason for poor performance (Oshima, 1987).

In the context of excessive population and limited resources in land there is growing need for governments to create non-farming opportunities to employ surplus labour that cannot be gainfully employed to exploit existing agricultural resources. The agricultural sector is thus faced with three options: (1) to increase productivity through the use of technology and economic incentives, (2) to create greater equity in land owning through land reforms, and (3) to encourage a variety of rural development programmes to promote alternative sources of rural development

Three alternative strategies for development of TW agriculture have been advocated. The first leaves agriculture to the dictates of markets where resource flows generally move from agriculture to industry. That approach generally reflects the current state of the FW where agriculture plays a limited role. The second, the 'interrelated strategy', encourages the growth of agriculture by investments in related areas like nutrition, technology and infrastructure. In such a strategy, government plays a major role in policy design and programme implementation. In adopting such a strategy governments recognize the linkage between agriculture and rural development. The third strategy, distinct from the free market and the interrelated strategy in that it calls for government policy intervention, uses markets to promote agricultural development. The dilemma of such a strategy is the existence of market failure. In such a situation government policy intervention is also likely to result in government failure (Meier, 1995).

In this chapter I examine these issues in detail. In section III attempt a discussion on traditional societies and their reaction to strategies of agricultural modernistion. In section III I look at types of political regimes and the type of strategies adopted linked to types of agricultural enterprise. In section IV I focus on the state-directed strategy for agriculture adopted by South Korea and Taiwan. An analysis of the fundamentals of the 'green revolution' follows in section V. In section VII examine further the impact of the green revolution and discuss the prospects for land reform to overcome the consequences of the green revolution. Section VII is an exploration of opportunities for non-farm-based incomes in rural communities. The final section sums up the experience of the TW in the development and management of agriculture.

II THE NATURE OF TW AGRICULTURAL SOCIETIES

In traditional societies land is inherited and its cultivation is based on local conditions and practices. Water for cultivation, if received, is looked upon gratefully 'as a gift of life from the gods of old, whom they still honor in accordance with folk traditions' (Weitz, 1986, 25). The socio-economic stability enjoyed by such pre-modern societies poses a challenge to policy-makers who are concerned about improving living standards without disrupting stability. While such fundamental changes did occur during colonialism, they were however not entirely irreversible. Unfortunately that trend has been perpetuated by post-colonial regimes.

The first goal of economic growth is to provide primary material needs to the population, for no society can hope to industrialize or automate its economy if it cannot feed and shelter and educate its citizens. Since agriculture is the main economic sector of Third World countries, and is necessary to meeting the first goal, it plays a critical role in the development process. The potential contributions of agriculture to the economy are: increasing the food supply, providing productive work to a rapidly increasing rural population, creating capital for investment, and supporting industrial development (Weitz, 1986, 40).

Any attempts to transform TW rural societies carry the inherent danger of uprooting traditional institutions of peasant economy which are socially embedded in the form of community. Such social embeddedness, according to the 'moral economists', is the reason for political conflict caused by the intrusion of the market economy. According to them, efforts to transform the rural community must be achieved without disrupting the institutions of the community, or the corporate village which is central to rural life. By adopting the embodied – disembodied distinction, the moral economist questions the relevance of economic analysis in attempting to understand pre-market societies (Booth, 1994). While that aspect of limited market penetration is recognized, one cannot overlook different images of rural life and the coexistence of harmony and conflict and, even exploitation. Generally characterized as peasant economies which grow food for consumption, entry into market transactions is undertaken only occasionally for sale of produce in return for basic necessities of life. The pre-capitalist idea of agrarian societies is reflected in the natural economy with limited market transactions and a peasant society which gradually undertakes increased interaction with markets. This idea of agrarian societies associated with TW (particularly Africa) is questioned by Bates (1984–85), who states that the characteristics of withdrawal from markets, subsistence and powerlessness are joint consequences of the manipulation of markets by states (253).

The existence of a dominant agricultural sector which has been exploited for centuries without significant technological change helps to explain the low economic performance of TW economies and their characterization as traditional societies. Throughout this study I make a distinction between traditional and modern, distinguishing societies in which religious, cultural, linguistic, ethnic and tribal influences play a more significant role from those where such influences are less pronounced in the behaviour and attitudes of people. In no way does that distinction suggest that traditional is bad or that modern is good. I have cited several examples to show how countries like Japan and Turkey have succeeded in introducing change within traditional norms and values.

When asked about their awareness of the Japanese system of cultivation, 90 per cent of farmers in the Indian state of Bihar indicated their knowledge of the system. They were however reluctant to adopt it because of the hard work involved. In citing this evidence, Deutsch (1971) is emphasizing the importance of one's own belief in the future. That belief in the future for peasants in Bihar is bleak because of their susceptibility to illness and their consequent mortality, which has its effects on the village economy. Such evidence has led to the comment: 'There is no place for a puritan ethic unless one believes in the future'. This illustrates the validity of Deutsch's (1971) statement that 'Health and vigour of the country's population is one of the preconditions for agricultural development and in the long run, also for political stability' (29).

While French impressionists and Elizabethan poets presented the rural scene as idyllic, the reality of rural life is that it is lonely and isolated and the farmer is often a victim of nature's fury in the form of floods, drought or famine. The harshness of their environment and adverse circumstances are reflected in the behaviour of rural people, described by Foster (1973) as 'image of limited good'. Rural people work on the land to grow food for their subsistence and enter into contact with the outside world only when necessary. Constant exploitation by local traders, middle men and money lenders has resulted in a fear of the outside world. Foster cites the case of Yucatan potters who feel obliged to return to their village before nightfall after a visit to the town to sell their pots (1973).

For rural people land constitutes the only good in life, and it is limited. Cultivating it in a harsh and hostile environment in which others control prices for produce leaves them at the mercy of the middlemen and economic dependence on the nearest town makes them powerless. Any changes to their existing state initiated by outsiders raise fears of instability and uncertainty.

Notwithstanding the rural perception of the outside world as hostile, there still exist a variety of factors that hinder the co-operation of rural communities against the world outside. Apart from the mistrust and suspicion that act as an obstacle (Banfield, 1958), there is the feeling that the good in life – i.e. prosperity in a closed environment with limited land – can come only at the cost of others. This leads to an atmosphere of mistrust which becomes an obstacle to co-operating against the outside world. Within such a limited view of good, any visible prosperity invites gossip and suspicion and tends to encourage people either to hide wealth (Foster, 1973) or to adopt an egalitarian sharing of poverty through community festivities. The above factors that I have discussed help to understand behavioural problems associated with rural people and explains their resistance to change.

If the selective evidence I have used conveys the impression that rural society is complex, it is intended to convey the significance of incorporating attitudes, values and culture when introducing technological change (Foster, 1973). As rural people tend to continue practices adopted by their forebears, any change with a view to improving efficiency must adopt, as suggested by Korten (1981) a process of social transformation using the learning process in preference to the technocratic approach adopting the blueprint approach. Typical of the technocratic approach is the practice advocated by a technical assistance expert in castrating young bulls in the interest of improved health among indigenous draught animals. Castration resulted in the disappearance of the hump and rendered the bulls useless as working animals. In South Asia the hump of the bull is an essential part of the plough and the bullock cart as it is used to hold the yoke (Foster, 1973, 97–98). Another example is the effort to introduce cooking stoves using kerosene to replace the earthen oven of old in which cow dung cakes were burnt as fuel. While smoke-free stoves made cooking much easier for village women, the absence of smoke denied villagers of their natural disinfectant against white ants which thrived under smokefree conditions, resulting in villagers having to replace their thatched roofs more frequently than before (Foster, 1973, 96).

Traditional societies are characterised by stability. Further, they are strongly influenced by social and religious values. Individuals are seen as part of an organic whole and membership is based on assigned roles. One's duty is to perform that role to maintain harmony, and violation of that role is open to punishment (Hegginbotham, 1975). Within such societies, stability, if used positively, can be used to enhance development. This historical evolution of grafting newer forms of agricultural or rural enterprise on traditional foundations is nowhere more pronounced than in India.

While the 'Dharmic' ideal advocates stability with rigidity, the Gandhian ideal sees the interests of the individual and those of society as identical. Dharma, the link between the individual and his or her social obligation, can hold society together harmoniously and act as a balance between individual freedom and social restraint (Tickner, 1987, 138). The Gandhian approach aims at reconstructing society on the basis of self-sufficient village communities organized on the family model where wealth is shared in common and public decisions are taken unanimously adopting consensus. Gandhians believe rural development must be consistent with the genius of Indian social organization, where organic self-regulation of society is based on the concept of Dharma (Narayan, 1961)).

III   POLITICAL REGIMES AND AGRICULTURAL TRANSFORMATION

In comparing the developmental performance of the two Asias in earlier chapters of this study, a factor that was noted as distinguishing the two was the emphasis laid by East Asia on agricultural transformation as a foundation for development. Governments generally adopt strategies for agricultural development depending on how much political support they need for their policies. For analytical purposes two possible options are open for political regimes. The first is where a regime controls total political authority and does not rely on the co-operation of rural elites to promote and implement policies. These regimes are identified as separate, i.e. they have acquired their power by dislodging existing power groups or are non-indigenous like the mainland Chinese in Taiwan. The second option is where a regime relies on the support of rural elites to promote and implement rural development policies. These are described as 'dominant elites' (Tai, 1974). Governments reliant on such support adopt a reformist agricultural strategy which attempts a combination of growth with distribution. Dominant elites, by adopting a selective growth strategy, are likely to enhance the power of rural elites who prove to become an obstacle to any efforts at land reform (Varshney, 1995), while separated elites are in a position to promote a technocratic growth strategy, having first achieved equity through a programme of land reform.

In linking regime composition to the type of agricultural strategy, Griffin (1974) attempts to relate government policies in the context of the prevailing agrarian social structure. Government policies in TW countries generally aim at increasing agricultural production and at reducing existing social and economic inequities, and, in so doing, respond to various powerful groups and their demands. When countries are faced with two distinct pressures of growth and equity, some opt for growth without redistribution while others opt for redistribution with no growth. The first seeks both growth and redistribution and is categorized as 'reformist'; the second lays exclusive emphasis on growth and is categorized as 'technocratic', and the last stresses redistribution and is characterized as 'radical'. All three types of regimes adopting distinctive agricultural strategies are prevalent in TW countries and have had distinctive outcomes.

Technocratic strategy is possible in countries where power and land is concentrated in the hands of a minority, as in Latin America where the concepts of private property and free market reign. Here the objective is growth and productivity through the use of modern technology. A radical strategy of land redistribution based on co-operative or collective ownership is possible in post-revolutionary regimes where land owners have been displaced through social upheavals, as in China and Vietnam. The options here are clear-cut, unhampered by tangible opposition to the regime and its policies. By contrast, reformist regimes continuously vacillate between options of growth with equity and are unable to make significant progress in conditions where both options have support from different groups, thus ending up with policies riddled with inconsistencies and contradictions.

In this study I place significant emphasis on regime composition (Raj, 1973, Rudolphs, 1987, Griffin, 1974) to highlight the importance of their role in promoting different strategies of development. In East Asia displacement of the landed elite was a significant factor in the emergence of an independent semi-authoritarian regime promoting a clear development strategy. Contrast this with South Asian economies, where notwithstanding the dominant role played by the rural elite a clear development strategy has yet to emerge. The policy of land distribution, which has been on the agenda of these countries for over four decades, is still ineffective owing to a lack of political will on the part of governments heavily dependent on the support of rural elites to remain in power (Mascarenhas, 1975). Instead the mid-1960s witnessed a distinct shift from a policy of land redistribution to one of agricultural modernization which had the opposite effect of enhancing the power of 'bullock capitalists' (Rudolphs, 1987, Varshney, 1995).

IV STATE-DIRECTED AGRICULTURAL DEVELOPMENT IN EAST ASIA

South Korea and Taiwan fortuitously achieved a level of agricultural modernization under Japanese colonialism. In Taiwan, Japan replicated some of its own experience of land reform undertaken during the Meiji period. Land rights were transferred from absentee to local landlords. A communications infrastructure with the objective of increasing small-holder rice and sugar production for markets in Japan was established. Other policies were implemented for enhancing production, such as improved irrigation, improved seeds, the use of fertilizers and the set-ting-up of farmers' co-operatives, irrigation associations and landlord-tenant associations. These policies had the cumulative affect of leading to greater knowledge and awareness and increased production and even-tually became a form of control over local population (Wade, 1990, 73). The benefits were many: easy accessibility to remote regions through extensive transportation and communication, the emergence of modern business and commercial centres, promotion of industrial processing of products, and the eradication of epidemic diseases. In effect these changes transformed Taiwan from a backward to a thriving region (Wade, 1990, 75).

In both South Korea and Taiwan, a strong state-directed programme of agricultural development was achieved without incurring political or economic costs. Several factors contributed to the evolution of that rela-tionship between state and agriculture: the legacy of Japanese colonial rule, density of agricultural populations, the prevalence of small family rice farms and finally the highly statist regimes established after World War II.

Rapid development of their economies and increasing industrializa-tion has led to a decline in agriculture. In 1953 the agricultural sector contributed to 34 per cent of Taiwan's Gross National Product. By 1981 this had fallen to seven per cent. Comparable figures for South Korea were 46 per cent and 18 per cent respectively (Moore, 1995). While the importance of agriculture within the overall economy has declined, there has been a distinct shift from grains to livestock and horticulture. This response of farmers in shifting from grains to livestock is reflected in changes in consumer demands resulting from increased incomes. This pattern is observed in South Asia, too, where similar diversification in agricultural production has been taking place. Such changes in agrarian structure in the TW have brought about closer links between industry and agriculture and with it the opportunity for non-farm incomes as a proportion to farm incomes to increase dramatically. In the context of limited land, such diversification, termed 'pluralistic realism' was advocated by Chambers (Mascarenhas, 1988).

Building on the foundation for agricultural modernization laid in South Korea and Taiwan by the Japanese, the newly established governments, with United States support, moved into a programme of land reform. An egalitarian distribution of land achieved through post-war land reform programmes has generally been identified as the foundation for NIE performance. The effects of egalitarian distribution of land are many: (a) the transfer of assets generates incomes and spreads the benefits of growth to those at the bottom of the economic scale; (b) higher yields from small farms result in higher agricultural productivity, and (c) land redistribution does away with the power of landed oligarchies who are capable of influencing public decisions (Gary Fields, 1995, 87).

There is considerable debate on the advisability of adopting land reform as a foundation for agricultural growth (particularly on arriving at an optimal size of holding). Recent studies of Taiwan's first land reform of 1949–53 reveal that the small size of land holdings is the basic cause of present agricultural inefficiency (Bain, 1993).

The 1949–53 land reforms in Taiwan were implemented in three phases: (1) rents were restricted to 37.5 per cent, (2) tenants were allocated public land held by Japanese nationals, and (3) landlords were required to hand over land above a minimal size to be distributed under a Land to the Tiller Act. Landlords whose land was taken over were compensated in the form of bonds and stocks in public enterprises. In the case of Taiwan, as the policy was implemented by a mainland government which had migrated to the island (Taiwan), there was no inherent obligation to the agricultural elite. South Korean and Taiwanese agriculturalists were completely excluded from the ruling coalition and from any influence on the policy-making process (Moore, 1995). The small class of landlords virtually disappeared, transforming Taiwan's agrarian economy into a large number of owner-operators with extremely small holdings (Amsden, 1995).

In South Korea, the 'land to the tiller' programme, as in Taiwan, was relatively successful. It however had some weaknesses which caused concern in later years. The small size of holdings eventually became economically unviable. The other problem with land distribution was that tenants who had recieved land had to pay 30 per cent of the produce for five years, were taxed at a rate between 8 per cent and 25 per cent of agricultural taxes and had to borrow working capital at high rates of interest (Rashid and Quibria, 1995).

In establishing the important role of agricultural modernization in the economic development of Taiwan, Amsden (1995) comments that:

Fast growth and a transfer of agricultural resource to the towns, however, were neither the outcome of free market forces nor the automatic result of purely technical phenomena – the green revolution. Rather they reflected the structure of ownership in the countryside and state management of almost every conceivable economic activity (85).

Unlike some political regimes that view land reform as a distributive strategy and an alternative to the technocratic approach, governments in South Korea and Taiwan have combined redistribution with growth. The Green Revolution, which in other countries has benefited large farmers, has in Taiwan benefited all farmers. 'It is then a defining characteristic of Taiwan's agriculture that a multiplicity of small peasant proprietors exist in conformity with the bourgeois model of individualistic family farming, whereas directing this drama is a highly centralized government bureaucracy' (Amsden, 1995, 85).

This result has been achieved by providing farmers with direct access to a range of government services which include credit, monopoly of fertilizer by the state to ensure adequate distribution and enhance productivity, procurement of surplus and the avoidance of price risks. Small holdings place limits on scientific farming and farmers generally produce for subsistence. However, through education the government in Taiwan was able to encourage farmers to break from tradition and produce for the market. In exchange for fertilizer, government entered into a barter arrangement whereby farmers paid in kind. This method to extract surplus by having farmers pay taxes and fertilizer costs in kind was popularly known as 'hidden rice taxes' because farmers paid over 40 per cent more than farmers in other countries for fertilizer.

During the 1970s rice productivity in South Korea increased as a result of the expansion of irrigation, the use of fertilizers and chemicals, the planting of high yielding varieties of rice (HYV) and better cultivation practices. Such policies marked a turnaround from the government focus of the 1960s when the bias towards industry and the urban sector resulted in a neglect of agriculture, increasing the gaps between rural and urban incomes, food shortages and rural migration. In the 1970s, a concerned government introduced agricultural and rural development policies whose objectives were: self-sufficiency in foodgrains (especially rice), parity in rural and urban incomes, low urban food prices to restrain wage demands, and finally stabilization of agricultural prices (Song and Ryu, 1992). The model of state-directed agriculture that remained intact until partial democratization in the 1990s could be successfully implemented only by an authoritarian regime. Farmers were obliged to grow rice on designated land, avail credit from state agencies, purchase fertilizer from a government monopoly, and pay for the fertilizer and agricutural taxes in kind. Rice thus procured was distributed to state, military and educational personnel. The entire structure of statist agriculture provided an organizational set-up for the exercise of political authority in the regions through an extensive surveillance system (Moore, 1995).

V   TECHNOLOGY FOR MODERNIZATION OF AGRICULTURE: THE GREEN REVOLUTION

The technocratic strategy for modernization of traditional agriculture focuses on (1) encouraging the use of a package of techniques based on the new technology, (2) providing a set of economic incentives to encourage the use of the technology to improve productivity, and (3) creating a set of public and private sector organizations to support the strategy. Such a strategy, with exclusive emphasis on agricultural growth based on the concept of private property, is feasible only in countries with large land holdings whose owners enjoy considerable political power. Considering the prevailing agrarian social structure, the above strategy for agricultural development is feasible in Latin American countries like Argentina, Peru and Chile. Most TW governments prefer to adopt a mix of policies which aim at encouraging agricultural growth and productivity and reducing existing social and economic inequalities. I intend to focus on the latter, i.e. countries which have implemented a combination of strategies resulting in mixed fortunes.

This approach to modernizing agriculture, termed the 'green revolution', centred around a major breakthrough in the development of 'high-yielding varieties' (HYV) of seeds – wheat, rice, maize and other cereals. The effectiveness of these HYVs depends on the judicious and timely use of a package of inputs combined with a range of organizations (public or private) to support the new technology. Accused by western economists of neglecting agriculture, India in the mid-1960s was well placed, because of its agricultural (research) and industrial (fertilizers) infrastructure, to exploit the potential of the HYVs. Adoption of the new agricultural strategy by countries like India, Philippines, Mexico and Pakistan indicated their move from an institutional approach (changing agrarian institutions and attitudes) to a technocratic approach using technology based on a new package of inputs and better management of agriculture.

A major player in the new agricultural development strategy is the government, which has to develop a price strategy to encourage farmers to adopt the new technology as well as provide inputs to farmers. A more important aspect of this strategy is for government to ensure that excess production is procured, stored and distributed through a public distribution system at subsidized prices to protect poor urban consumers. These issues are likely to create conflicts between different interests in a democracy. 'In the early stages of development resource transfers from agriculture are expected to finance industrialization but raising food prices and financing the technology in agriculture entail an investment shift away from industry, including the possibility that a surplus from other sectors might have to be raised to finance agricultural development' (Subramaniam, 1995).

When government has to play a major role in developing the agricultural infrastructure to promote research and adopt a price support policy to encourage the use of the technology, it also has to procure, store and distribute excess grain production through a chain of public and private sector organizations. The downside to this policy, however, is that it assists prosperous farmers who already have access to irrigation. They are also in a better position to receive scarce inputs for which farmers need to establish links with dispensing bureaucracy. This dependency on the outside world suggests that those capable of manipulating the links between the local community and the state or local market are more likely to succeed.

VI   IMPACT OF THE AGRICULTURAL STRATEGY: INDIA

The new agricultural strategy was adopted selectively in most countries and its impact on overall agricultural growth was impressive in countries like India, Pakistan, Mexico and the Philippines, where governments adopted the total range of policies supported by a network of agencies geared for the purpose. Despite a consistent growth in production, India's inability to eliminate hunger is due not to a case of shortage of food but to the absence of purchasing capacity among the rural and urban poor. However, the policies adopted over the years to sustain the green revolution have, according to researchers, enhanced the power of the countryside. A plausible explanation offered for the empowerment of the rural sector in the polity (Varshney, 1995, 3) is the fact that democracy preceded industrialization. It is difficult to interpret government strategy of raising procurement price of foodgrains, providing subsidized inputs and writing off loans as an indication of rural power. When viewed in pragmatic terms, it appears more like a response to the voting strength of rural India. Governments that adopt policies to gain support of significant groups like landowners are described as intermediate regimes. TW governments in their bid to placate the peasantry and lower middle class often fall into this category (Raj, 1973).

While the increase in India's agricultural production from 82 million tonnes in 1970–71 to 190 million tonnes in 1995–96 (see Table X-1) is a direct result of this strategy, there is evidence to show that it has been achieved at considerable social cost (Frankel, 1968). As the strategy was selective and could succeed only in areas already bestowed with irrigation, the existing gap between regions was further widened. The intensive agricultural development programme which laid the foundation of the green revolution involved extensive investment and, in the view of its critics, was a case of 'betting on the strong', exacerbating the inequalities that the policy on land distribution had hoped to avoid. As a result, regions with appropriate ecological conditions have prospered under the green revolution, while other parts, generally rain-fed, have stagnated. 'The growing prosperity and accumulations in political power have led to a vicious circle. Research and investment favour irrigated areas; farmers come to power and demand further research and investment soon the inequities within regions are overshadowed by regional differences. To date interregional differences have not yet led to any organised rebellion, but the political debates have been acrimonious, and violence may not be far behind' (Schusky, 1995, 139).

Apart from the proliferation of inequalities between regions, the new agricultural strategy has, by encouraging excessive use of chemical fertilizers, had negative consequences on soil depletion and salination. Tubewell irrigation has resulted in a declining water table. Further, the initial expectation that the new technology was resistant to plant pests and easily adaptable to different agricultural conditions is now being questioned as farmers resort increasingly to the use of insecticides and pesticides in areas now under HYVs. The new agricultural strategy is now seen as fraught with risk, involving greater reliance on external knowledge than traditional forms of agriculture. Critics suggest that a return to traditional agriculture and the replacement of fertilizers with composting can halt the decline in productivity of land.

Table X-1   Agricultural Production in India 1950–51 to 1995–96
(in million tones)

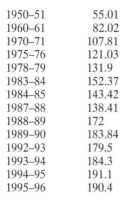

1950–51	55.01
1960–61	82.02
1970–71	107.81
1975–76	121.03
1978–79	131.9
1983–84	152.37
1984–85	143.42
1987–88	138.41
1988–89	172
1989–90	183.84
1992–93	179.5
1993–94	184.3
1994–95	191.1
1995–96	190.4

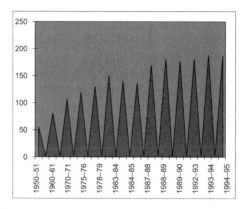

Source: *The Hindu*, July 1996.

Of far greater consequence is the question raised by the new agricultural strategy: that of growth with social inequity versus no growth with equity. To overcome the social consequences of the green revolution and compensate those unable to benefit by it, governments have introduced poverty amelioration programmes.

VII   DEVELOPMENT WITH REDISTRIBUTION

Land reform as a strategy of agricultural development is generally adopted by reformist regimes which seek to overcome some of the existing inequalities in land ownership and combine it with modernization of agriculture by initiating a green revolution. Such political regimes generally vacillate between conflicting objectives of increasing agricultural production and equitable distribution and adopt this dual strategy in order to avoid concentration of wealth in rural areas. India, which fits this description, had hoped to achieve social transformation through political democracy. Its leaders assumed that a 'well informed and organized peasantry could build direct relationships with outside centres of power in both the administration and the political parties, to convert its strength of numbers under a democratic political system into a non-violent sanction for radical reform' an approach that has been characterized as 'a political compromise with powerful propertied interests' (Frankel,

1979, 217). That expectation of emerging rural power has eventuated and has been effectively used to prevent the implementation of land reform (Mascarenhas, 1975; Varshney, 1995).

Frankel distinguishes the direct from the indirect obstacles to economic development. Existing land distribution and tenure relations are classed by her as direct constraints while cultural attitude, caste structures and power groups are termed indirect obstacles. India's agrarian pattern of land distribution and land tenure relations are based not on religious beliefs or cultural attitudes but on a system of individual proprietory land rights introduced by the British in the mid-nineteenth century. While the former are easier to resolve, it is the indirect factors that stand in the way of reform (Frankel, 1979, 226). The unfavourable ratio of land to rural population of 0.71 acre per capita continues to be an overriding constraint. Such scarcity, combined with inequalities in the distribution of land, is further accentuated by the complex tenurial relationships. Together they place obstacles to increases in agricultural productivity, even under HYV programmes. In such a context Frankel favours 'a change of the agrarian pattern rather than an undifferentiated assault on the entire social system' (Frankel, 1979, 230). Although ceilings on land holding have existed in most states since the 1960s, in reality only 4.1 million acres of surplus land have been transferred by private owners to the government (Frankel, 1979, 233).

In relating the nature of regime composition to the type of agricultural strategy adopted, it is significant to note that land reform of the type advocated by Frankel (1979) has only been successfully adopted by non-indigenous or separated elites who do not rely on the support of dominant rural interests. This is directly related to their adoption of authoritarian political systems to promote radical social change. Countries like India which have adopted political democracy are unable to achieve such reform through the political and administrative process or through compulsion. The existence of various social and religious divisions within rural society renders it even more difficult to mobilize rural support in favour of radical land reform (Mascarenhas, 1975, Frankel, 1979).

Whether it instigates reform from above or below, an authoritarian form of government is therefore not likely to be any more successful than the 'soft' democratic state in carrying out institutional change-given practical political constraints on the use of compulsion for this purpose. On the contrary, an authoritarian political system might be counter-productive at this time, by creating even more unfavourable

conditions for social reform because it may freeze existing power relationships at the local level while dominant landowning castes still have
the upper hand (Frankel, 1979, 238).

There is evidence to show how a properly organized and managed
programme of land reform implemented through devolution (allocation
of administrative authority) can benefit both peasants and tenants
by increasing their income and power. Non-adoption, however, would
have the opposite effect of enhancing the power of bureaucratic agencies
(Montgomery, 1972).

Such assessments on the feasibility of land reform are more like an
article of faith than a realistic appraisal. The real issue in the case of TW
countries in South Asia is the availability of excess land for distribution
to meet the demands of the landless. Some consider the excess land to be
insufficient and predict that a programme of land distribution will only
result in increased poverty. A crucial aspect of such cynicism is the quality
of land that is collected by governments for distribution. Consideration
of such factors renders any programme of land reform less attractive,
particularly in the context of political and administrative obstacles to
successful implementation.

While there is increasing evidence of rural power making demands
on the political system through mobilization of numbers and demon-
strations at centres of power (Varshney, 1995), it is equally significant to
note the inability to mobilize rural discontent against landed interests
who use their power to suppress sporadic expressions of discontent. As
noted earlier, the difficulty in mobilizing support for any programme of
land reform is related to internal divisions, and this is a product of an
agrarian social structure which is vertically divided (Mascarenhas, 1975,
Frankel, 1979).

Recognition of the various impediments in adopting a realistic programme of land reforms leads one to conclude that governments are left
with two options: either a programme of land distribution or tenancy
reform. In the context of the existing agrarian social structure land distribution would be easier to implement, as it could be undertaken as a
one-off programme for which an effective administrative system could
be established with the required authority. Regulating tenancy would
be far more complicated as systems vary between countries and within
regions.

When choosing between the various land reform programmes, importance should be given to (1) the type of political support to be mobilized
in support of the programme and (2) whether the programme can be

implemented without such support. The evidence available thus far reveals both succcsscs and failures. Countries listed as successful are those which do not require support, either because political elites have been displaced or the ones that have assumed power have eliminated likely opposition to the regime. Countries regarded as failures are those in which dependence on rural support by the political elite makes it difficult to successfully implement a land reform programme. It has been noted, however, that over the years enthusiasm for land reform has gradually declined (Rashid and Quibria, 1995).

VIII   OPPORTUNITIES FOR NON-FARM INCOME GENERATION

The outcome of the dual strategy of agricultural modernization and land reform has been twofold.While the first has resulted in an increase in the incomes of farmers with large landholdings, the limited success of land reform has meant that governments need to create alternative sources of rural income for those not entirely dependent on land. In the context of large populations with insufficient land for cultivation, the option open to governments is to adopt what Robert Chambers calls 'pluralistic realism'. This involves three principles: (1) to seek change in which the poor can gain overall, (2) to concentrate attention on common property resources like land, water, grasslands, fisheries and forests, which the poor can control and benefit from, and (3) to examine the scope and concern of existing professions and departments and ask what potential is being consistently overlooked in rural development (Chambers, 1984).

The need for such opportunities for non-farm incomes seems less in East Asia when compared to South Asia, as governments in East Asia have, over a long period, promoted such opportunities by incorporating them in their agricultural and rural development policies. That the policies have borne fruit is evident from the gradual increase in the ratio of non-farm to farm incomes in South Korea and Taiwan. By contrast the absence of proper integration between agricultural and industrial policies in South Asia has yielded disappointing results, necessitating specific programmes for poverty alleviation. Any policy to generate non-farm incomes has to examine options taking into consideration equity–efficiency trade-offs, the nature of the delivery system and the extent of beneficiary participation. As this aspect of rural development has received sufficient attention, I intend to explore the prospects for the use of local-level organizations that offer opportunities for investment of government resources, opportunity for entrepreneurial skills and self-initiative, enable the democratic participation of beneficiaries and avoid all the negative attributes of traditional development bureaucracy. Only development that is centred around people meets the above criteria.

Notwithstanding the enormous investment in agriculture and rural development, the extent of rural poverty in South Asia is an issue that demands special attention from governments. (see Table X-2).

There are two distinct views on tackling poverty. While the first, attributed to Schultz, is that the objective of development should be to enhance the opportunities for the poor, the second directs our attention to the poor. Asserting his belief that political and administrative system is incapable of administering poverty alleviation programmes, Bhagwati (1988) favours a growth strategy with a built-in pro-poor bias built into policies in place of the direct poverty alleviation strategy. Similarly Bardhan (1996) maintains that government interference with the market process to promote redistributive policies is the reason for such negative outcomes. While the capability of administrative systems in India is justifiably questioned, the approach to setting the poverty line has been highly acclaimed. Gary Fields (1995) states:

In India, the poverty line was set in a scientific way. The caloric and nutrient values of various foods consumed by the poor were measured. The cost of an adequate diet was then calculated. To this was added the cost of shelter, clothing, and other basic necessities of life. Separate poverty lines were set up for urban and rural India, reflecting differences in the cost of the basic market basket of goods. Each year, these poverty lines are increased in proportion to changes in consumer prices. Thus, the poverty line changes in nominal terms but is constant in real terms (79).

Using the poverty line as a guideline, governments in South Asia have developed a series of programmes to alleviate poverty. Of these, the earliest and most extensive is the Integrated Rural Development Programme (IRDP) which has been followed by several other employment-generating and social assistance programmes. The IRDP, however, has suffered owing to lack of information on the poor, the absence of effective administrative machinery and (most important) the lack of participation from proposed beneficiaries. The Integrated Rural Development Programme in India was designed to provide credit for asset building while the other policies were intended to assist small and marginal farmers and landless labourers who had been sidestepped by the green

Table X-2   India: Data on Poverty (% below the offical poverty line)
1951–52 to 1993–94

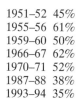

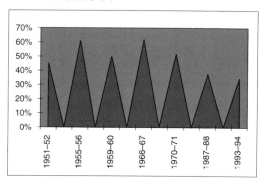

Source: India at Fifty – A Statistical Comparison I in *The Hindu*, July 21, 1997.

revolution. Unfortunately, the machinery for implementing the programme was so cumbersome that the poor were unable to access the subsidised credit without the assistance of intermediaries. It meant they had to incur an initial investment which was in some cases burdensome to begin with (Sunderam and Tendulkar, 1985). On the basis of longitudinal studies, Ravallion and Datt (1996) come to the conclusion that:

Fostering the conditions for growth in the rural economy – both primary and tertiary sectors – must be considered central to an effective strategy for poverty reduction in India. At the same time, the relative failure of India's industrialization strategy from the perspective of the poor points to the importance of successful transition to a strategy capable of absorbing more labour particularly from rural areas (2484).

While touching on the failure of direct programmes of poverty alleviation, I am inclined to advocate the more successful programmes of rural development like the Grameen Bank in Bangladesh and the Anand-type dairy co-operatives, whose success has now been well recorded. Essentially their strength lies in having evolved a distinctive programme of rural development, in providing incentives for active democratic participation and in establishing accountability based on a clear lines of responsibility and a highly routinized and reliable service (Mascarenhas, 1988, 1993).

Bardhan (1996) advocates a move away from both state paternalism and harsh market processes to local self-governing institutions and community involvement to enhance conditions of the poor and to build up their autonomy. Very little of state expenditure on anti-poverty programmes actually reaches the poor because of 'corrupt, unaccountable, insensitive bureaucracy'. Handouts also perpetuate a sense of dependency among the poor and encourage a tendency to exploit the state. Those who benefit are politicians, bureaucrats and middlemen who have the skills to manipulate the system (Bardhan, 1996, 1354).

IX CONCLUSION

Current research on TW economies, particularly the NIEs, is contributing to knowledge of how the process of structural transformation based on successful agricultural modernization works. Recognition of such a interrelationship prompted the following newspaper headline: 'Does agricultural growth still influence industry?' (*The Hindu*, June 19, 1997). To answer that question I have explored the strategies for agricultural and rural development in both East and South Asia.

Two important characteristics of East Asian agriculture are the impact of Japanese modernization under colonial rule and the subsequent state-directed strategy based on a successful programme of land reform. The absence of these factors in South Asia, where traditional agriculture stagnated during British colonialism, where the existence of internal political and social divisions of rural society were further accentuated through the democratic process, and where the failure of land reform and the inequalities caused by the green revolution were further compounded by the adoption of a basic and heavy industry strategy ahead of agricultural development, account for the difference in development performance.

11 Conclusion

In this study of development policy and management in East and South Asia I have adopted the institutionalist approach to examine the political and administrative capability of TW countries. It is a study in the comparative political economy of two regions with distinct historical experiences, cultural influences and different political and economic systems. Their development performance has been compared in that context. In line with the interdisciplinary studies that emerged in the late 1960s, this study takes a broad-based perspective of development. It focuses on both political and economic development with emphasis on values, freedom, quality of life and well-being. It acknowledges such development objectives as goals that TW countries aspire to and concludes that attempts to achieve them will depend on their political and administrative capability.

The progress of TW countries on that path towards development following decades of colonialism appears to have been uniquely influenced by each one's historical experience. The extraordinary economic performance of East Asian economies and the relatively indifferent performance of South Asian and other TW countries has created much interest in comparative studies of TW development. In attempting to explain or understand such a gap in performance I focus on the quality of policies and their effective management. In the case of East Asian economies the policies were the product of a 'developmental state' comprised of technocrats with authority and independent of the political regime. Such a strong state evolved out of historical circumstances influenced by Confucian values, the achievement of social and economic equality through agricultural modernization during Japanese colonization and through a programme of land reform.

The East Asian experience signifies the importance of a homogeneous society with greater equality for the effective formulation and implementation of development policy. By contrast, South Asia a heterogeneous society with social and economic inequality, installed a constitutional democracy with an elected government and an elitist 'bureaucratic state'. While the political and administrative system adopted seemed appropriate to a developed polity, its establishment in a large, overpopulated society divided on the basis of religion, language, caste, regions and income became a serious impediment to formulating and implementing policy. There is no doubt that India, by adopting a democratic political system, encouraged active political mobilization through mass demon-strations, organized trade unions, political parties, periodic elections and a free press. That this has been sustained over a period of 50 years in conditions of poverty and low literacy speaks volumes. However, the very strengths of Indian political development have become obstacles to effective policy formulation and execution. That inequality allows power to be concentrated in the hands of an elite is exemplified in the failure to implement land reforms. This failure has left the rural power structure intact, thus thwarting government efforts in other areas of agricultural development and economic policy-making. While the decline in power of the landowning groups was instrumental in disciplining business in both Korea and Taiwan, the opposite has occurred in India with the suc-cess of the 'green revolution' (Varshney, 1995). In the context of demo-cratic politics the dominant power of rural elites virtually constrains the ability of any government to carry out serious reform.

Having discussed the core theme of this study, the types of political and administrative systems and their capability to formulate and imple-ment policies, it may be worthwhile to look at the criticism of state inter-vention. Observers of the East Asian miracle alternate between different systems of economic management and credit their success to efficient markets and the failures of other TW countries to state intervention. Such an interpretation has led to the revival of interest in development studies. Identified as 'revisionist', these studies credit East Asian success to effective state intervention (Amsden, 1989, Wade 1990, Fields, 1995) thus providing a balanced view to the debate between market and state. In the process such studies have also enriched the content with variations of state-market mix like 'disciplined state' (Amsden, 1989) 'governed market' (Wade, 1990), 'embedded enterprise' (Fields, 1995) and 'synergy and complementarity' (Evans, 1996). Therefore East Asian success is not an issue between market versus state; rather it symbolizes the difference between effective and ineffective state intervention.

If TW governments need to adopt appropriate types of state interven-tion then they need to enhance their political and administrative capability. This view does not reject the relevance of markets, but only recognizes the reality of TW countries where such markets are incomplete and their development rests on effective state intervention. Forcing that process under duress through structural adjustment can result in setbacks like that in Mexico in the early 1990s, the recent Southeast Asian and East Asian financial crisis and some outcomes being seen in India. A functioning mar-ket does not merely consist of a developed private sector and an open invitation to foreign private investment. The institutional foundations of a market rest on a stable political system and an efficient administrative system, coupled with firm rules and regulations that support open transactions. Further, a functioning market relies on rules and regulations drawn up and implemented by the state. Only then can entrepreneurs and investors confidently and freely transact business.

Mere reduction of the role of the state does not result in the immediate emergence of the market. This can only occur during the process of differentiation. The level of differentiation varies, depending upon the capacity of a society to match organizations to changing needs. Specialized agencies are created (differentiated) to manipulate the physical, social and economic environment as a society develops. TW countries need to develop that capability, either through institution-building or through training, education, new technology. The creation of new capability has to be seen as building on existing institutions, where traditions, values, culture and religion play a crucial part. The creation of the capacity for improving health or family planning has different implications depending upon the depth of feeling or intensity of feeling one has for culture, religion or family values. This varies between countries or within a country, where caution demands a blending of traditional values with modern technology. It is easier to overlook this in authoritarian political systems than in democratic political systems. Likewise, the attitude of people to primary education in East Asia is different from South Asia. With 70 per cent of the population living in rural areas, efforts at population control and increased enrolment in primary education within the existing democratic process will be a challenging task. Unless India tackles these two basic problems the current abnormal economic growth rates of six to seven percent will only exacerbate existing inequalities, resulting in concentration of power in rural and urban elite.

The culture of elitism is more pronounced in a society like India with inherent inequalities than in East Asian countries. Such elitism is reflected in India's science and technology policy and its policy on industrialization. The objective of creating a sophisticated science and technology establishment that is a replica of the west is a product of such thinking. While I am understandably sympathetic to India's industrial strategy at the neglect of agriculture on the grounds of its geopolitical status in the 1950s and 1960s, I cannot at the same time condone its neglect of basic education, health, sanitation and housing. Such basic necessities are fundamental and neglect in these areas provides ammunition to those who condone the sacrificing of democracy for basic necessities. Notwithstanding the validity of such criticisms, India's progress on the industrial front is outstanding and its science and technology manpower is known internationally. To promote industrialization through state intervention India had to establish a large number of public enterprises. Some were located by politicians in areas of doubtful political support. Others had defeated politicians appointed to their boards, while graduates from the lower middle class coming from the newly established institutions of learning secured positions within. While public enterprises provided cheap inputs like power and fertilizer to rich farmers and to small businesses, they also offered opportunities to indigenous business enterprises as suppliers of inputs and a source of collaboration for foreign technology. Despite these negative aspects, public enterprises contribute to over 50 per cent of Indian industrial production. Their overall cost to the economy, however, is difficult to establish easily. While they undoubtedly laid the foundation for building an industrialized economy, their entire establishment and management under bureaucratic control has operated inefficiently. Too many vested interests in that sector have restricted the scope for any meaningful reform.

Likewise, the agricultural sector of the economy since the green revolution of the mid-1960s has shown extraordinary progress. Apart from the negative effects of technological inputs into farming, the green revolution perpetuated existing inequalities in the countryside. The revolution has only touched large farmers with irrigation and not others, leaving small farmers without irrigation virtually unchanged. Several programmes intended to alleviate poverty have suffered from poor management and execution and failed to have any impact on poverty in rural areas. Although land reforms have never been implemented in most states, rural development has had successful programmes such as the Anand-type dairy co-operatives.

If East Asia has achieved an economic miracle without political development, South Asia has achieved a political miracle with mixed fortunes on the economic and social fronts. In line with the theme of this study, both regions – East Asia and South Asia – need to strive for greater balance.

References

REFERENCES: CHAPTER 1

Amsden, Alice H. (1989) *Asia's Next Giant: South Korea and Late Industrialisation*, New York and Oxford, Oxford University Press.

Bartlett (1996) "The Decline of Development Studies", *Review of Politics*, Vol. 58, 269–298.

Blomkvist, Hans (1992) "The Soft State: Making Policy in a Different Context" in Douglas Ashford (ed.) *History and Context in Comparative Public Policy*, Pittsburgh, University of Pittsburgh Press, 117–150.

Booth, William James (1994) "On the idea of the Moral Economy" *American Political Science Review*, Vol. 88, 653–667.

Coleman, James S. (1988)"Social Capital in the Creation of Human Capital" *American Journal of Sociology*, Vol. 94 Supplement S95–S120.

Evans, Peter (1996) "Government Action, Social Capital and Development: Reviewing the Evidence on Synergy", *World Development*, Vol. 24, 1119–1132.

Fields, Karl J. (1995) *Enterprise and the State in Korea and Taiwan*, Ithaca and London, Cornell University Press.

Granovetter, Mark (1985) "Economic Action and Social Structures: The Problem of Embeddedness"*American Journal of Sociology*, Vol. 91, 481–510.

Hamilton, Gary G. and Nicola Woolsey Biggert (1988) "Market, Culture, and Authority: A Comparative Analysis of Management and Organisation in the Far East", *American Journal of Sociology*, Supplement Vol. 94, S52–S94.

Hall, Peter A. (1986) *Governing the Economy: The Politics of State Intervention in Britain and France*, Oxford, Oxford University Press.

Haggard, Stephan and Chung In Moon (1989–90) "Institutions and Economic Policy", *World Politics*, Vol. 42, 210–237.

Johnson, Chalmers (1982) *MITI and the Japanese Miracle: The Growth of Industrial Policy 1925–1975*, Stanford, Stanford University Press.

Lal, Deepak and H. Myint (1996) *The Political Economy of Poverty, Equity, and Growth: A Comparative Study*, Oxford, Clarendon Press.

Mascarenhas, Reginald C. (1982) *Public Enterprise in New Zealand*, Wellington, New Zealand Institute of Public Administration.

Mascarenhas, Reginald C. (1993) "Explaining Success in South Asian Rural Development: the Importance of Routine" *Public Administration and Development*, Vol. 13, 475–487.

Mascarenhas, Reginald C. (1996) *Government and the Economy in Australia and New Zealand: The Politics of Economic Policy Making*, San Francisco and Bethesda, Austin & Winfield.

Myrdal, Gunnar (1968) *Asian Drama: An Inquiry into the Poverty of Nations*, London, Penguin.

Pontusson, Jonas (1995) "From Comparative Public Policy to Political Economy: Putting Political Instituions in their Place and Taking Interests Seriously" *Comparative Political Studies*, Vol. 28, 117–147.

Sachs, Wolfgang (1988) "The Economist's Prejudice" in Paul Ekins and Manfred Max-Neef (eds.) *Real Life Economics: Understanding Wealth Creation*, London, Routledge.
Schatzher, Michael G. (1995) Review of Robert H. Bates (1989) *Beyond the Miracle of the Market: The Political Economy of Agrarian Development in Kenya*, Cambridge University Press, in *American Political Science Review*, Vol. 84, 1414–1415.
Sen, Amartya (1994) *Resources, Values and Development*, London, Basil Blackwell.
Smith, Tony (1984–85) "Requiem or New Agenda for Third World Studies", *World Politics*, Vol. 37, 532–562.
Wade, Robert (1990) *Governing the Market: Economic Theory and the Role of Government in East Asian Industrialisation*, Princeton, Princeton University Press.

REFERENCES: CHAPTER 2

Amsden, Alice H. (1989) *Asia's Next Giant: South Korea and Late Industrialisation*, Oxford, Oxford University Press.
Arndt, Heinz W. (1987) *Economic Development: The History of an Idea*, Chicago, Chicago University Press.
Arndt, Heinz W. (1988) "Market Failure and Underdevelopment", *World Development*, Vol. 16, 219–232.
Bhagwati, Jagdish (1988) "Poverty and Public Policy", *World Development*, Vol. 16, 539–555.
Bierstakes, Thomas J. (1994) "The Triumph of Neoclassical Economics in the Developing World: Policy Convergence and bases of Governance in the International Economic Order" in James N Rosenau and Ernst-Otto Czempiel (eds) *Governance Without Government: Order and Change in World Politics*, Cambridge, Cambridge University Press.
Biswas, Ajit (ed.) (1984) *Climate and Development*, Natural Resources and Environment Series, Vol. 13, Dublin, Tycooly International Publishing Ltd.
Booth, William James (1994) "On the Idea of the Moral Economy" *American Political Science Review*, Vol. 88, 653–667.
Brockway, Lucile (1996) "Plant Imperialism" in Kenneth P. Jameson and Charles W Wilbur, (eds) *The Political Economy of Development and Underdevelopment*, New York, McGraw Hill, Sixth Ed, 116–124.
Brusser-Periera, Luis Carlos (1994) "Economic Reforms and Cycles of State Intervention" *World Development*, Vol. 21, 1337–1353.
Darling, Frank C. (1979) *The Westernisation of Asia: A Comparative Political Analysis*, Boston, G K Hall & Co.
Dube, S. C. (1984) *Development Perspectives for the 80s*, Kuala Lumpur, Asian Centre for Development Administration.
Evans, Peter (1996) "Government Action, Social Capital, and Development: Reviewing the Evidence on Synergy" *World Development*, Vol. 24, 1119–1132.
Fields, Karl J. (1995) *Enterprise and the State in Korea and Taiwan*, Ithaca, Cornell University Press.
Fishlow, Albert (1991) "Review of Handbook of Development Economics" *Journal of Economic Literature*, Vol. 29, 1728–1737.

Foster, George (1973) *Traditional Societies and Technological Change*, New York, Harper & Row.

Goulet, Denis (1992) "Development: Creator and Destroyer of Values" *World Development*, Vol. 20, 467–475.

Grindle, Merillee and John W. Thomas (1991) *Public Choices and Policy Change: The Political Economy of Reform in Developing Countries*, Baltimore, Johns Hopkins University Press.

Hagen, Everett (1962) *On the Theory of Social Change: How Economic Growth Begins*, Bombay, Vakils.

Hall, Robert E. and Charles I. Jones (1997) "What Have We Learned From Recent Empirical Growth Research? Levels of Economic Activity Across Countries" *The American Economic Review*, Papers and Proceedings, Vol. 87, 173–177.

Havinden, Michael and David Meredith (1995) *Colonialism and Development: Britain and its Tropical Colonies 1850–1960*, London/ New York, Routledge.

Jagannathan, Vijay (1987) *Informal Markets in Developing Countries*, New York, Oxford University Press.

Johnson, Gale D. (1997) "Agriculture and the Wealth of Nations" *The American Economic Review*, Papers and Proceedings, Vol. 87, 1–12.

Kilksberg, Bernardo (1994) "The Necessary State: A Strategic Agenda for Discussion" *International Review of Administrative Sciences*, Vol. 60, 183–196.

Myrdal, Gunnar (1968) *Asian Drama: An Inquiry into the Poverty of Nations*, London, Penguin.

Oshima, Harry T. (1987) *Economic Growth and Monsoon Asia: a Comparative Survey*, Tokyo, University of Tokyo Press.

Przeworski, Adam and Fernando Limongi (1997) "Modernization Theories and Facts" *World Politics*, Vol. 49, 155–183.

Panickar, K. M. (1953) *Asia and Western Dominance*, London, Allen & Unwin.

Raj, K. N. (1973) "The Politics and Economics of Intermediate Regimes," Kale Memorial Lecture, Pune.

Ram, Rati. (1997) "Tropics and Economic Development: an Empirical Investigation" *World Development*, Vol. 25, 1443–1452

Sen, Amartya K. (1983) "Development: Which Way Now?" *Economic Journal*, Vol. 93, 145–162.

Smith, Tony (1984–85) "Requiem or New Agenda for Third World Studies", *World Politics*, Vol. 37, 532–561.

Snider, Lewis A. (1990) "The Political Performance of Third World Governments and the Debt Crisis" *American Political Science Review*, Vol. 84, 1263–1280.

Solomon, Morton (1995) "The Structure of the Market in Underdeveloped Economies" in V. Pillai and L. Shanon (eds) *Developing Areas*, New York, Berg Publishers, 86–94.

Stern, Nicholas (1989) "The Economics of Development" *Economic Journal*, Vol. 99, 597–685.

Subrahmanyam, Sanjay (1996) "Institutions, Agency and Economic Change in South Asia" in Burton Stein and Sanjay Subrahmanyam (eds) *Institutions and Economic Change in South Asia*, Delhi, Oxford University Press.

Sundrum, R. M. (1983) *Development Economics: a Framework for Analysis and Policy*, Chichester, John Wiley and Sons.

Tabb, William (1995) *The Post-War Japanese System: Cultural Economy and Economic Transformation*, New York, Oxford University Press.

Wade, Robert (1990) *Governing the Market: Economic Theory and the Role of Government in East Asian Industrialisation*, Princeton, Princeton University Press.

Weber, Max (1958) *The Protestant Ethic and the Spirit of Capitalism*, New York, Charles Scribner.

Williamson, John (ed.) (1994) *The Political Economy of Reform*, Washington DC, Institute of Intenational Economics.

World Bank (1993) *The East Asian Miracle*, New York, Oxford University Press.

REFERENCES: CHAPTER 3

Bagchi, Amiya Kumar (ed.) (1992) *Democracy and Development*, Proceedings of the IEA Conference held in Barcelona, New York, St Martins Press.

Bardhan, Pranab ((1988) "Dominant Proprietory Classes and India's Democracy" in Atul Kohli (ed.) *India's Democracy: An Analysis of Changing State Society Relations*, Princeton, Princeton University Press.

Bartlett, Robert C. (1996) "The Decline of Development Studies" *The Review of Politics*, Vol. 58, 269–298.

Bhatt, V. V. (1977) *Development Perspectives: Problems, Strategy and Policies*, Oxford, Pergamon

Colclough, Christopher and James Manor (eds) (1991) *States or Markets? Neoliberalism and the Development Policy Debate*, Oxford, Clarendon.

Collier, David and Stevewn Livitsky (1997) "Democracy with Adjectives: Conceptual Innovation in Comparative Research" *World Politics*, Vol. 49, 430–451.

Das Gupta, A. K. (1988) *Growth, Development and Welfare*, London, Blackwell.

Dreeze, Jean and Amartya K. Sen (1996) *Economic Development and Social Opportunuity*. New Delhi, Oxford University Press.

Economist, The, London, August 27, 1994.

Evans, Peter (1996) "Government Action, Social Capital and Development: Reviewing the Evidence on Synergy" *World Development*, Vol. 24, 1119–1132.

Fields, Karl J. (1995) *Enterprise and the State in Korea and Taiwan*, Ithaca, Cornell University Press.

Foster, George (1973) *Traditional Societies and Technological Change*, New York, Harper & Row.

Goulet, Denis (1989) "Participation in Development: New Avenues" *World Development*, Vol. 17, 165–178.

Goulet, Denis (1992) "Development: Creator and Destroyer of Values" *World Development*, Vol. 20, 467–475.

Hadenius, Axel and Fredrik Uggla (1996) "Making Civil Society Work, Promoting Democratisation and Development: What Can States and Donors Do?", *World Development*, Vol. 24, 1621–1639.

Hart, Henry C. (1988) "Political Leadership in India: Dimension and Limits" in Atul Kohli, (ed.) *India's Democracy: An Analysis of Changing State–Society Relations*, Princeton, Princeton University Press.

Huntington, Samuel (1966) *Political Order in Changing Societies*, New Haven, Yale University Press.

Humphrey, John (1995) "Industrial Reorganisation in Developing Countries: From Models to Trajectories" *World Development*, Vol. 23, 149–162.

Khilnani, Sunil (1997) *The Idea of India*, London, Hamish Hamilton.

Korten, David (1986) "The Management of Social Transformation", *Public Administration Review*, Vol. 41, 609–618.

Landes, David (1995) "Why are we so Rich and They so Poor?" in V. Pillai and L. Shannon (eds) *Developing Areas*, New York, Berg Publishers.

Lane, Robert (1996) "The Quality of Life and the Quality of Persons: A New Role for Government" in Avner Offer (ed.) *In Pursuit of the Quality of Life*, Oxford, Oxford University Press.

Leftwitch, Adrian (1996) "Two Cheers for Democracy" *The Political Quarterly*, Vol. 67, 334–339.

Lijphart, Arend (1996) "The Puzzle of Indian Democracy: A Consociational Interpretation" *American Political Science Review*, Vol. 90, 258–268.

Lipset, Seymour Martin (1994) "The Social Requisites of Democracy Re-visited" *American Sociological Review*, Vol. 59, 1–22.

Lipson, Leslie (1995) "Democracy: The First Twenty Five Centuries" in John A Koumoulides (ed.) *The Good Idea: Democracy in Ancient Greece*, New York, Aristede d Caratzas, 133–146.

Mascarenhas, Reginald C. (1975) Land Reforms in India: The Problems of Implementation, Indian Institute of Management Calcutta Working Papers No. 11.

Mascarenhas, Reginald C. (1988) *A Strategy for Rural Development: Dairy Cooperatives in India*, New Delhi/ London, Sage.

Mascarenhas, Reginald C. (1993) "Explaining Sucess in South Asian Rural Development: the Importance of Routine" *Public Administration and Development*, Vol. 13, 475–487.

Moore, Barrington Jr. (1966) *The Social Origins of Dictatorship and Democracy: Lord and Peasant in the Making of the Modern World*, London, Penguin.

Myrdal, Gunnar (1968) *Asian Drama: An Inquiry into the Poverty of Nations*, London, Penguin Press.

Oakerson, Ronald J. (1987) "Reciprocity: A Bottomup View of Political Development" in Vincent Ostrom et al. (eds) *Rethinking Institutional Analysis and Development*, San Francisco, International Center for Economic Growth, 141–158.

Olson, Mancur "Diseconomies of Scale and Development" in L. Shannon and V. Pillai (eds) *Developing Areas*, New York, Berg Publishers, 95–103.

Ostrom, Elinor (1988) *Governing the Commons: The Evolution of Institutions for Collective Action*, Cambridge, Cambridge University Press.

Pourgerami, Abbas (1994) *Development and Democracy in the Third World*, Boulder, Westview Press.

Przeworski, Adam and Fernando Limongi (1997) "Modernisation: Theories and Facts" *World Politics*, Vol. 49, 155–183.

Pye, Lucien (1985) *Asian Power and Politics: The Cultural Dimensions of Authority*, Cambridge, Belknap Press of Harvard University Press.

Qizilbash (1996) Ethical Development, *World Development*, Vol. 24 July 1996, 1209–1221.

Raj, K. N. (1973) The Politics and Economic of Intermediate Regimes, Kale Memorial Lecture, Poona.

Riggs, Fred W. (1992) "Bureau Power: South East Asia" Paper Prepared for the IPSA/SOG Seminar, Chiangma, Thailand.

Rudolph, Lloyd I, and Susan Hoeber Rudolph (1987) *In Pursuit of Lakshmi: The Political Economy of the Indian State*, Chicago, Chicago University Press.

Ruttan, Vernon W. (1991) "What Happened to Political Development" *Economic Development and Cultural Change*, Vol. 39, 265–296.

Sen, Amartya K. (1984) *Resources, Values and Development*, London, Basil Blackwell.

Shin, Do Chull (1994) "On the Third Wave of Democratisation: A Synthesis and Evaluation of Recent Theory and Research", *World Politics*, Vol. 47, 135–170.

Sirowy, Larry and Alex Inkeles (1993) "The effects of Democracy on Economic Growth and Inequality" in Selignon, Mitchell and T. Passe Smith (eds) *Development and Underdevelopment: The Political Economy of Inequality*, Boulder, Lynne Reinner Publishers.

Smith, Tony (1984–85) "Requiem or New Agenda for Third World Studies", *World Politics*, Vol. 37, 532–561.

Snider, Lewis A. (1990) "The Political Performance of Third World Governments and the Debt Crisis" *American Political Science Review*, Vol. 84, 1263–1280.

Streeton, Paul (1975) *The Limits of Development Research*, Oxford, Pergamon Press.

Streeton, Paul (1995) "Human Development: The Debate about the Index" *International Social Science Journal*, No. 143, 25–37.

Tabb, William (1995) *The Post-War Japanese System: Cultural Economy and Economic Transformtion*, New York, Oxford University Press.

Varshney, Asutosh (1995) *Democracy, Development and the Countryside: Urban-Rural Struggles in India*, London, Cambridge University Press.

Weiner, Myron and Ergun Ozbuden (eds) (1987) *Competitive Elections in Developing Countries*, AEI Publishers, Duke University Press.

Wignaraja, Ponna (1995) "Towards a Theory and Practice of Rural Development" in V. Pillai and L. Shannon, (eds) *Developing Areas*, New York, Berg Publishers.

REFERENCES: CHAPTER 4

Abegglan, James C. (1994) *Sea Change: Pacific Asia as the New World Centre*, New York, Free Press.

Amsden, Alicse H. (1989) *Asia's Next Giant: South Korea and Late Indusrialisation*, New York, Oxford University Press.

Arendt, Hannah (1988) "Market Failure and Underdevelopment" *World Development*, Vol. 16, 219–229.

Batley, Richard (1994) "The Consolidation of Adjustment: Implications for Public Administration" *Public Administration and Development*, Vol. 14, 489–505.

Bernard, Mitchell and John Ravenhall (1995) "Beyond Product Cycles and Flying Geese: Regionalisation, Hierarchy and the Industrialisation of East Asia", *World Politics*, Vol. 47, 171–209.

Bhagwati, Jagdish (1988) "Poverty and Public Policy", *World Developmnent*, Vol. 16, 539–555.

Biersteker, Thomas J. (1992) "The 'Triumph' of Neoclassical Economics in the Developing World: Policy Convergence in the International Economic Order" in James N. Rosenau and Ernest-Otto Czempiel (eds) *Governance Without Government: Order and Change in World Politics*, New York, Cambridge University Press.

Darling, Frank 1979) *The Westernisation of Asia: A Comparative Political Analysis*, Boston, G K Hall.

Dong, Kim Kyong (1994) "Confucianism and Capitalist Development" in Leslie Sklair (ed.) *Capitalism and Development*, London, Routledge, pp. 72–85.

Dore, Ronald (1992) "Reflections on Culture and Social Change" in Gary Gereffi and Donald L. Wyman (eds) *Manufacturing Miracles: Paths of Industrialisation in Latin America and East Asia*, Princeton, Princeton University Press.

Dreeze, Jean and Amartya Sen (1996) *Economic Development and Social Opportunity*, New Delhi, Oxford University Press.

Evans, Peter (1996) "Government Action, Social Capital and Development: Reviewing the Evidence on Synergy" *World Development*, Vol. 24, 1119–1132.

Fields, Karl J. (1995) *Enterprise and the State in Korea and Taiwan*, Ithaca and London, Cornell University Press.

Friedman, Edward (1996) "Learning from East Asian Economic Success: Avoiding the Soviet-Style Developmentalist Deadends" *Economic Development and Cultural Change*, Vol. 44, 879–889.

Ghosh, Jayati, Abhijit Sen and C. P. Chandrasekhar (1998) "East Asian Dilemma: Is there a Way Out?" *Economic and Political Weekly*, January 24, 143–146.

Granato, Jim *et al.*, (1996) "The Effect of Cultural Values on Economic Development: Theory, Hypotheses and Some Empirical Tests" *American Journal of Political Science*, Vol. 40, 607–631.

Grindle, Merilee and John W. Thomas (1991) *Public Choices and Policy Change: the Political Economy of Reform in Developing Countries*, Baltimore, Johns Hopkins University Press.

Grabowski, Richard (1994) "The Successful Developmental State: Where does it come from?" *World Development*, Vol. 22, 413–422.

Hagen, Everett (1962) *On the Theory of Social Change: How Economic Growth Begins*, Bombay, Vakils.

Jenkins, Rhys (1994) "Capitalist Development in the NICs" in Leslie Sklair (ed.) *Capitalism and Development*, London, Routledge, 72–95.

Johnson, Chalmers (1982) *MITI and the Japanese Miracle: The Growth of Industrial Policy 1925–1975*. Stanford, Stanford University Press.

Kang, David C. (1995) "South Korean and Taiwanese Development and the New Institutionalist Economics", *International Organisation*, Vol. 49, 555–588.

Kilskberg, Bernardo (1994) "The 'Necessary State': A Strategic Agenda for Discussion" *International Review of Administrative Sciences*, Vol. 60, 183–196.

Krugman, Paul (1994) "The Myth of the Asian Miracle" *Foreign Affairs*, Vol. 73, 77–80.

Mascarenhas, Reginald C. (1982) *Public Enterprise in New Zealand*, Wellington, New Zealand Institute of Public Administration.

Mascarenhas, Reginald C. (1992) "State Intervention in the Economy: Why is the United States Different from other Mixed Economies?", *Australian Journal of Public Administration*, Vol. 51, 385–397.

Mascarenhas, Reginald C. (1996) *Government and Economy in Australia and New Zealand: The Politics of Economic Policy Making*, San Francisco/Bathesda, Austin & Winfield.

Moore, Mick (1997) "The Identity of Capitalists and the Legitimacy of Capitalism: Sri Lanka since Independence" *Development and Change*, Vol. 28, 331–360.

Myrdal, Gunnar (1968) *Asian Drama: An Inquiry into the Poverty of Nations*, London, Penguin.

Poulson, Barry W. (1995) *Economic Development: Private and Public Choice*, New York, West Publishing Company.

Pye, Lucian W. (1985) *Asian Power and Politics: the Cultural Dimension of Authority*, Cambridge, Belknap Press of Harvard University.

Raj, K. N. (1973) The Politics of Intermediate Regimes, Kale Memorial Lecture, Pune.

Rangarajan, C. Indian Economic Planning, H. C. Mathur Memorial Lecture, *The Hindu*, April 24, 1996, 22.

Ravi, N. (1996) *The Hindu*, December 25, Chennai.

Rondinelli, Denis and John D. Montgomery (1989) "Managing Economic Reform: An Alternative Perspective on Structural Adjustment Policies" *Policy Sciences*, Vol. 22, 73–93.

Rozman, Gilbert (ed.) (1991) *The East Asian Region: Confucian Heritage and its Modern Adaptation*, Princeton, Princeton University Press.

Sen, Amartya (1984) *Resources, Values and Development*, London, Basil Blackwell.

Streeton, Paul (1993) "Markets and States: Against Minimalism", *World Development*, Vol. 21, 1281–1298.

Wade, Robert (1990) *Governing the Market: Economic Theory and the Role of Government in East Asian Industrialisation*, Princeton, Princeton University Press.

Williamsons, John (ed.) (1994) *The Political Economy of Reform*, Washington DC, Institute of International Economics.

REFERENCES: CHAPTER 5

Abegglan, James C. (1994) *Sea Change: Pacific Asia as the New World Centre*, New York, Free Press.

Amsden, Alice H. (1989) *Asia's Next Giant: South Korea and Late Industrialization*, Oxford, Oxford University Press.

Amsden, Alice H. (1992) "A Theory of Government Intervention in Late Industrialization" in Louis Patterson and Dietrich Rueschemeyer (eds) *State and Market in Development: Synergy or Rivalry*, London/ Boulder, Lynne Reinner Publishers.

Amsden, Alice H. (1995) "The State and Taiwan's Economic Development" in John Revenhill (ed.) *The Political Economy of East Asia 2: China, Korea and Taiwan* Vol. II, Aldershot, Elgar Reference Collection, 78–106.

Amsden, Alice *et al.* (1996) "Strategies for a Viable Transition: Lessons from the Political Economy of Renewal", *Economic and Political Weekly*, Vol. 31, December 28, 3383–3390.

Bhagwati, Jagdish (1988) "Public Policy and Poverty" *World Development*, Vol. 16, 539–555.

Bhagwati, Jagdish (1993) *India in Transition: Freeing the Economy*, London, Clarendon Press.

Blomkvist, Hans (1992) "The Soft State: Making Policy in a Different Context" in Douglas E. Ashford (ed.) *History and Context in Comparative Public Policy*, Pittsburgh, Pittsburgh University Press, 117–150.

Bose, Sugato and Ayesha Jalal (eds) (1997) *Nationalism, Democracy and Development: State and Politics in India*, New Delhi, Oxford University Press.

Bruton, Henry J. (1992) "International Aspects of the Role of Government in Economic Development" in Louis Patterson and Dietrich Rueschmeyer (eds) *State and Market in Development: Synergy or Rivalry*, London/Boulder, Lynne Reiner Publishers, 101–129.

Clark, Cal and Steve Chan (1994) "The Developmental Roles of the State: Moving Beyond the Developmental State in Conceptualising Asian Political Economies" *Governance*, Vol. 7, 332–359.

Chung-in Moon and Rashemi Prasad (1994) "Beyond the Developmental State: Networks, Politics, and Institutions" *Governance*, Vol. 7, 360–386.

Curle, Adam (1963) *Educational Strategy for Developing Societies: A Study of Educational and Social Factors in Relationship to Economic Growth*, London, Tavistock.

Darling, Frank (1979) *The Westernisation of Asia: A Comparative Political Analysis*, Boston, G K Press.

Dobbs-Higginson, Michael S. (1993) *Asia Pacific: Its Role in the New World Disorder*, Boston, Houghton Mifflin.

Dore, Ronald (1992) "Reflections on Culture and Social Change" in Gary Gereffi and Donald L. Wymer (eds) *Manufacturing Miracles: Paths of Industrialization in Latin America and East Asia*, New Jersey, Princeton, Princeton University Press, 353–367.

Dreeze, Jean and Amartya Sen (1996) *Economic Development and Social Opportunity*, New Delhi, Oxford University Press.

Dubey, Vinod (1994) "India: Economic Policies and Performance" in Enzo Grilli and Dominick Salvatore (eds) *Economic Development*, Westport, Greenwood Press, 420–485.

Evans, Peter B. *et al.* (eds) (1985) *Bringing the State Back In*, Cambridge, Cambridge University Press.

Evans, Peter B. (1996) "Government Action, Social Capital and Development: Reviewing the Evidence on Synergy" *World Development*, Vol. 24, 1119–1132.

Fields, Gary S. (1995) "Income Distribution in Developing Economies: Conceptual, Data and Policy Issues in Broad-based Growth" in M. G. Quibria (ed.) *Critical Issues in Asian Development: Theories, Experiences and Policies*, Hong Kong, Oxford University Press, 75–107.

Fields, Karl J. (1995) *Enterprise and the State in Korea and Taiwan*, Ithaca, Cornell University Press.

Friedman, Edward (1996) "Learning from East Asian Economic Success: Avoiding the Pitfalls of Soviet-style Developmentalist Dead Ends" Review Article, *Economic Development and Cultural Change*, Vol. 44, 879–889.

Galbraith, John Kenneth (1964) "Development Planning in Principle and Practice" in Jawaharlal Nehru Memorial Volume: *The Emerging World*, Bombay, Asia Publishing, 61–71.

Gershenkron, Alexander (1988) "Economic Backwardness in Historical Perspective" in Mark Granovetter and Richard Swedberg (eds), *The Sociology of Economic Life*, Boulder, Westview Press, 111–130.

Goulet, Denis (1992) "Development: Creator and Destroyer of Values" *World Development*, Vol. 20, 467–475.

Grabowski, R. (1994) "The Successful Developmental State: Where Does it Come From?" *World Development*, Vol. 22, 413–422.

Hagen, Everett E. (1962) *On the Theory of Social Change: How Economic Growth Begins*, Bombay, Vakils.

Heller, P. "Social Capital as a Product of Class Mobilization and State Intervention: Industrial Workers in Kerala, India" *World Development*, Vol. 24, 1055–1071.

James, William E. *et al.* (1989) *Asian Development: Economic Success and Policy Lessons*, Urbana, University of Wisconsin Press.

Johnson, Chalmers (1982) *MITI: The Japanese Miracle*, Stanford, Stanford University Press.

Kang, David C. (1995) "South Korean and Taiwanese Development and the New Institutional Economics" Review Essay, *International Organisation*, Vol. 49, 555–587.

Khilnani, Sunil (1997) *The Idea of India*, London, Hamish Hamilton.

Kohli Atul (1994) "Where Do High Growth Political Economies come From? The Japanese Lineage of Korea's Developmental State" *World Development*, Vol. 22, 1269–1293.

Krugman, Paul (1995) "The Myth of the Asian Miracle", *Foreign Affairs*, Vol. 73, 77–80.

Larsen, Gerald J. (1995) *India's Agony over Religion*, Albany, New York University Press.

Lewis, John P. (1995) *India's Political Economy: Governance and Reform*, Delhi, Oxford University Press.

Lim, David (1994) *Explaining Economic Growth: A New Analytical Framework*, Cheltenham, Edward Elgar.

Maddison, Angus (1995) *Explaining the Economic Performance of Nations: Essays in Time and Space*, Cheltenham, Edward Elgar.

Mascarenhas, Reginald C. (1975) *Land Reforms in India: Some Problems in Implementation*, Indian Institute of Management Calcutta Working Papers, No. 11.

McClelland, David (1961) *The Achieving Society*, Princeton, Van Nostrand.

Moore Jr, Barrington (1966) *Social Origins of Dictatorship and Democracy: Lord and Peasant in the Making of the Modern World*, London, Penguin.

Moore, Mick (1997) "The Identity of Capitalists and the Legitimacy of Capitalism: Sri Lanka since Independence" *Development and Change*, Vol. 28, 331–360.

Myrdal, Gunnar (1968) *Asian Drama: An Inquiry into the Poverty of Nations*, London, Penguin.

Oshima, Harry T. (1987) *Economic Growth and Monsoon Asia: A Comparative Survey*, Tokyo, University of Tokyo Press.

Pye, Lucian W. (1985) *Asian Power and Politics: The Cultural Dynamics of Authority*, Cambridge, Belknap Press of Harvard University.

Raj, K. N. (1971) The Politics and Economics of Intermediate Regimes, Pune, Kale Memorial Lecture.

Ranis, Gustav (1992) "The Role of Governments and Markets: Comparative Development Experience" in Louis Patterson and Dietrich Rueschmeyer (eds) *State and Market in Development: Synergy or Rivalry*, London/Boulder, Lynne Reiner Publishers, 84–99.

Root, Hilton L. (1996) *Small Countries, Big Lessons: Governance and the Rise of East Asia*, Honk Kong, Oxford University Press.

Royle, Trevor (1997) *The Last Days of the Raj*, London, John Murray.

Rozman, Gilbert (ed.) (1991) *The East Asian Region: Confucian Heritage and its Modern Adaptation*, Princeton, Princeton University Press.

Sen, Amartya (1986) "How is India Doing?" in Dilip K. Basu and Richard Sisson (eds) *Social and Economic Development in India: a Reassassment*, New Delhi, Sage, 28–42.

Sudarshan, Ramaswamy (1997) "Law and Democracy in India" *International Social Science Journal*, No. 152, 271–278.

Varshney, Asutosh (1995) *Democracy, Development and the Countryside-Urban-Rural Struggles in India*, Cambridge, Cambridge University Press.

Wade, Robert (1990) *Governing the Market: Economic Theory and the Role of Government in East Asian Industrialization*, Princeton, Princeton University Press.

Weiss, Linda and John M. Hobson (1995) *States and Development: A Comparative Historical Analysis*, London, Polity Press.

World Bank (1993) *The East Asian Miracle*, New York, Oxford University Press.

REFERENCES: CHAPTER 6

Bhagwati, Jagdish (1988) "Poverty and Public Policy" *World Development*, Vol. 16, 539–555.

Grindle, Merilee S. (ed.) (1980) *Policies and Policy Implementation in the Third World*, Princeton, Princeton University Press.

Grindle, Merilee S. (1997) "Divergent Cultures? When Public Organisations Perform Well in Developing Countries" *World Development*, Vol. 25, 481–495.

Grindle, Merilee S. and John Thomas(1991) *Public Choices and Policy Change: The Political Economy of Reform in Developing Countries*, Baltimore, Johns Hopkins University Press.

Gross, Bertram G. (1965) "National Planning: Findings and Fallacies" *Public Administration Review*, Vol. 25, 263–273.

Hart, Henry (1971) "The Village and Development Administration" in J. Heapey (ed.) *Spatial Dimensions of Development Administration*, Durham, Duke University Press.

Horowitz, Donald L. (1989) "Is there a Third World Policy Process" *Policy Sciences*, Vol. 22, 197–212.

Illchman, Warren and Norman Uphoff (1976) *The Political Economy of Change*, Berkeley, University of California Press.

Korten, David (1981) "The Management of Social Transformation" *Public Administration Review*, Vol. 41, 608–618.

Mascarenhas, Reginald C. (1975) Land Reforms in India: Problems of Implementation, Indian Institute of Management Calcutta Working Paper Series, No. 11.

Mascarenhas, Reginald C. (1982) *Technology Transfer and Development: India's Hindustan Machine Tool Company*, Boulder, Westview Press.

Montgomery, John D. (1974) *Technology and Civic Life*, Cambridge, MIT Press.

Montgomery, John D. (1979) "Decisions, Non-Decisions and other Phenomena: Implementation Analysis for Development Administration" *Hong Kong Journal of Public Administration*, Vol. 1, 2–21.

Montgomery, John D. and Denis Rondinelli (1989) "Managing Economic Reform: An Alternative Perspective on Strutural Adjustment Policies" *Policy Sciences*, Vol. 22, 73–93.

Myrdal, Gunnar (1968) *Asian Drama: an Inquiry into the Poverty of Nations*, London, Penguin.

Pyle, David F. (1980) "From Pilot Project to Operational Program in India: The Problems of Transition" in Merilee S. Grindle (ed.) *Politics and Policy in the Third World*, Princeton, Princeton University Press.

Rondinelli, Denis (1982–83) "Dilemma of Development Administration: Complexity and Uncertainty in Control-Oriented Bureaucracies" *World Politics*, Vol. 35, 43–72.

Rondinelli, Denis A. (1993) *Development Projects as Policy Experimenta*, London, Routledge.

Rudolph, Lloyd I. and Susan Hoeber Rudolph (1987) *In Pursuit of Lakshmi: The Political Economy of the Indian State*, Chicago, University of Chicago Press.

Sagasti, Francisco (1988) "National Development Planning in Turbulent Times: New Approaches and Criteria for Institutional Design" *World Development*, Vol. 16, 431–448.

Varshney, Asutosh (1995) *Democracy, Development and the Countryside: Urban-Rural Struggles in India*, Cambridge, Cambridge University Press.

Weiner, Myron (1962) *The Politics of Scarcity*, Chicago, University of Chicago Press.

REFERENCES: CHAPTER 7

Arkadie, Brian Van (1990) "The Role of Institutions in Development" Proceedings of the World Bank Conference on Development Economics, 153–175.

Bhagwati, Jagdish (1988) "Poverty and Public Policy" *World Development*, Vol. 16, 539–555.

Bjur, Wesley E. and Gerald E. Caidemn (1978) "On Reforming Institutional Bureaucracies", *International Review of Administrative Sciences*, Vol. 44, 359–365.

Blomkvist, Hans (1992) "The Soft State: Making Policy in a Different Context" in Douglas E. Ashford (ed.) *History and Context in Public Policy*, Pittsburgh, University of Pittsburgh Press, 117–150.

Blunt, P. and P. Collins (1994) "Introduction" to the Special Issue on Institution-Building, *Public Administration and Development*, Vol. 14, 111–120.

Darling, Frank (1979) *The Westernisation of Asia: A Comparative Political Analysis*, Boston, G K Press.

Drucker, Peter (1985) *Innovation and Entrepreneurship*, New York, Harper & Row.

Esman, Milton J. (1972) "Elements of Institution Building" in Joseph W. Eaton (ed.) *Institution-Building and Development*, Beverly Hills, Sage, 21–39.

Esman, Milton J. (1980) "Development Assistance in Public Administration: Requiem or Renewal" *Public Administration Review*, Vol. 40, 426–432.

Esman, Milton J. (1991) *Management Dimensions of Development: Perspectives and Strategies*, Westport, Kumarian Press.

Friedman, John (1987) *Planning in the Public Domain: From Knowledge to Action*, Princeton, Princeton University Press.

Gawthrop, Louis C. (1983) "Organising for Change" *Annals*, Vol. 466, 19–34.

Gross, Bertram G. (1965) "National Planning: Findings and Fallacies" *Public Administration Review*, Vol. 25, 263–273.

Gross, Bertram G. (1969) *Appraising Administrative Capability for Development*, New York, United Nations.

Grindle, Merilee S. (1997) "Divergent Cultures? When Public Organisations Perform Well in Developing Countries" *World Development*, Vol. 25, 481–495.

Ho, Samuel P. S. (1987) "Economics, Economic Bureaucracy, and Taiwan's Economic Development" *Pacific Affairs*, Vol. 60, 226–247.

Im, Hyug Baeg (1986–87) "The Rise of Bureaucratic Authoritarianism in South Korea" *World Politics*, Vol. 39, 231–257.

Israel, Arturo (1987) *Institutional Development: Incentives to Performance*, World Bank, Baltimore, The Johns Hopkins University Press.

Jayal, Niraja Gopal (1997) "The Governance Agenda: Making Democratic Development Dispensable" *Economic and Political Weekly*, Vol. 32, 407–412.

Kapp, William (1960) "Economic Development: National Planning and Public Administration" *Kyklos*, Vol. 13, 172–204.

Kohli, Atul (1994) "Where Do High Growth Economies Come From? The Japanese Lineage of Korea's "Developmental State" *World Development*, Vol. 22, 1269–1293.

Korten, David (1981) "The Management of Social Transformation" *Public Administration Review*, Vol. 41, 609–618.

La Palombara, Joseph (1971) "Developing Administrative Capability" in Fred W. Riggs (ed.) *Frontiers of Development Administration*, Durham, Duke University Press.

Leftwitch, Adrian (1994) "Governance, the State and the Politics of Development" *Development and Change*, Vol. 25, 363–386.

March, James C. and Johan Olsen (1989 *Re-discovering Institutions: The Organisational Basis of Politics*, New York, The Free Press.

Montgomery, John D. and Denis Rondinelli (1989) "Managing Economic Reform: An Alternative Perspective on Structural Adjustment Policies" *Policy Sciences*, Vol. 22, 73–93.

Morgan, Phillip E. (1996) "Analysing Fields of Change: Civil Service Systems in Developing Countries" in Hans A. G. M. Bekke *et al.* (eds) *Civil Service Systems in Comparative Perspective*, Bloomington, Indiana Press, 227–243.

Riggs, Fred W. (1964) *Administration in Developing Countries: A Theory of Prismatic Society*, Boston, Houghton Miffin.

Riggs, Fred W. (ed.) (1971) *The Frontiers of Development Administration*, Durham, Duke University Press, 72–107.

Root, Milton L. (1996) *Small Countries, Big Lessons: Governance and the Rise of East Asia*, Hong Kong, Oxford University Press.

Selznick, Philip (1957) *Leadership in Administration: A Sociological Interpretation*, New York, Harper and Row.
Weick, Karl (1995) "Organisational Culture as a Source of High Reliability" in Haridomos Tsoukas (ed.) *New Thinking in Organisational Behaviour: From Social Engineering to Social Action*, New York, Butterworth-Heinemann.
Williams, David and Tom Young (1994) "Governance, The World Bank and Liberal Theory" *Political Studies*, Vol. 42, 84–100.
World Bank (1993) *The East Asian Miracle*, New York, Oxford University Press.

REFERENCES: CHAPTER 8

Amsden, Alice (1989) *Asia's Next Giant: South Korea and Late Industrialisation*, New York, Oxford University Press.
Amsden, Alice (1997) "Editorial: Bringing Production Back in-Understanding Government's Economic Role in Late Industrialisation", *World Development*, Vol. 25, 469–480.
Balasubramaniam, D. (1996) "Rid Polio for a Dozen Rupees" *The Hindu, Science and Technology*, December 19.
Bernard, Mitchell and John Ravenhill (1995) "Beyond Product Cycles and Flying Geese: Regionalisation, Heirarchy and the Industrialisation of East Asia" *World Politics*, Vol. 47, 171–209.
Bhagwati, Jagdish (1988) "Poverty and Public Policy" *World Development*, Vol. 16, 539–555.
Bhagwati, Jagdish (1993) *India in Transition-Freeing the Economy*, Clarendon Press.
Bhatt, V. V. (1980) *Development Perspectives: Problems, Strategy and Policies*, Oxford, Pergamon Press.
Deutsch, Karl W. (1971) "Developmental Change: Some Political Aspects" in J. Paul Leagans and Charles P. Loomis (eds) *Behavioural Change in Agriculture: Concepts and Strategies for Influencing Transition*, Ithaca, Cornell University Press.
Dreeze, Jean and Amartya Sen (1996) *Economic Development and Social Opportunity*, New Delhi, Oxford University Press
Dore, Ronald (1989) "Technology in a World of National Frontiers" *World Development*, Vol. 17, 1665–1675.
Dore, Ronald (1992) "Reflections on Culture and Social Change" in Gary Gereffi and Donald Y. Wyman (eds) *Manufacturing Miracles: Paths of Industrialisation in Latin America and East Asia*, Princeton, Princeton University Press.
Dubey, Vinod (1994) "India's Economic Policies and Performance" in Enzo Grilli and Dominic Salvatore (eds) *Economic Development: Handbook of Comparative Economic Policies*, Vol. 4, Westport, Greenwood Press.
Ekins, Paul and Manfred Max-Neef (1990) *Real-life Economics: Understanding Wealth Creation*, London, Routledge.
Fallows, James (1994) "How the World Works" *Atlantic Monthly*, January, 61–85.
Foster, George M. (1973) *Traditional Societies and Technological Change*, New York, Harper and Row.
Gershenkeron, Alexander (1988) "Economic Backwardness in Historical Perspective" in Mark Granovetter and Richard Swedberg (eds) *The Sociology of Economic Life*, Boulder, Westview Press.

Hayashi, Takashi (1990) *The Japanese Experience in Technology: From Transfer to Self-Reliance*, Tokyo, United Nations University Press.

Hveem, Helge (1983) "Selective Dissociation in the Technology Sector" in Gerald Ruggie (ed.) *The Anti-monies of Interdependence: National Welfare and the International Division of Labour*, New York, Columbia University Press.

Kumar, Krishna (1996) "Agricultural Modernisation and Education: Contours of a Point of Departure" *Economic and Political Weekly*, Special Number, September, 2367–2373.

Larsen, Gerald J. (1995) *India's Agony over Religion*, Albany, New York University Press.

Lewis, John P. (1995) *India's Political Economy: Governance and Reform*, Delhi, Oxford University Press.

MacMahon, Arthur W. (1961) *Delegation and Autonomy*, New Delhi, Asia Publishing.

Mascarenhas, Reginald C. (1982) *Technnology Transfer and Development: India's Hindustan Machine Tool Company*, Boulder, Westview Press.

Mascarenhas, Reginald C. (1988) *A Strategy for Rural Development: Dairy Cooperatives in India*, London/New Delhi, Sage.

Moore, Mick (1997) "The Identity of Capitalists and the Legitimacy of Capitalism: Sri Lanka since Independence" *Development and Change*, Vol. 28, 331–366.

Montgomery, John D. (1974) *Technology and Civic Life*, Cambridge, MIT Press.

Pitroda, Sam (1993) "Development, Democracy and the Village Telephone" *Harvard Business Review*, November–December, 66–79.

Roemer, Michael (1981) "Dependence and Industrialisation Strategies" *World Development*, Vol. 9, 429–434.

Simon, Denis Fred (1995) "Taiwan's Emerging Technological Trajectory: Creating New Forms of Competitive Advantage" in John Ravenhill (ed.) *China, Korea and Taiwan, Vol. II The Political Economy of East Asia* 2, Aldershot, Elgar Reference Collection, 123–147.

Tickner, Ann J. (1987) *Self-Reliance versus Power Politics: The American and Indian Experience in Building Nation States*, New York, Columbia University Press.

Ungson, Gerardo R. *et al.* (1997) *Korean Enterprise: The Quest for Globalisation*, Boston, Harvard Business School Press.

Wade, Robert (1990) *Governing the Market: Economic Theory and the Role of Government in East Asian Industrialisation*, Princeton, Princeton University Press.

REFERENCES: CHAPTER 9

Alice, Amsden (1985) "The State and Taiwan's Economic Development" in Peter Evans *et al.* (eds) *Bring the State Back In*, Cambridge, Cambridge University Press.

Dinavo, Jacques V. (1995) *Privatization in Developing Countries: Its Impact on Economic Development and Democracy*, Westport, Praeger.

Evans, Peter B. *et al.* (eds) (1985) *Bring the State Back In*, Cambridge, Cambridge University Press.

Gross Bertram (1965) "What Are Your Organisations Objectives: A General Systems Approach to Planning" *Human Relations*, Vol. 18, 195–216.

Hying, KI Kim (1988) "Institutional Framework for Decision Making in Korean Public Enterprises: Some Implications for Developing Countries" in Paul Streeton, (ed.) *Beyond Adjustment: The Asian Experience*, Washington, International Monetary Fund, 212–225.

Mahashwari, S. R. (1995) "Public Enterprise: Privatisation and Beyond" *The Hindu Business Review*, May 25, 17.

Mascarenhas, Reginald C. (1972) "A Conceptual Framework for Understanding Autonomy for Public Enterprises in India", *Academy of Management Journal*, Vol. 15, 65–75.

Mascarenhas, Reginald C. (1974) "A Systems Approach to the Measurement of the Performance of Public Enterprises in India, *Policy Sciences*, Vol. 5, 75–95

Mascarenhas, Reginald C. (1982a) *Public Enterprise in New Zealand*, Wellington, New Zealand Institute of Public Administration.

Mascarenhas, Reginald C. (1982b) *Technology Transfer and Development: India's Hindustan Machine Tool Company*, Boulder, Westview Press.

Mascarenhas, Reginald C. (1996) "The Evolution of Public Enterprise Organisation" in John Halligan, (ed.) *Public Administration Under Scrutiny: Essays in Honour of Roger Wettenhall*, Canberra, University of Canberra.

Olson, Mancur (1995) "Diseconomies of Scale and Development" in V. Pillai and L. Shannon (eds) *Developing Areas*, Berg Publishers.

Raj, K. N. (1973) The Politics of Intermediate Regimes, Kale Memorial Lecture, Pune

Roemer, Michael (1981) "Dependence and Industrialisation Strategies" *World Development*, Vol. 9, 429–434.

Riggs, Fred W. (1964) *Administration in Developing Countries*, Boston, Houghton Mifflin.

Sherwood, Frank P. (1971) "The Problem of Public Enterprise" in Fred W. Riggs (ed.) *The Frontiers of Development Administration*, Durham, Duke University Press, 348–372.

World Bank (1995) *Bureaucrats in Business*, New York, Oxford University Press.

REFERENCES: CHAPTER 10

Amsden, Alice (1995) "The State and Taiwan's Economic Development" in John Ravenhill (ed.) *China, Korea and Taiwan – Vol. II Political Economy of Asia 2*, Aldershot, An Elgar Reference Collection, 78–86.

Bain, Irene (1993) *Agricultural Reform in Taiwan*, Taipeh, The Chinese University Press.

Bardhan, Pranab (1996) "Efficiency, Equity and Poverty Alleviation: Policy Issues in Less Developed Countries" *Economic Journal*, Vol. 106, 1344–1356.

Banfield, Edward C. (1958) *The Moral Basis of a Backward Society*, New York, Free Press.

Bates, Robert H. (1984–85) "Some Conventional Orthodoxies in the Study of Agrarian Change" *World Politics*, Vol. 37, 234–254.

Bhagawati, Jagdish (1988) "Poverty and Public Policy" *World Development*, Vol. 16, 539–555.

Booth, William James (1994) "On the Idea of the Moral Economy" *American Political Science Review*, Vol. 88, 653–667.

Chambers, Robert (1984) "Beyond the Green Revolution: A Selective Essay" in Tim Bayliss-Smith and Sudhir Wanmali (eds) *Understanding the Green Revolution*, Cambridge, Cambridge University Press, 362–379.

Deutsch, Karl W. "Development Change: Some Political Aspects" in J. Paul Leagans and Charles P. Loomis (eds) *Behavioural Change in Agriculture: Concepts and Strategies for Influencing Transition*, Ithaca, Cornell University Press, 27–50.

Fields, Gary S. (1995) "Income Distribution in Developing Economies Conceptual, Data, and Policy Issues in Broad based Growth" in M. G. Quibria (ed.) *Critical Issues in Asian Development: Theories, Experiences Policies*, Hong Kong, Oxford University Press, 75–107.

Frankel, Francine (1978) "Compulsion and Social Change: Is Authoritarianism the Solution to India's Economic and Development Problems?" *World Politics*, Vol. 30, 215–240.

Foster, George M. (1973) *Traditional Societies and Technological Change*, New York, Harper & Row.

Griffin, Keith (1974) *The Political Economy of Agrarian Change: An Essay on the Green Revolution*, London, Macmillan.

Hegginbotham, Stanley (1979) *Conflict of Cultures: Four Faces of Indian Bureaucracy*, New York, Columbia University Press.

Johnson, Gale D. (1997) "Agriculture and the Wealth of Nations" Richard T. Ely Lecture, *The American Economic Review*, Papers and Proceedings, 1–12.

Korten, David C. (1981) "The Management of Social Transformation" *Public Administration Review*, Vol. 41, 609–618.

Oshima, Harry T. (1987) *Strategic Processes in Monsoon Asia's Economic Development*, Baltimore, Johns Hopkins University Press.

Mascarenhas, Reginald C. (1975) *Land Reforms in India: Some Problems in Implementation*, Indian Institute of Management Calcutta Working Paper Series, No. 11.

Mascarenhas, Reginald C. (1988) *A Strategy for Rural Development: Dairy Cooperatives in India*, New Delhi/ London, Sage.

Mascarenhas, Reginald C. "Explaining Success in South Asian Rural Development: the Importance of Routine" *Public Administration and Development*, Vol. 13, 475–487.

Montgomery, John D. (1972) "Allocation of Authority in Land Reform Programs: A Comparative Study of the Administrative Processes and Outputs" *Adminstrative Science Quarterly*, Vol. 17, 62–75.

Moore Jr, Barrington (1966) *Social Origins of Dictatorship and Democracy: Lord and Peasant in the Making of the Modern World*, Harmondsworth, England, Penguin Books.

Moore, Mick (1995) "Economic Growth and the Rise of Civil Society: Agriculture in Taiwan and South Korea" in Gordon White (ed.), *Development States in East Asia*, London, Macmillan, 113–152.

Narayan, Jaiprakash (1961) "A Communitarian Society for India" in Myron Wiener (ed.) *Introduction to the Civilization of India* Vol. 2, Chicago, University of Chicago Press.

Raj, K. N. (1973) The Politics of Intermediate Regimes, Kale Memorial Lecture, Pune.

Rashid, Salim and M. G. Quibria "Is Land Reform Passe? With Special Reference to Asian Agriculture" in M. G. Quibria (ed.) *Critical Issues in Asian Development: Theories Experiences Policies*, Hong Kong, Oxford University Press, 127–159.

Ravallion, Martin and Gaurav Dutt (1996) "India's Checkered History in Fight Against Poverty" *Economic and Political Weekly*, Special Number, 2479–2485.

Rudolph, Lloyd I. and Susan Hoeber Rudolph (1987) *In Pursuit of Lakshmi: The Political Economy of the Indian State*, Chicago, Chicago University Press.

Schusky, Ernest L. (1995) *Culture and Agriculture: An Ecological Introduction to Traditional and Modern Farming Systems*, New York, Bergin & Garvey Publishers.

Song, Dae-Hee and Byung Seo Ryu (1992) "Agricutural Policies and Structural Adjustment" in Vittoria Corbo and Song-Mok Suh (eds) *Structural Adjustment in a Newly Industrialised Country: The Korean Experience*, World Bank, Baltimore, John Hopkins University.

Subramaniam, C. (1995) "From Steel to Food" *The Hindu*, May 14.

Sunderam K. and Suresh D. Tendulkar (1985) "Integrated Rural Development Programmes in India: a Case Study of Poverty Eradication Programme" in Swapna Mukhopadhyay (ed.) *Case Studies in Poverty Programmes in Asia*, Kuala Lumper, Asian and Pacific Development Centre, 201–243.

Tai, Hung Chao (1974) "The Political Process of Land Reform: A Comparative Study" in Norman Uphoff and Warren Ilchman (eds) *The Political Economy of Development*, Berkeley, University of California Press, 295–305.

Tickner, J. Ann (1987) *Self-Reliance versus Power Politics: The American and Indian Experiences in Building Nation States*, New York, Columbia University Press.

Varshney, Asutosh (1995) *Democracy, Development and the Countryside: Urban-Rural Struggles in India*, Cambridge, Cambridge University Press.

Wade, Robert (1990) *Governing the Market: Economic Theory and the Role of Government in East Asian Industrialisation*, Princeton, Princeton University Press.

Weitz, Raanan (1986) *New Roads to Development*, New York, Greenwood Press.

REFERENCES: CHAPTER 11

Amsden, Alice (1989) *Asia's Next Giant: South Korea and Late Industrialization*, Oxford, Oxford University Press.

Evans, Peter (1996) "Government Action, Social Capital and Development: Reviewing the Evidence on Synergy" *World Development*, Vol. 24, 1119–1132.

Fields, Karl (1995) *Enterprise and the State in Korea and Taiwan*, Ithaca, Cornell University Press.

Varshney, Asutosh (1995) *Democracy, Development and the Countryside: Urban-Rural Struggles in India*, Cambridge, Cambridge University Press.

Wade, Robert (1990) *Governing the Market: Economic Theory and the role of Government in East Asian Industrialization*, Princeton, Princeton University Press.

Bibliography

Abegglen, James C. (1995) *Sea Change: Pacific Asia as the New World Industrial Center*, New York, The Free Press.

Amsden, Alice H. (1989) *Asia's Next Giant: South Korea and Late Industrialisation*, Oxford, Oxford University Press.

Bhagwati, Jagdish (1993) *India in Transition: Freeing the Economy*, London, Clarendon Press.

Bhatt, V. V. (1977) *Development Perpectives: Problems, Strategies and Policies*, Oxford, Pergoman.

Bose, Sugato and Ayesha Jalal (eds) (1997) *Nationalism, Democracy and Development: State and Politics in India*, New Delhi, Oxford University Press.

Cho, Lee-Jay and Yoon Hyung Kim (eds) (1994) *Korea's Political Economy: An Institutional Perspective*, Boulder, Westview Press.

Colclough, Christopher R. and James Manor (eds) (1991) *States or Markets? Neo-liberalism and the Development Policy Debate*, Oxford, Clarendon Press.

Darling, Frank (1979) *The Westernisation of Asia: A Comparative Political Analysis*, Boston, G K Press.

Dreeze, Jean and Amartya Sen (1996) *Economic Development and Social Opportunity*, New Delhi, Oxford University Press.

Esman, Milton J. (1991) *Management Dimension of Development: Perspectives and Strategies*, Westport, Kumarian Press.

Evans, Peter *et al*. (eds) (1985) *Bringing the State Back In*, Cambridge, Cambridge University Press.

Evans, Peter (1995) *Embedded Autonomy: State and Industrial Transformation*, Princeton, Princeton University Press.

Fields, Karl (1995) *Enterprise and the State in Korea and Taiwan*, Ithaca, Cornell University Press.

Friedmann, John (1987) *Planning in the Public Domain*, Princeton, Princeton University Press.

Foster, George M. (1973) *Traditional Societies and Technological Change*, New York, Harper & Row.

Goulet, Denis (1992) "Development: Creator and Destroyer of Values" *World Development*, Vol. 20, 467–475.

Granovetter, Mark and Richard Swedberg (ed.) *The Sociology of Economic Life*, Boulder, Westview Press

Grilli, Enzo and Dominick Salvatore (eds) (1994) *Economic Development: Handbook of Comparative Economic Policies*, Westport, Greenwood Press.

Grindle, Merilee S. (1980) *Policies and Policy Implementation in the Third World*, Princeton, Princeton University Press.

Grindle, Merilee S. and John W. Thomas (1991) *Public Choices and Policy Change: The Political Economy of Reform in Developing Countries*, Baltimore, Johns Hopkins University Press.

Hegginbotham, Stanley (1979) *Conflict of Cultures: Four Faces of Indian Bureaucracy*, New York, Columbia University Press.

Johnson, B. L. C. (1983) *Development in South Asia*, London, Penguin.

Joshi, Vijay and I. M. D. Little (1996) *India: Macroeconomics and Political Economy– 1964–1991*, Washington, DC, The World Bank.

Khilnani, Sunil (1997) *The Idea of India*, London, Hamish Hamilton.

Kohli, Atul (ed.) (1988) *India's Democracy: An Analysis of Changing State-Society Relations*, Princeton, Princeton University Press.

Korten, David C. (1981) "The Management of Social Transformation" *Public Administration Review*, Vol. 41, 609–618.

Lewis, John P. (1995) *India's Political Economy: Governance and Reform*, Delhi, Oxford University Press.

Lal, Deepak and H. Myint (1996) *The Political Economy of Poverty, Equity, and Growth: a Comparative Study*, Oxford, Clarendon Press.

Lewellen, Ted C. (1995) *Dependency and Development: An Introduction to the Third World*, Westport, Bergin & Garvey.

Maddisson, Angus (1995) *Explaining the Economic Performance of Nations: Essays in Time and Space*, Cheltenham, Edward Elgar.

Mascarenhas, Reginald C. (1982) *Technology Transfer and Development: India's Hindustan Machine Tools Company*, Boulder, Westview Press.

Mascarenhas, Reginald C. (1988) *A Strategy for Rural Development: Dairy Cooperatives in India*, London/New Delhi, Sage.

Meier, Gerald M. (ed.) (1995) *Leading Issues in Economic Development*, New York, Oxford University Press.

Moore Jr, Barrington (1966) *Social Origins of Dictatorship and Democracy: Lord and Peasant in the Making of the Modern World*, Hamondsworth, Penguin.

Mosley, Paul, Jane Harrigan and John Toye (1992) *Aid and Power: The World Bank and Policy Based Lending*, London, Routledge.

Myrdal, Gunnar (1968) *Asian Drama: An Inquiry into the Poverty of Nations*, Harmondsworth, England, Penguin.

Oshima, Harry T. (1987) *Strategic Processes in Monsoon Asia's Economic Development*, Tokyo, University of Tokyo Press.

Patterson, Louis and Dietrich Rueschmeyer (eds) (1992) *State and Market: Synergy or Rivalry*, London/Boulder, Lynne Reiner Publishers.

Pillai, V. and L. Shannon (eds) (1995) *Developing Areas*, New York, Berg Publishers.

Poulson, Barry W. (1995) *Economic Development: Private and Public Choice*, New York, West Publishing Company.

Pye, Lucien (1985) *Asian Power and Politics: The Cultural Dynamics of Authority*, Cambridge, MA, Belknap Press.

Raj, K. N. (1973) The Politics of Intermediate Regimes, Kale Memorial Lecture, Pune.

Ravenhill, John (ed.) (1995) *The Political Economy of East Asia 2: China, Korea and Taiwan* – Vol. II, Aldershot, An Elgar Reference Collection.

Riggs, Fred W. (1964) *Administration in Developing Countries: A Theory of Prismatic Society*, Boston, Houghton Mifflin.

Rhee, Jong-Chan (1994) *The State and Industry in South Korea*, London, Routledge.

Riggs, Fred W. (ed.) (1971) *The Frontiers of Development Administration*, Durham, Duke University Press.

Rozman, Gilbert (ed.) (1991) *The East Asian Region: Confucian Heritage and its Modern Application*, Princeton, Princeton University Press.

Rudolph, Lloyd H. and Susan Hoeber Rudolph (1987) *In Pursuit of Lakshmi: The Political Economy of the Indian State*, Chicago, Chicago University Press.

Sen, Amartya (1994) *Resources, Values and Development*, London, Basil Blackwell.

So, Alvin Y. and Stephen W. K. Chiu (1995) *East Asia and the World Economy*, London, Sage.

Stein, Burton and Sanjay Subramanyam (eds) (1996) *Institutions and Economic Change in South Asia*, Bombay, Oxford University Press.

Sundrum, R. M. (1983) *Development Economics: A Framework for Analysis and Policy*, London, Wiley.

Tabb, William K. (1995) *The Postwar Japanese System: Cultural Economy and Economic Transformation*, New York, Oxford University Press.

Tickner, Ann J. (1987) *Self-Reliance versus Power Politics: The American and Indian Experience in Building Nation States*, New York, Columbia University Press.

Varshney, Asutosh (1995) *Democracy, Development and the Countryside: Urban-Rural Struggles in India*, Cambridge, Cambridge University Press.

Wade, Robert (1990) *Governing the Market: Economic Theory and the Role of Government in East Asian Industrialisation*, Princeton, Princeton University Press.

Weiss, Linda and John M. Hobson (1995) *States and Economic Development: A Comparative Historical Analysis*, London, Polity Press.

Williamson, John (ed.) (1994) *The Political Economy of Policy Reform*, Washington DC, Institute for International Economics.

World Bank (1993) *The East Asian Miracle: Economic Growth and Public Policy*, New York, Oxford University Press.

Index